Internet Books for Educators, Parents, and Students

Internet Books for Educators, Parents, and Students

Jean Reese

1999
Libraries Unlimited, Inc.
and Its Division
Teacher Ideas Press
Englewood, Colorado

LIBRARIES UNLIMITED, INC.
and Its Division
Teacher Ideas Press
P.O. Box 6633
Englewood, CO 80155-6633
1-800-237-6124
www.lu.com

Library of Congress Cataloging-in-Publication Data

Reese, Jean.
    Internet books for educators, parents, and students / Jean Reese.
    xiii, 299 p.   22×28 cm.
    Includes bibliographical references and index.
    ISBN 1-56308-697-2 (pbk.)
    1. Education--Computer network resources--United States
Bibliography.   2. Internet (Computer network) in education--United
States Bibliography.   3. Internet (Computer network)--United States
Bibliography.   I. Title.
Z5814.C812R44   1999
[LB1044.87]
016.37133'44678--dc21   99-26463
                                                              CIP

In loving memory
of my father...thanks for everything, Pop.

Contents

Preface

Having access to electronic resources in the classroom allows teachers to provide and promote an exciting environment for learning. Electronic sources can give a currency and interactive feeling to lessons that make everyday classroom activities come alive. Discussions in classes, the writing of reports, and other special projects become more meaningful and alive with the ability to use electronic resources.

Online databases have been used in academic libraries in higher education institutions for many years and have provided libraries with the opportunity to offer up-to-date information to their patrons. Schools have incorporated some of the special online packages into their classrooms over the years as well. In the mid-1980s, along came CD-ROM, which provided educators and librarians another form of electronic access to information. Though perhaps not as timely, CD-ROMs do offer a way to know how much money to budget for electronic access, thus making their purchase easier in some cases. CD-ROM databases also created an environment in which the end-users could sit down and do their own searches.

And now we have the Internet! It not only provides up-to-the-minute information, but also offers it in an interactive, entertaining way. There are many exciting K-12 projects, programs, lesson plans, and guides "out there" which can help teachers with creative new ways to teach. The Internet is an exciting place today for schools.

Educators who have access to a computer, a modem, communication software, and online resources now have the world at their fingertips. But this also creates some considerations and concerns. Today's busy educator is faced with a difficult task of sorting through all the choices in education resources. There is so much, and it is growing daily. This guide provides a means of looking at the books available for educators and parents to learn more about the world of the Internet. *Internet Books for Educators, Parents, and Students* is one way to help locate valuable resources. It ties together a variety of topics for the education community.

Introduction

With new Internet books filling up bookstore shelves all the time, the need for a current guide to aid in selecting Internet books seems more obvious than ever. *Internet Books for Educators, Parents, and Students* is a reference guide to more than 100 Internet books. My primary goal in writing this book was to provide a one-stop source to help educators, parents, and students learn about the variety of Internet books available. The annotations are descriptive and provide evaluative comments as well. I hope these snapshots will provide enough information to help educators and librarians decide what titles might be best for them.

As Associate Director for the Education Library at Vanderbilt University, part of my responsibilities are in collection development. The library also has a youth collection and Curriculum Laboratory for teacher education students, area teachers, and administrators. I am always aware of the impact the Internet has on teaching and look for titles that might be useful for our collections. I am also the editor of "The Reference Shelf," a column for the magazine *Multimedia Schools*, which reviews professional materials of interest to educators in the area of technology in the schools.

Scope and Coverage

The book is divided into six chapters covering general Internet books; books for educators and librarians; books for students, parents, and children; books for use in curriculum development; fiction books for juvenile literature; and books about Web design and creating Web sites. Within each chapter, entries are in alphabetical order by title and include an annotation that describes as well as offers evaluative comments. Types of books include tutorials, guides, fiction works for children and adolescents, and curriculum resource collections, which are often compendiums of Web sites.

Because of the constantly changing nature of the Internet, resources appear and disappear every day. It is impossible to say that some of the sites in the books are not out of date or that a version of some piece of software has not been superseded. In every case I made the effort to review the latest edition of a title. Due to the nature of publication deadlines, new books are already being published as I type the last word of this manuscript, and many titles will have newer editions. Nevertheless, the annotations included with each book will give you an overview of what the book offers so that you can decide if it suits your needs. Then just locate the latest edition! Every effort was made to include the most prominent education resources. In many cases, I was able to obtain review copies from the publishers. When such copies were unavailable, I found our Interlibrary Loan Service here at Vanderbilt extremely helpful in providing me with titles. In general, years covered are 1996 to 1998, but an occasional title from 1995 may show up. The vast majority of these titles are still in print. If not, they are still available through sources such as Amazon.com or bookstores that specialize in locating hard-to-find titles. A few of the juvenile literature titles may be out-of-print, but these titles *are* available from public libraries.

In some cases titles could have been placed in more than one chapter. My choice boiled down to the emphasis in the book. For example, a book in the curriculum chapter may also present an introduction to the Internet and its tools. But the majority of the book is focused on the Web sites or lesson plans and activities and that's why it was put in the curriculum chapter rather than the educators chapter. If the majority of a book is an introduction to the Internet, with some pages devoted to Web sites, then that title went in the appropriate chapters for educators or librarians. If the book was devoted to kids' Web sites, I put it in the chapter for parents, children, and students rather than the curriculum chapter. In some cases books were written for both teachers and parents. If the emphasis was on using the sites in a classroom setting rather than at home, I put it in the curriculum chapter.

Selection Criteria

In selecting education resources for this book, I began with books I had reviewed for my "Reference Shelf" column. There is a note after each review indicating that they first appeared in *Multimedia Schools*. Whenever a newer edition came along, I re-reviewed the book for this guide. I reviewed education journals for new titles. I regularly visited Amazon.com and barnesandnoble.com, as they are two great sources for very current titles and even upcoming ones. I checked *Books in Print* online and in print to see what might be out there, and I used the Internet to visit publishers' sites.

I have tried to include a variety of materials, always thinking in terms of whether an item would be useful to an educator. Some of the titles in the general section do not address education issues, but contain a good look at the Internet or HTML or some aspect of the Internet and its resources. Therefore, if they were well written and easy to use, I felt they would be tools that educators might want to consider.

In 99% of the titles, I had the book in hand to review. If I was unable to obtain a copy from the publisher or through interlibrary loan, but felt that it deserved to be included in this book, I located a description of the contents. In these cases, I did not include evaluative comments.

Who Should Read This Book?

This book is written primarily for the K-12 education community, including educators, librarians, library media specialists, administrators, parents, students, children, and college faculty. But in reality, I believe anyone who might want to see what's available in the area of Internet books in education would benefit from reading it. For librarians, it may serve as an aid in selection of materials. Parents can learn about titles to help them become more aware of the Internet and more able to interact with their children on the Internet. Teachers can find some good resources for curriculum projects and lesson plans and sources for helping them get started creating Web sites for their classrooms.

Organization and Format

Within the six chapters, book entries are arranged alphabetically by title, followed by author's name, publisher information, date, Web address, number of pages, series title (if any), ISBN number, type of binding, cost, software information (when available), and annotation. I chose to list the title first because it seemed the most practical way to locate a book. Most people will choose a book in this guide by the title and so it seemed appropriate to put that piece of information first. The citations may include the URL of a Web site that belongs to the publisher or of a Web site that updates the material in the book. I tried to find a Web address for each entry, but in some cases no Web address was given for the publisher. The annotations are descriptive as well as evaluative.

Chapter 1://General Internet Books

Introduction

The books listed in this section are general books on the Internet, not necessarily written for or by educators. I have tried to include books that take a down-to-earth, practical approach to introducing the Internet. The idea of many is to introduce you to the Internet or World Wide Web in a user-friendly manner. Some books are very detailed, covering all aspects of the 'Net and its resources. Others are meant to provide a jump-start, a look at what's possible. Here you will find topics such as searching on the World Wide Web; quick guides to the Internet or Web; issues related to the Internet, such as copyright or technology planning; and software for searching, including Netscape and Internet Explorer. Each of the titles here has at least one Internet component among its chapters. In most cases the entire book is about the Internet or World Wide Web. Some of the titles are parts of a series such as The Complete Idiot's Guides or the Dummies guides, which take computer topics and present them in a nonthreatening and friendly manner. Other books take a more serious approach to a topic. Because the Internet is ever-changing, later editions may already be available. Use this guide to determine style and substance in selecting a book. Then just be sure to check what the latest edition is.

The ABCs of the Internet, 2d Edition

Christian Crumlish

Alameda, CA: Sybex, 1997. (http://www.sybex.com). 344p.
ISBN: 0-7821-2079-2. Softcover, $19.99.

The Internet is a hot topic, no doubt about it. There are literally hundreds of Internet books out there. According to the author of *The ABCs*, many are "pieces of puff" offering vague generalities. Not so with this book; Crumlish asserts that his book tells how to "get things done on the Internet." The book's 12 chapters do focus on practical uses of the Internet, including e-mail, how to browse the Web, locating resources, multimedia, push technology, using mailing lists, Usenet news, chat, FTP, and creating a basic Web page. Much of the information is hands-on. There is very little theory or history at all. Because the World Wide Web and electronic mail are the overwhelming choices of most Internet users, they receive a lot of attention in the book.

There's no real target audience except beginners who want to learn to use the Internet. However, at times it seems as though the author is speaking to the business community. Whether you need a complete guide or just want a reference tool, the material is presented in such a way as to be useful for either purpose. For example, if you are itching to get going with e-mail and don't really want to read an introductory chapter on the Internet, then just skip to the e-mail chapter.

The first of the 12 chapters is an introduction to the Internet, "The Internet Getting in Your Face?," and covers the obligatory topics of "What is the Internet?," the Web, getting connected, and finding a service provider. If you are completely new to computers as well, there is information about which ones to use and what you can do on the 'Net. Chapter 2 covers sending and receiving mail; choosing mail programs such as Eudora, MS Exchange, Pegasus, Pine, and others. Material is very detailed, especially concerning some of the mail programs, and gives step-by-step directions for using them. Chapter 3, "Making the Most of E-Mail," continues the discussion by presenting more advanced features, such as sending to multiple recipients, sending files, forwarding messages, and using your word processor to create mail. There are little details, such as how to filter your mail, attach a signature, and use mail from several accounts, that broaden the scope. Chapter 4, "Browsing the Web," exposes you to browsing basics, such as how to follow a link, making bookmarks and managing them, working with frames and image maps, plus a section on using Gopher. Additional topics cover how to access the Web via an online service such as America Online or CompuServe. One service (Cyberdog from Apple) is no longer available. There's a detailed section on Lynx for those who still use this text-only browser, and, of course, the two hottest browsers, Netscape and Internet Explorer are featured. Once you learn all about browsing, finding what you really want is the next step covered, in Chapter 5, "Finding Stuff on the Net." For anyone who is tired of surfing, Crumlish offers details on subject directories and search engines. Yahoo is featured with step-by-step directions that take you through its hierarchical structure.

Multimedia is one of the main reasons the Web has such appeal. Chapter 6, "The Multimedia Explosion," helps you understand the potential of sound, music, movies, and animation on the Web. Media viewing is discussed by describing plug-ins, viewers, and players, as well as helper applications. There's a good section on the various types of media, which will introduce you to the types of pictures, sounds, music, animations, movies, and 3D available on the Web. *Push technology* has become the new buzzword for the Web. Realizing this, Crumlish includes a chapter called "Push and the Desktop Web," highlighting push tools such as Microsoft Internet Explorer, PointCast, and Netscape Newscaster.

The final chapter is "Making a Home Page or Web Site." There's not enough here to let you become a Web author, but it will introduce you to some basic ideas about creating pages and putting together a Web site. Appendices include "Getting Connected and Getting Started," with information about modem connections and direct connections as well as finding a service provider. Appendix B is a "Glossary of Internet Terms."

The author's goal of producing a practical, easy-to-understand guide to the Internet is reached, but there's nothing really outstanding about the presentation of the material—the material is somewhat disorganized. Electronic mail is discussed in the first couple of chapters, then mailing lists aren't featured until the end of the book. The writing is straightforward but not outstanding.

The AltaVista Search Engine Revolution

Richard Seltzer, Deborah Ray, and Eric J. Ray

Berkeley, CA: Osborne McGraw-Hill, 1997. (**http://www.osborne.com**). 274p. ISBN: 0-07-882235-1. Softcover, $16.99.

Let's face it, finding information on the Internet can still be a challenging endeavor for even the most skilled "surfer." There are certainly help screens and online articles comparing search engines that can get you going, but reading the information on a computer may not be the best way for some people to learn. Along comes an entire book devoted to one search engine. But make no mistake, it's not just any search engine. AltaVista is (at this writing) the most popular choice among Internet searchers.

The AltaVista Search Revolution covers everything needed to get up to speed and search effectively with AltaVista. The book is divided into seven chapters: "Introduction to AltaVista," "Getting Started with AltaVista," "Advanced Search," "Searching Usenet Newsgroups," "Providing Information the AltaVista Way," "Using the AltaVista Search A to Z Reference," and "The AltaVista Story." The authors state that their book is for "anyone who uses the Internet to locate resources."

To get the most out of much of the material, it's necessary to be connected to the Internet to follow the step-by-step directions for various topics. Material includes Boolean operators as well as limiting operators, with examples of how they work on AltaVista. Besides searching tips, the book also discusses how AltaVista gathers information, ranks sites, and indexes them, as well as what it does not index. All of this information can help you better understand what's going on in the background, as well as help Webmasters figure out how to get more hits from an AltaVista search.

An interesting chapter is the "AltaVista A to Z Reference." Here you'll find out what can make a successful search, with a look at some successful AltaVista searches and results. Essentially, it's a "how to find information" chapter. To use the reference, look up a topic under the equivalent letter of the alphabet. Because there is a wide range of topics, it's a good idea to browse the chapter first. A number of education-related subjects are available. For example, there are entries for child development, colleges and universities, day care, copyright, parenting, and lesson plans, to mention a few.

In each chapter you can find icons highlighting tips that point out important ideas you should be aware of, troubleshooting tips, and notes, as well as a reminder of some things you were supposed to have learned in a previous chapter.

Appendices include "The Top 1,000 Most Common Words on the Web," "A Sample of 1,000 Queries," and "A Frequency of Words Used in AltaVista Search Queries."

With simple language and an enthusiastic writing style, it sometimes feels as though the authors are trying to sell AltaVista. Still, if AltaVista is your main search tool and you want an in-depth book about this popular search engine, you will find all you need in this guide.

BeginnerNet: A Beginner's Guide to the Internet and World Wide Web, 3d Edition

Brian Pomeroy

Thorofare, NJ: SLACK, 1997. (http://www.slackinfo.com). 144p.
ISBN: 1-55642-355-1. Softcover, $18.95.

If you are intimidated by the Internet and technology in general, most likely you want a resource that will address the main issues in simple terms with jargon-free language. *BeginnerNet* is written for any beginner wishing to learn about the Internet and especially those with no computer experience. The third edition of *BeginnerNet* includes the following chapters: "Anatomy of a Computer," "What Is the Internet?," "What Is the World Wide Web?," "How to Connect to the Internet and World Wide Web," "Surfing the Web for the First Time," "Test Your Web Skills," "Troubleshooting," and "Using Other Internet Features." Two chapters new to this edition include "The Internet and Society" and "Launching Your Own Web Site." They discuss social issues, crime, privacy, free speech, and how to set up a Web site.

The book covers essential information about the Internet and World Wide Web, such as what they are, how they can be used, getting connected, what sets the Web apart, basics of navigating with a browser, Web addresses, bookmarks, and more. Web directories for searching on the Internet are also covered and updated in the new version. Five appendices include "Internet Glossary," "Major Internet Service Providers," "How and Where to Download Popular Net Software...For Free," "International Top-Level Domain Names," and a bibliography. An "Internet Resource Directory" lists general-interest sites as well as health-related sites. There is a small education list, but those selected are fairly general in nature. This is really a simple guide to the Internet with basic information organized so that a complete novice can learn the essentials.

The Big Guide to Netscape Communicator 4

Bill Harris and Bill Vernon

Indianapolis, IN: Sams.net Publishing, 1997.
(http://www.samspublishing.com). 848p. ISBN: 1-57521-301-X.
Softcover, $29.99.

At more than 800 pages, "Big" is a good word to use for this thick tome. Today Netscape is still the most popular Web browser (at this writing), and has grown bigger by offering more features than just being able to browse on the Web. Today Netscape is called Netscape Communicator, because it allows you to do so much more than just explore the Internet.

The Big Guide is an easy-to-read book divided into 10 main parts. It's designed to be a handy reference tool for anyone who needs to look up something about Communicator or as a complete guide to the computer novice. Everything you could ever want to know about Netscape is covered. Each of the more than 50 chapters covers a single subject, making it easier to learn the information you need.

The authors make it a point to say that the only real skill needed is being able to move a mouse. A nice feature is that both Windows and Macintosh platforms are taken into account. When a feature is different in one, it is mentioned.

Part One begins with an introductory look at Netscape Communicator and its components, what's needed to connect, and requirements for your computer to run Netscape, as well as installing it. Part Two looks into Navigator essentials such as navigating, bookmarks, searching, getting files, saving, and printing pages, as well as how to customize your browser. Parts Three through Eight cover the major components, including Messenger (e-mail), Collabra (newsgroups), Composer (Web page creation), Netcaster, and the Professional Edition. Part Nine shows you how to extend the capabilities of Netscape through graphics, video, sound, plug-ins, helper applications, and more.

The chapters are well laid out and organized with a similar format for each one. "In This Chapter" outlines the basics to be covered. The "Introduction" sets the stage for the subject under discussion. The various sections of the chapter are in bold letters and interspersed throughout are figures that illustrate Netscape. Also included are boxes that contain tips or hints and suggestions for important points. "What's Next" concludes each chapter with a look at what was covered and what is coming up. It's very easy to find the chapter or subtopic you want if you are using the book as a reference tool. The many screen shots help illustrate points made so that it's possible to have good visual cues for learning. Step-by-step directions help you work through the book and learn as you practice. Part

Ten is a Yellow-Pages-style directory of InfoSeek's Web Hot Spots. Each one has a brief description along with the title and URL (uniform resource locator or Web address). Sites are arranged by broad subject areas such as Arts and Entertainment, Business, Finance, Shopping, Sports, etc.

Why should you buy this "big" Netscape book? Well, if you use Netscape Communicator as your primary tool for searching the Web, sending electronic mail, reading newsgroups, and composing Web pages, then you will have everything you need. It can be frustrating sometimes to use downloadable products that don't come with manuals. But if you buy this book, you'll have a complete reference tool for learning all about the capabilities of Netscape Communicator. Although it's not something you'll carry around with you for lunchtime reading, it is a resource you can keep and refer to whenever you need some help on a particular topic or as you move through learning the various Netscape components.

The Complete Idiot's Guide to the Internet, 5th Edition
Peter Kent

Indianapolis, IN: Que, 1998. (**http://www.mcp.com/publishers/que/**).
409p. ISBN: 0-7897-1690-9. Softcover, $16.99.

This is the fifth edition of this book in five years. The author, Peter Kent, has written all four of the other best-selling editions, as well as articles for magazines such as *Internet World*. The material is geared to the beginner as well as the intermediate user who wants to learn about the powerful tool called the Internet and perhaps have a little fun along the way. The author writes with a humorous style that makes learning fun. He also interjects his experiences with various tools so that you get a personal insight into them. For example, when discussing chat rooms, he states that he's not a big fan of them. He gives his reasons why, but also presents informative material on using them.

The book assumes basic computer skills and does not go into using a mouse or changing windows, etc. There are four parts. Part One, "Start at the Beginning," is where you can learn all about e-mail; what the Internet and World Wide Web are; how to connect, set up your equipment, choose an online service, and use multimedia on the Web; the basics of using a browser; and more. Part Two, "There's Plenty More," continues with other Internet tools such as e-mail, push technology, discussion groups, newsgroups, FTP, chat rooms, Internet conferencing, file types, Gopher, and Telnet. Part Three, "Getting Things Done," helps you learn how to use search engines and subject directories to locate information and how to set bookmarks; it also covers safety on the Internet, how to make your own Web page, the future of the Web, Web Television, and more, along with a complete frequently asked questions chapter. Part Four, "Resources," provides appendices on Windows 98, software you'll need, finding Internet access, the e-mail responder, and a glossary of important terms.

Liberally illustrated with screen shots and cartoons, as well as "techno talk" and "check this out" features along the way, this guide provides a complete look at the Internet. Humor and good writing offer a winning combination for anyone who may still be a bit wary about getting on this information superhighway.

The Complete Idiot's Guide to Netscape Communicator 4

Joe Kraynak

Indianapolis, IN: Que, 1997. (**http://www.mcp.com/publishers/que**). 310p. ISBN: 0-7897-1029-3. Softcover, $19.99.

Here's another in the Idiot's series of computer books, and it follows a style very similar to the others in presenting the material. There are basically two Web browsers that have the lion's share of the browser market today: Netscape and Internet Explorer from Microsoft. Internet Explorer comes bundled with most Windows 95/98 machines today. Netscape 4.xx is the latest version as of this writing.

This guide from Que covers all about setting up and working with Netscape Communicator 4. It assumes a Windows platform, so if you use a Macintosh, some of the screens for setup and installation will look different.

As an all-in-one Internet tool, Communicator has a lot to offer. There are six components that make up the browser. Que's guide takes a basic look at all the components in an introductory chapter. This is a good way to see how they all work together before you venture into the details of each one. If you are like a lot of people, you may only have used the navigator component for browsing and not even realize the capabilities the whole package provides. This guide will certainly get you going, with essential information presented in a friendly, non-threatening way.

The various conventions used in the book will give you some added information as you move through the material. "Check This Out" contains tips, warnings, and other tidbits; "Techno Talk" presents some high-tech stuff that the author feels is important to present. "Frequently Asked Questions" contains—what else?—common questions that arise. Of course, you may choose to skip these boxes and read only the main material. Written in 1997, some information has changed, at least as far as obtaining the software. Netscape Communicator is available free from Netscape's Web site. Netscape's site has changed completely since this book was written. If your connection is slow and downloading is excruciatingly tedious, you may want to consider purchasing a copy.

As a Macintosh user, it's always interesting to me how many people "assume" a certain platform without ever mentioning that fact. When discussing installation, it's assumed you are using Windows. Then, at the end, there is some information in a "Check This Out" box for Mac users—but nowhere is it actually stated that the book is for Windows. There are some differences between platforms with Communicator, so just keep this in mind if you use a Macintosh.

The book is organized to move through the various components and master some of the details of each. First Navigator, the browser, is discussed. All kinds of information about setting it up and customizing it for personal use shows how to make the most of it. Anyone can point and click, but by taking the time to learn some of the special features, browsing will take on an added dimension. At the end of each chapter is a summary of the important facts presented. The author recognizes that in some cases there may be a bit of information overload, so he presents the "points you should never forget."

Within the chapter on Navigator, various search engines are explored. Though not a feature of Communicator, except for accessing them, it's useful to know what's available.

Netcaster is Netscape's component that allows you to subscribe to various Web sites and receive updated pages delivered directly to your computer. *Push technology* is the technical name of this function. After a brief description of push content, there is a detailed look at how it operates within Netscape. To get the most out of this section (and others), it's recommended that you run Netscape Communicator 4 as you read parts of the book. Step-by-step directions take you through the process of setting up channels.

Saving and printing graphics found along the way, as well as how to use Navigator to explore Gopher and FTP sites, are covered. Customizing Navigator can create a good working environment, and adding plug-ins and ActiveX Controls as well will "beef up" Navigator. From looking at multimedia to learning to interact with Java applets and VRML, this book rounds out the tour of Navigator.

Netscape Messenger is the electronic mail component that allows you to send and receive e-mail through Netscape Communicator. Setting it up is a prerequisite to successful use of it. The step-by-step directions take you through the process. Another chapter explores how to set up and use an address book. For those already using another e-mail program, just skip this information. The same holds true for Netscape Collabra, the component for accessing newsgroups. If you don't have a newsgroup reader, take a look at what Collabra has to offer. Netscape Conference, another component, allows you to set up and interact in a conference setting. By following the directions, it's easy to get going and learn to place calls to interact with others in real time on the 'Net. Finally, if you have a yen to create your own Web page, then learn how Composer works. It's Netscape's program for generating Web pages and no HTML is required. There are lots of details for creating various kinds of Web pages, ranging from beginning to more advanced.

For people who have decided that Netscape Communicator is their choice for Internet access, this guide covers almost anything you'd like to learn. Start out with the basics and then move on to additional components as needed. By the way, a newer edition is probably out by now.

Copyright for Schools: A Practical Guide, 2d Edition

Carol Mann Simpson

Worthington, OH: Linworth Publishing, 1997. (**http://www.linworth.com/**). 116p. ISBN: 0-938865-57-9. Softcover, $24.95.

Technology use, including multimedia and the Internet, has changed copyright issues dramatically. Simpson's notebook is directed at school librarians who must deal with copyright issues. Her knowledge comes from much research resulting from her own experiences with copyright problems at her school. *Copyright for Schools* is loaded with everything you need to know about fair use, the history of copyright, print materials, computer software, audiovisual materials, distance learning, the Internet, plus interlibrary loan, facsimile, and document delivery—really the whole spectrum found in the educational environment. You will find some redundancies between chapters because the same laws may apply to several formats. The work is meant to be a handy tool for busy librarians. It is easy to locate the format you want to learn about, and the examples provide a very clear view of what is acceptable and what isn't. Appendices include a sample compliance agreement, copyright do's and don'ts, useful sources of information, copyright warning notices, copyright policy, release forms, and plagiarism guidelines for students.

If you've been blissfully ignorant of copyright laws or perhaps keeping your blinders on about it, you'll find your eyes wide open as you thumb through and learn what's "not acceptable." I know I did. *(Courtesy of Multimedia Schools Magazine, Information Today, Inc., Medford, NJ).*

Dan Gookin's Web Wambooli

Dan Gookin

Berkeley, CA: Peachpit Press, 1997. (http://www.peachpit.com).
368p. ISBN: 0-201-88597-2. Softcover, $22.95.

The title is a bit weird. What is a Wambooli? Dan Gookin, a well-known author of computer books, came up with the made-up term a few years ago when he tried to cover his lack of knowledge about the Web during a conversation. It stuck and it's now the name of his Web site as well as of this book.

Even though he is a computer guru, Gookin writes in a lighthearted manner to teach about the World Wide Web. It's fun to read. No technical jargon here; just the facts explained in a straightforward but humorous way. The author makes certain assumptions, such as that you have a computer and a modem, that you know how to use a mouse with Windows, and the obvious one, that you wish to learn about the Internet. That's about it. Beginners are welcome here.

It's possible to treat this book as a tutorial, reading it cover-to-cover, or to use it as a reference tool. The chapters are created so that those in a hurry can read only the important text and skip the rest. For example, the bold arrow and bold heading mean "here's the necessary information to be able to follow the exercises or directions to move along."

The book is divided into four parts. Part One, "Dull, Boring, Setup Information," takes you through the beginning stages of preparation, including setting up the computer, installing the software, and connecting to the Internet. The three chapters include step-by-step directions to install Netscape on a Windows machine and move through the process of dialing up and getting familiar with a browser. Part Two, "Wild, Wild Web," is the heart of the book, with 10 chapters. Here's a sampling of some of them: "Going Places, Hither, Thither and Yon," "Finding the Stuff They Tell You Is Out There," "Having Fun Mit Sound," and "The Fine Art of W-W-Waiting." As you can see, humor is a large part of this book. Among the material covered are topics such as getting around; all about home pages; bookmarks; and how to find people, places, and things. There are also chapters on using sounds, forms, frames, animation, and Java, plus error messages that crop up. Many newcomers to computers and the Internet will be reassured by the chapter titled "Has This Ever Happened to You?" Here you'll learn that all those things that go wrong when online also happen to other people, not just you. Modem problems, error messages from your browser, keeping safe, and broken graphics—they're all covered.

Part Three, "Conquering E-mail," makes the exciting world of electronic mail understandable to the newcomer. Topics covered are learning about e-mail addresses, getting mail and reading it, sending and receiving attachments, joining mailing lists, and more. A Frequently-Asked-Questions section covers some of the typical problems people encounter. Part Four, "News, Information and Folly," teaches you all about newsgroups, Usenet, and how to read and post messages, as well as problems to avoid.

Appendix A, "Some Items Your Internet Provider Should Provide You With," is a very helpful section. Keep this handy if you are new to the Internet. It has technical facts that will help translate the process of choosing an Internet service provider (ISP) so that you can make an informed decision. Appendix B is "General Info on the Online Services' Browsers," containing facts about the major services such as America Online. Appendix C provides a list of the country extensions found in URLs (for example, .au means Australia). A glossary with many helpful terms, along with an index, complete the book.

Because it is so liberally interspersed with tips, hints, and suggestions, along with screen prints, learning to navigate the World Wide Web is fun with this book. Though not geared specifically to educators, the numerous step-by-step directions and friendly writing style make this guide a fun tool for anyone who wants a bit of humor along with their learning.

Discover the World Wide Web

John Ross

Indianapolis, IN: IDG Books Worldwide, 1997.
(**http://www.idgbooks.com**). 331p. ISBN: 0-7645-3060-7.
Softcover, $19.99.

Written for beginners who want to learn to use the Internet but don't want to get into all that techno-jargon, this is another practical, user-friendly book from the IDG folks who are responsible for the Dummies series. The Discover series teaches the basics of technology topics with "real-world" examples that allow you to get going quickly. Each Discover book is similarly organized and features the following components: "Discovery Central," a tear-out card that acts as a quick reference to the important ideas expressed in the book; a "Quick Tour" to get you started right away; "Real-Life Vignettes," one-page scenarios that apply a real-life situation; "Goals" expected to be achieved by the chapter; "Side Trips" that include information about other ways to approach the topics; "Bonuses," time-saving tips and some other advanced techniques; "Discovery Center," a guide that illustrates important procedures; and a "Visual Index," which includes documents and page numbers pointing you to information you can use to achieve the effect under discussion.

The book's four major parts include "An Introduction to the Web," "Navigating the World Wide Web," "World Wide Web Destinations," and "Beyond Browsing."

The book begins by showing how a trip from San Francisco can be planned using nothing but information found on the World Wide Web. From airline reservations to weather reports to car rentals, sightseeing trips, restaurants, and hotels, the Web has a great deal to offer. The point of the book is to discover the Web and be able to make use of its many features. Therefore, the chapters take you through a logical organization for figuring out what kind of hardware and software are needed, suggest places to buy them, and then move on to finding an Internet service provider. The book is very good about offering all the possibilities, ranging from online services, to large service providers like MCI, to the smaller, local ones, as well as mentioning network connections some people may already have through a LAN. Next, getting a browser and then configuring it are discussed. Both Internet Explorer and Netscape are featured. The logical next step is to get familiar with using a browser, so there are sections on links, moving around, and setting bookmarks or lists. Several helpful features from Internet Explorer are described. There are step-by-step directions when applicable to guide you through the process. Screen shots help illustrate the points under discussion.

Finding things is the ultimate goal of anyone using the Web, but doing that can be problematic. The author discusses the main search tools, including the ever-popular Yahoo, AltaVista, and others. There's a very helpful part that lists certain Web "guides," as they are called here, to start out with. These include such well-known ones as The Scout Report and EINet Galaxy, among others.

Once you are up and running, the remainder of the book focuses on the kinds of resources and information available to you. With more than a hundred sites, including newspapers, weather, sports, business news, and all kinds of specialized sources, there's something for everyone. These resource chapters often have screen shots of a Web page and may have directions to access the site, or at the very least the Web address and a description of the site's main features. There's also a chapter on electronic mail, including how it works with Netscape, plus some other important programs like Eudora.

As mentioned earlier, the Discovery Center is a nice way to find out the important topics and return to them. It's more than an index, because it lists by chapter, with a paragraph or so about the topic and then a page number.

Though not geared to educators, this is a practical and easy-to-follow tour of the World Wide Web, with very down-to-earth examples. You'll get a good all-around view of what the Web has to offer, along with tutorials for getting your newly acquired skills up to speed.

Easy Internet, 3d Edition

Joe Kraynak

Indianapolis, IN: Que, 1998. (**http://www.mcp.com/publishers/que/**).
207p. ISBN: 0-7897-1639-9. Softcover, $19.99.

Easy Internet takes a visual approach to teaching how to use the Internet.
Using a series of short lessons with lots of color illustrations, the concept is to
keep the narrative short and learn by looking at the photos. The eight parts cover
the basics of topics like connecting to the Internet, the World Wide Web, e-mail,
newsgroups, FTP, chat, Internet phone calls, and creating and publishing Web
pages.

Each chapter lists the various tasks covered. In the "How to Use This Book"
introduction, the various icons used throughout are illustrated. Rather than
words, the icons express the task performed, whether it's clicking the mouse,
selecting an onscreen area, typing a word, or dragging and dropping. Perhaps a
better name for this book is "Easy Internet with Internet Explorer": even though
the author never states it, Microsoft products are used throughout and Microsoft
Internet Explorer is the featured browser for all the screen shots. Although
Netscape is mentioned at times, it's not really featured as a choice for learning to
use the Internet.

There are step-by-step directions for various activities, such as accessing the
Internet with America Online. Microsoft Network is also described. Perhaps the
section on browsing the Web makes the best use of the visual environment, showing how you move around on a Web page using links and buttons.

The concept of using a visual approach will appeal to many. The Peachpit
Press Visual Quickstart guides also use this approach. For some reason, their
guides just work better than this one; in this book the photos almost seem distracting. Reading the text may tell you all you need to know. Certainly, if you
aren't using Internet Explorer or Windows, this book won't be one you'll want to
buy. It would be extremely helpful for guides like this to state on the cover what
platform is used. The book includes a glossary of terms from the chapters.

The Essential Netscape Communicator Book

Rob Tidrow and Greg Robertson

Rocklin, CA: Prima Publishing, 1997. (**http://www.primapublishing.com**).
672p. ISBN: 0-76150733-7. Softcover, $24.99.

This is not a book you'll grab off your night table to do a little light reading.
At almost 700 pages, the book is full of anything and everything you'd want to

know about using Netscape Communicator. It's intended to be an all-in-one resource that can be used cover-to-cover or as a reference source. For those just starting out, who don't have much experience with the Internet or World Wide Web, it's best to start from Chapter 1. Anyone who feels comfortable with the Web can skip the introductory material and locate the chapter needed to begin.

The Essential Netscape Communicator Book's audience is businesspeople as well as the average user at home. That's a wide range to satisfy. But this book does it by presenting the material in a way that allows you to choose your starting point. A "Where to Start" table lists which chapter to begin with according to certain skill levels. This is very helpful because the book contains so much material.

There are 25 chapters in 8 parts. The eight parts are: "Netscape Communicator Basics," "Netscape Navigator Essentials," "Netscape Composer Essentials," "Netscape Messenger Essentials," "Netscape Collabra Essentials," "Netscape Conference Essentials," "Netscape Constellation Essentials," and "Appendices." (Netscape Constellation is the beta version name of Netcaster.) Each component contains several chapters.

The book is written with the Windows 95 platform in mind and uses the Netscape Communicator Standard software. If you use another platform, the installation and setup instructions will be different. So will the screen shots that go along with the hands-on exercises. There are some differences in options and features between the platforms. A "Hands-On Topics" table of contents lists all the hands-on exercises in the book. This is a nice feature that lets you look up a specific topic or feature you may want to master right away.

As you move through the chapters, you'll find certain icons that contain some helpful information. "Note" is a discussion about how best to use a particular feature. "Tip" is a helpful shortcut or recommendation. "Cautions" are just what they seem to be: warnings about some procedures or features that may cause problems. "Sidebars" provide additional information about a topic that doesn't really fit in naturally with the discussion.

Each of the components is covered in detail. There are many screen shots that help illustrate the material, as well as exercises for practice. It will probably be a good idea to have Netscape Communicator open even when just reading some of the chapters. It's often difficult to visualize what is going on if you can't see the screen.

Most people will want to get started with the Navigator component. This is one of the largest sections of the book, with 10 chapters devoted to learning all about how to set up, customize, and use Navigator. A couple of chapters also cover more general topics, such as browsing the Web, learning about hyperlinks and what makes up a Web page, entering URLs, and setting bookmarks. Netscape Composer has a large section as well, with individual chapters on fundamentals of Web page creation; creating a new page; adding hyperlinks, images, and tables; and getting your pages published. This is not just a quick look at the subject. There are hands-on exercises and many screen shots that take you through the process of creating pages in step-by-step fashion.

Netscape Messenger is the e-mail component of Netscape and the book covers all about how to configure it and send, reply to, and receive mail, as well as manage e-mail. With Collabra, the newsgroup component, subscribing and posting to newsgroups as well as to Collabra servers are discussed. Netcaster is also introduced. For some reason, the old name "Constellation" is used in the table of contents.

This combination tutorial and reference guide has a lot of information. If all you want is to scratch the surface and learn a few things about Netscape Communicator, you may want to stick with the manual and online help. But if you need to know a lot about the subject to put all the components into use, this guide takes a well-organized and detailed look at the subject.

Eudora for Windows & Macintosh

Adam Engst

Berkeley, CA: Peachpit Press, 1997. (http://www.peachpit.com).
198p. (Visual Quickstart Guide series). ISBN: 0-201-69663-0.
Softcover, $16.95.

Eudora is one of the most popular e-mail programs used today. It's available for both Windows and Macintosh platforms. The author of this Visual Quickstart guide, from Peachpit Press, is an enthusiastic user of the program. Admittedly, it's pretty easy to send mail with Eudora without buying a book like this, but if you want to learn how to get the most out of the program, this handy, step-by-step guide will take you through everything from beginning to end. The book uses the commercial version of the program, Eudora Pro. Many people use the free version, Eudora Lite, rather than the commercial one. The versions covered are 3.0/Windows and 3.1 Macintosh.

You can use this guide whether you are a Windows or Mac person. The directions are clearly marked when necessary to indicate a Windows or Mac environment. As with other guides in this series, the author's style is very user-friendly and the directions are clear and easy to follow. Anyone who already has a foundation in using Eudora can go to the table of contents, locate the desired activity, and proceed from there. Beginners should go through the book and use it as a tutorial.

Even if you have used Eudora for a while, this book can still help you learn all those extra features you've never bothered with before. Although there is good online help with Eudora, this guide is a good tool to have with you as you work through the various components of the program.

From creating new messages, replying, forwarding, and redirecting, you'll be able to apply all the possibilities that come up when receiving or sending mail. For anyone who has to send out the same message over and over, Eudora Pro's stationery message feature is a must. It allows you to create and send the same information again and again without having to type it again. This is even better than copying and pasting. You'll also learn how to reply to the same questions over and over using stationery. These features can help busy people save time with their e-mail. Other topics covered include "Writing Messages," which covers how to use the toolbar menus and attachments, using signatures, and more. An exciting new plug-in from Qualcomm (the producer of Eudora), called PureVoice, lets you send voice messages with your e-mail. "Sending and Receiving Messages" explores how to queue up your messages, send them immediately, or send them at a later date.

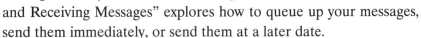

Most people probably spend more time working with messages they receive, so there's a very helpful chapter on all kinds of possibilities for making life easier when selecting messages, changing message priority, changing text, navigating between messages, and more. Often it's necessary to save mail, and to do so effectively you need a place to store the messages so that you can retrieve them easily. Eudora's mailboxes let you perform all kinds of tasks to manage your mail. And what about a way to filter some of your messages? For anyone who subscribes to mailing lists that are very active, learning how to keep them from coming to your "In" box is essential. It's possible to have them go to an appropriately named mailbox to access later. There are also chapters on using the Address Book, customizing the toolbar in Eudora, and working with directory services such as Ph and Finger. There is an appendix with the keyboard shortcuts for both the Macintosh and Windows versions and an e-mail glossary in Chapter 1 to help you learn some of the jargon used in the book.

All in all, the material covered in this book presents anyone with all the information they need to become a power user of Eudora. You may find that after reading all the nifty little things you can do with the Pro version, Eudora Lite is just not going to cut it anymore.

Field Guide to Internet Explorer 4

Stephen L. Nelson

Redmond, WA: Microsoft Press, 1998. (**http://mspress.microsoft.com**).
180p. ISBN: 1-57231-741-8. Softcover, $12.99.

It's not always necessary to have a 400-page book to learn how to use an Internet tool. If you want a source for learning Internet Explorer that gives quick, easy answers, this field guide will serve your purpose. Divided into four sections—"Environment," "Internet Explorer A to Z," "Troubleshooting," and "Quick Reference"—the book's goal is to help you find the information you need quickly and easily.

The "Environment" portion covers basics about the Internet, providing a background to get the most out of Internet Explorer. There are diagrams of key concepts and terms, with definitions and cross-references. The format is very easy to read and the diagrams help teach the concept in a visual way. Some of the topics are connecting to the Internet, e-mail, newsgroups, mailing lists, Telnet, FTP, and the Web.

The lion's share of the book is "Internet Explorer A to Z," an alphabetical list of commands, terms, tasks, and procedures. This section covers all the things you need to set up Explorer and begin using its features on the Internet. There are numerous cross-references and screen shots that illustrate the concept. The "Troubleshooting" section offers helpful information on some typical problems that may turn up as you learn how to use Internet Explorer. The "Quick Reference" part presents details on the commands and toolbar buttons.

This field guide makes finding those quick answers easy if you know what you want to look up. If you are completely new to using the Web or browsers, you may also want to find a more detailed book that gives you more step-by-step directions. Keep this one next to your computer as a reference tool.

FrontPage for Windows 98

Phyllis David and Deborah Craig

Berkeley, CA: Peachpit Press, 1998. (**http://www.peachpit.com**).
338p. (Visual Quickstart Guide series). ISBN: 0-201-69694-0.
Softcover, $17.95.

The Visual Quickstart series from Peachpit Press is known for its straightforward and simple approach in teaching software programs. The visual approach allows pictures to guide you through the software's features. Along with step-by-step directions, the total effect is nonthreatening, clear, and easy to

follow. For those who want a lot of theory or history along with learning to operate the software program, this isn't the series for you. The good thing about this
guide (as with others in this series) is that you can proceed through the chapters
one at a time or use it as a reference tool. Simply locate what you need to know
and go to it.

Creating Web pages is a lot different today than it was a couple of years ago.
It's no longer necessary to know Hypertext Markup Language (HTML) to create
professional-looking Web sites. There are sophisticated packages that do all the
encoding behind the scenes. One of the leaders of the pack is Microsoft's
FrontPage. This guide covers FrontPage 98.

The nine chapters teach all you need to know to get a full-blown Web site
up and running, or as little as you want, which might be to create a series of pages
linked together. The first chapter, titled "The Basics," is an introductory explanation of how FrontPage works, some terminology for the Web and FrontPage,
and all about the Explorer toolbar, screens, and views, as well as the six Editor
toolbars. System requirements are detailed at the end of the chapter.

FrontPage consists of two programs: Microsoft Explorer and Microsoft
Editor. You'll learn what each does; look at their screens to see how to use menus
and toolbars; and learn how the different views, such as Navigator view or the
Hyperlinks view, contribute to your Web site development. If you are familiar
with Microsoft products such as Office, it should be a simple process to transfer
learning to FrontPage. Illustrations will help visualize the results as you move
through the tutorial. After the basics of FrontPage, Chapter 2, "Web Concepts,"
moves on to more introductory material for sprucing up your knowledge of the
World Wide Web—or, if you choose, just skip this part. It isn't absolutely necessary to know what goes on behind the scenes on the Web to create sites with
FrontPage. Covered in this chapter are basic Web concepts such as addresses,
servers, and clients; viewing an HTML document in a browser (along with a
touch of HTML and its tags); plus browsers and finding an Internet service
provider. In keeping with all of the changes occurring, there's even a little about
push technology—where content providers bring information to your desktop
rather than you having to go out and browse sites to find what you want.

Chapter 3 introduces "Principles of Web Design." FrontPage makes it easy
to add a lot to Web pages, but the layout, design, and continuity are all up to you.
Knowing a few tips about good design will go a long way toward creating a successful Web site. Topics include naming Web pages, planning Web site flow, using
graphics, and the importance of narrative to a page. Chapter 4, "Installing
FrontPage 98," takes you through the installation process step-by-step. It even
considers if you have a previously installed version and has instructions for load-

ing it with or without a previous version. Beginning with Chapter 5, "Getting Started with Explorer," you begin to put the program to use by learning how to launch it and start a new Web site.

The rest of the chapters progress through topics that include working with text; having some fun with text; using graphics, multimedia, tables, and forms; and more. There is also a chapter to help keep up with any tasks to be done, via a list that lets you assign tasks and shows what has to be done. This feature is a great way to keep organized as you work through your site. For those interested in administering a Web site, Chapter 16 covers the basics. It describes how you assign levels of access and tells all about adding users and groups. These topics are a bit more technical and may not be something everyone wants to do. Nevertheless, the information is here and available should you find that Web administration is something you want to add to your assortment of skills.

How to Search the Web: A Quick-Reference Guide to Finding Things on the World Wide Web

Robert S. Want, ed.

New York: WANT Publishing, 1998. (**http://www.wantpublishing.com**). 59p. ISBN: 0-942008-88-X. Spiral notebook, $12.95.

As the Web expands and grows, with more and more sites and sources for information, it's even more difficult to find that precise piece of information you want. Knowing the basics of searching on the Web can help you increase your chances of locating relevant resources in an efficient and time-effective manner. "How to Search the Web" is a nice little spiral notebook that provides details on eight of the most popular and important search engines used today. It doesn't try to tell you everything about each one, nor does it attempt to give you any background on the Web or the Internet. Nor does it discuss details about subject directories versus search engines versus mega-search engines. But tucked away in its 59 pages are a Boolean Logic primer, search basics, how to conduct searches using the eight top engines, and some advanced search tips, along with additional resources for further learning. Researchers, librarians, students, executives, and anyone who wants to find things on the Web can use this guide.

If you are a complete search novice, then the "Boolean Basics" chapter will help you understand how to construct searches using the Boolean operators "or," "and," and "not." There are no long-winded explanations. The language is straightforward, with an example of a search statement to illustrate each concept. If you are already proficient at Boolean logic, just skip to the "Conducting Searches" section.

In the section on "Search Basics," the two types of Web searches—keyword and concept—are discussed. For anyone not familiar with the idea of concept searching, this section explains how it works, along with some pluses and minuses. Keyword searching is the most popular method of finding sources on the Web. After reading this material, you should be more aware of why you so often get some of those absolutely irrelevant sites. Relevancy ranking of results is also an important point to understand. It's covered well, with some key points that help to understand how search engines rank their results.

If you are used to sitting down and just typing in a word or two, then the "How to Formulate Queries" can provide insight into creating a useful search strategy before you go online. A successful search is only as good as the strategy you come up with. Taking a couple of minutes to read the information here can get you started on the right foot. "Search Engine Basics" is a short section covering some of the more general ideas behind search tools, such as how search tools index, some general search engine features, and the importance of understanding rankings.

The eight search engines covered are Yahoo, Infoseek, AltaVista, HotBot, Excite, Lycos, Northern Light, and MetaCrawler. Each entry contains a screen shot of the opening page with the Web address, and the descriptions offer basic search examples, advanced searches, and some of the additional search options available for each. "Basic and Advanced Search Tips" is a section offering 10 tips for conducting basic and advanced searches on the Web.

Much of the information about the specific search engines can be found online with the Help functions. But how many people take the time to read those screens? If you want to learn how to search the Web and don't have a lot of time, then keep a copy of this by your computer. It's a good reference to learn the important features of the most popular search engines used today.

How to Use Netscape Communicator 4.0: The Complete Visual Solution

Rebecca Tapley

New York: Ziff-Davis, 1997. (**http://www.mcp.com**). 228p.
(How to Use...series). ISBN: 156276-467-5. Softcover, $24.99.

First, this is a guide to using Netscape Communicator 4 with Windows. It doesn't say so anywhere on the cover. But when you open and read the first few pages, it only gives requirements for equipment for PCs, not Macintoshes; and in the "How to Install Communicator" section, it says, "After you've turned on your computer, starting Windows 95...." If you use a Macintosh and have some experience, then you can learn how to use Netscape Communicator with this book.

Just remember, the visual approach means that screen shots are from Windows, and they will look different if you use a platform other than Windows. So, if you are a beginner and don't use Windows, you may want to opt for a book that covers the Macintosh. One more point: the installation instructions assume that you are using a version of Netscape on a CD-ROM rather than downloading a copy from Netscape's Web site.

With step-by-step directions, this seven-part tutorial guide covers all the components of Netscape Communicator, including Navigator, Messenger, Collabra, Conference, and Composer. Beginning with detailed installation instructions for registering the software, and moving to setting preferences and then on to navigating and searching for information, the visual approach in this guide shows color screen shots of the points under discussion so that you can follow along with your computer. The screen shots are rather small, but someone with good eyes probably won't need to pull out a magnifying glass.

In each case, the component's menus, toolbars, and preferences are discussed and illustrated. You'll learn how to place a "phone call" or chat using Conference; how to create Web pages with Composer; and how to subscribe to and use newsgroups in Collabra. There is also a section on multimedia, security issues, and additional plug-ins such as Shockwave and RealAudio.

This is a very easy-to-follow guide for learning Netscape Communicator 4.0. It's simple but doesn't talk down to beginners. The visual approach helps you to see what is happening. The only drawback is when your screen doesn't match the one in the book, which could be frustrating for a complete novice. If you are a Macintosh user, you should probably look for a book that at least mentions Macs, especially if you are a real beginner. My suggestion for any future editions is to mention what platform is being used.

The Internet for Dummies, 4th Edition

John R. Levine, Carol Baroudi, and Margaret Levine Young

Indianapolis, IN: IDG Books Worldwide, 1997.
(http://www.idgbooks.com). 374p. (... for Dummies series).
ISBN: 0-7645-0106-2. Softcover, $19.99.

Using the same lighthearted approach to teaching computer topics as others in the series, this beginner's guide to the Internet has all the flavor of other Dummies books. Humor and a nontechnical writing style, along with good solid information, make it an appealing resource for anyone who may be intimidated about learning to use the Internet. Icons along the way guide you through the important points made. A new feature called "Whoosh" tells you there is more current information at the Web site; "Warning" is for those tricky situations; and "Technical Stuff" lets you know there's some "nerdy" stuff coming up.

The five parts making up the book include "Welcome to the Internet," which explores what the Internet is, why it's such a success, and safety issues, as well as other introductory material. One chapter, titled "The Net, Your Kids, and You," explores how families can benefit from the 'Net. Guidelines, mailing lists, newsgroups, and Web sites for children are also discussed.

Part Two, "Using Your Internet Account," covers basic Internet skills necessary to become a true surfer and Web user, including all about the Web and browsers, search tools to help locate information, Internet addresses, using e-mail, newsgroups, FTP, and downloading files. There's something here for everyone who wants to use the Web. Step-by-step directions take you through learning to read mail with several programs, including Eudora, Pine Mail, Internet Mail, and others. Useful information abounds. Remember, you can skip to the part you are really interested in. Just locate the topic you are interested in, whether it's searching for information or learning how to download files.

Part Three, "Getting an Internet Account: Some Popular Entrance Ramps," tackles the process of getting connected. Whether it's PPP or SLIP or a direct connection, there are directions for specific platforms such as Windows and Mac, as well as how to connect with an online service such as America Online or CompuServe.

Part Four is the familiar "Part of Tens" seen in most Dummies books, reserved for those intangible topics that just don't seem to fit anywhere else. Covered are "Ten Frequently Asked Questions," which is general stuff about the Internet, e-mail, etc.; "Ten Ways to Find E-Mail Addresses," to help you find those elusive friends in cyberspace; "Ten Types of Files and What to Do with Them," which helps you understand the array of files found on the Internet and how to make sense of them; and "Ten Ways to Avoid Looking Like a Klutz," to help the novice learn the rules of the road, so to speak, covering newsgroups, e-mail, and Web pages. Part Five, "Resource Reference," provides some details on locating Internet providers, Internet software, and magazines for additional information (in case you didn't get enough with this book). A glossary is also included.

After much experience, the writers of these Dummies books know just the right combination of style and substance to keep putting out successful books. For anyone who likes a more lighthearted approach to learning, you can't go wrong with this book.

The Internet Glossary and Quick Reference Guide

Alan Freedman, Alfred Glossbrenner, and Emily Glossbrenner

New York: American Management Association, 1998.
(http://www.amanet.org). 385p. ISBN: 0-8144-7979-0. Softcover, $24.95.

Alan Freedman is the best-selling author of *The Computer Glossary and the Computer Desktop Encyclopedia*, now in its eighth edition. Between them, Friedman and Alfred Glossbrenner have more than 75 years of computer, online, and Internet experience to share in this book.

It is written as a glossary and intended as a reference tool. The process of determining what should go into a book like this is not easy. In this case, terms were chosen for two basic reasons. Any terms that a new user would most likely encounter when preparing to connect to the Internet are included, along with terms all users are most likely to encounter when using the 'Net. There are also terms related to cyber culture and Internet slang. The audience is anyone in business, education, government, or at home who wants a resource for Internet terms.

Because this reference tool covers a very broad range of terms, there are some you may never need to know about, depending on your level of Internet use and reasons for using the Internet. Many are technical terms; some are abbreviations, along with other very practical and everyday concepts and terms. From *geek* to *IGRP* (Internet Gateway Routing Protocol), there is something here for everyone. The definitions range from a sentence or two to most of a page. Illustrations and screen prints are used to help illustrate definitions when applicable.

Internet in a Nutshell

Valerie Quercia

Sebastopol, CA: O'Reilly & Associates, 1997. (http://www.ora.com). 450p.
ISBN: 1-56592-323-5. Softcover, $19.95.

Internet in a Nutshell sounds like a brief guide—but at more than 400 pages, it's a large nutshell. Intended for the surfer who has already tested some of the waves on the Internet, this is really a "second-generation" book to follow Ed Krol's highly successful *The Whole Internet User's Guide & Catalog*. Following an introductory chapter on the basics of the Internet—what it is and how to navigate—the rest of the book takes an in-depth look at Web browsers and their main features, e-mail, Usenet news, files, plug-ins, Web authoring, Internet Relay Chat, and more.

More of a reference tool than a tutorial or step-by-step guide, there is a lot of information packed into this book. Beginning with an orientation tour for some of the terms and concepts you may run into and explaining tools you need along the way, the author mentions some technical components that most introductory books don't: authentication and cookies, as well as privacy issues.

Part Two is an in-depth look at Web browsers. In particular, it covers Netscape and Internet Explorer. The "tips, tricks and hidden stuff" features shortcuts, tips on customizing a browser, and a chart of preference features to refer to later on. It's possible to get a good sense of what each browser's strengths and weaknesses are from reading this section. In a later chapter, the mail features of both browsers are discussed in detail.

After browsing successfully, the next step is to "find stuff" out there on the Web, beginning with understanding URLs and how to recognize them and continuing with Internet resources arranged by subject. "Landmark" sites help you identify those of special value and interest, according to the author. Educational sites are featured in a section on "kids, parents and teachers." To be an effective searcher today, you have to understand the basics of search engines. The author has included a list of the top ones—where to find them as well as an explanation of what they do and how they work. Web design is covered, from the basics of HTML to more complex Web authoring skills such as JavaScript.

Though not a book for real beginners, anyone looking for a handy desktop reference book that cuts right to the heart of matters will find this book a good resource.

Internet 101: A Beginner's Guide to the Internet and World Wide Web

Wendy G. Lehnert

Reading, MA: Addison Wesley Longman, 1998. (http://www.awl.com). 534p. ISBN: 0-201-32553-5. Softcover, $35.95.

Internet 101 is a guide to the Internet written primarily as a textbook for an undergraduate course on the Internet, geared to students who know little or nothing about computers. But as the author states, it can also be used by *anyone* who wants to learn how to use the Internet and World Wide Web. What sets *Internet 101* apart from other Internet guides is that it is an integrated package— a course pack that includes a Web site with a teacher's manual. Most of the chapters are self-contained, so there are various options for incorporating the material into a course or just for use by an individual who wants to learn at his or her own pace.

The 13 chapters cover everything necessary to master the Internet and its applications. They include Chapter 1, "First Things First," which is all about getting started with your computer, setting it up, hooking up the modem, and creating a game plan for exploring online. Chapter 2 is "Networking Concepts and Facts," covering the details on what the Internet is, protocols necessary, host machines and host names, and some technical information on Internet architecture, packet switching, the client/server model, and more. Chapter 3, "Working with E-mail," covers all about how to use it, send it, and reply to it, as well as netiquette issues, folders, and some good management tips for taking care of your mail, along with some abuses found on the Internet. Chapter 4, "Mailing Lists and E-mail Archives," continues the concept of using electronic mail, but now covers discussion lists, LISTSERV commands, e-mail archives, and much more. Chapter 5, "The World Wide Web," takes you on a tour of the Web and explores hypertext, browsers, how to locate material, search engines and subject directories, evaluation of Web sites, and the basics of creating a Web page. Chapter 6 is "Gophers and Veronica," describing somewhat in-depth these two lesser-used Internet tools. Chapter 7, "Search Strategies for the Web," goes into more detail about locating information on the Web, to include the concepts of forming search strategies with Boolean logic. A nice section on "Search Expeditions" has guided exercises to explore the various types of search strategies for finding information. There are comparisons of various search engines and mega-search engines as well. "Usenet Newsgroups," in Chapter 8, describes what they are and how they work, and includes some frequently asked questions, as well as how to find them and use news readers. Chapter 9, "FTP and Computer Viruses," explores how to use FTP, file types and extensions, freeware, shareware, and risks of viruses when using FTP. Suggestions for some FTP clients are also included. "Telnet," another Internet tool, is discussed in Chapter 10. Also included in this chapter is a section on MUDs, MOOs, and MUSH. Chapter 11, "Web Page Construction," takes HTML a little further than the earlier chapter, with tips on effective Web pages, editors, more HTML tags, a bit about advanced features such as frames and tables, and an HTML reference list of tags. Chapter 12, entitled "Encryption on the Internet," explores cryptography as it relates to security and privacy on the Internet. Copyright issues, privacy, and free speech are several of the topics covered in Chapter 13, "Social Issues."

The focus is on nontechnical material, although some of the subjects are themselves technical in nature, such as cryptography or networking. When jargon is necessary, it is indicated by a special icon and introduced in the context of the topic under discussion. The language is in a simple, straightforward style. Throughout the book, the author inserts screen shots and other icons to indicate Web pages; helpful hints; "Heads-up Warnings" or useful definitions; "Software Checklists"; and "Real-World and the Internet" sections, which are anecdotes and historical notes of interest. Screen shots are used to reinforce important points and help illustrate the topic under discussion. Each chapter contains "Problems and Exercises," with both chapter questions to check on what you remember and hands-on practice that requires connecting to the Internet to locate resources or complete an exercise. The hands-on exercises are always marked as such.

Appendices include "Internet Service Providers," where the author offers some important considerations and tips concerning selection of an ISP. Appendix B is "Dial-Up Access," concerning what you need to access the Internet by phone lines; Appendix C is "When to Talk to Tech Support." Appendix D lists "Commands for Mailing Lists," a helpful compendium of the most important ones for LISTSERVs and LISTPROCs. Appendix E contains "Advanced Search Features" of three popular search engines. This information is taken from their online documentation. A bibliography and extensive list of credits, along with an index, complete the book.

The *Internet 101* Web pages are a valuable addition to keep the book current. Frequent updates will allow you to keep up with changes and newer information as it applies to the material in the book. It also provides a resource for practicing online as you go through the exercises in each chapter. This guide is a valuable source for anyone who needs to teach an Internet course. It's not exactly a book you would pull out and read during your lunch break, but is a more serious and comprehensive approach to learning how to use the Internet.

IRC & Online Chat

David Powers

Grand Rapids, MI: Abacus, 1997. (**http://www.abacuspub.com**).
238p. ISBN: 1-55755-333-5. Softcover, $29.95. (Includes CD-ROM for Windows).

Chat rooms can be a great place to meet people and discuss topics of mutual interest. There aren't very many books out on the topic of IRC/online chat, at least not compared to other Internet tools. Many Internet books include a paragraph or chapter about chat, but not many are comprehensive enough to really help you learn how to use it. David Powers has written a very readable book about online chat, with step-by-step directions that actually instruct you in how to download freeware, set it up, and get "chatting" online. The author's goals are to show how to use the tools (chat rooms, room commands, and more), help you learn the rules, and help you to be a "good chatter." The book is geared to the beginner, and its nine chapters cover topics such as tools used by Internet users; rules for chatting; what the emoticons (smileys) mean; how to tell which chat rooms are best suited to your needs; online games; and IRC, AOL, CU-SeeMe, and videophones. Beginning with an introduction for a novice, Powers goes over some important computer terms. If you already have some computer knowledge, just skip this section.

Chat rooms use a language all their own, so it's important to have a solid foundation in it to be successful communicating with others. This involves learning basic abbreviations used by chatters to simplify typing online. There are also many emoticons used to convey emotion in text.

Probably the best way to use the book is to install the software that comes on the CD and work with it as you go through the book. Unfortunately, if you're a Macintosh user, this won't be possible, as the CD is for Windows 95. The author does explain this up front in his discussion of what's on the CD. In fact, all instruction pertains to the Windows environment, so it won't be too helpful as far as learning to install software unless you use Windows. The easiest way to get started with online chat is through an online service. America Online is the online service used to demonstrate chat. If you are already familiar with AOL setup, you can skip that section as well. Directions are included for Internet Relay Chat for those not using America Online. There are plenty of screen shots to help illustrate what chat conversations might look like. Sometimes the examples seem pretty silly, but that's a real picture of some chat rooms.

Besides the mechanics of getting online and into a chat room, there are plenty of do's and don'ts associated with being a good "chatter." The chapters on "Rules" and "How Not to Be an Online Embarrassment" cover all the little things, written and unwritten, that you should and should not do in a chat room. Basically, if it's not something you would do in public, don't do it online.

The section called "Tips on Chatting Well" gives you lots of good advice about how to bring your personality into a chat session without being too overbearing or obnoxious. Learning to be conversational and typing the way you speak are also part of the chat culture. "Ways to Chat Poorly" focuses on pretending to be someone you aren't and flames or attacks online. As we all know, not everyone follows the rules online. The chapter on "Dealing with Inappropriate Behavior" covers the kinds of inappropriate behavior you might run into online and how to avoid them or handle them if you have to.

Have you ever wondered who's online and why? If so, the chapter titled "Who Are These People, Anyway?" will answer that question. The author's many experiences online provide a good source of information. Other forms of chat, such as MUDs, are also found here. Step-by-step directions will guide you through a Telnet session and show you how to use a MUD. Safety is also an issue that receives attention. Knowing the dangers and types of people to avoid will make your journey online safe and fun.

Chatting online requires some technical know-how to get connected and can be confusing. This book provides the necessary information to sort out the ins and outs of online chatting to give you a firm foundation and sense of self-confidence to get started. Appendix A is a glossary of useful terms, and the accompanying CD provides software (for Windows) that lets you test some of the popular freeware/shareware programs. The writing is user-friendly and easy to read.

Learning to Use the World Wide Web (Academic Version)

Ernest Ackermann

Wilsonville, OR: Franklin, Beedle & Associates, 1997.
(http://www.fbeedle.com). 406p. ISBN: 1-887902-28-7.
Softcover, $18.00.

The intent of *Learning to Use the World Wide Web* is to teach you (whether novice or beginner) how to use the World Wide Web, using Netscape; find what you want; create Web pages so you can publish your own; and learn to use various Internet tools, such as Telnet, Gopher, and FTP. No experience is required. However, many of the exercises require a connection to the Internet to get the most out of them.

The book is organized into nine chapters covering information about the World Wide Web and the Internet. Topics include Web browsers; electronic mail (using Netscape); discussion lists; Usenet news; finding information using search tools; writing Web pages; and Internet tools, such as Gopher, Telnet, and FTP; plus a chapter on legal and ethical issues, privacy, and security.

The text is intended as a self-paced guide or as a supplemental textbook for a class about the Internet/World Wide Web. Within each chapter, the material is presented in an easy-to-read manner, with figures to illustrate the concepts when applicable. Step-by-step examples allow you to follow and apply the material after reading the topic under discussion. Rounding out the chapters are exercises to practice the concepts learned in a chapter. Some exercises are meant to be completed in a classroom environment, with results discussed among members of the class. However, most can be done on your own as well.

If you are a true beginner, the amount of information covered may be a bit overwhelming. But hang in there and you will be able to surf with the best of them. Examples plus a readable style help make the material easy to follow. Appendices are a glossary, Netscape Options and Preferences, Unix electronic mail programs, Eudora, and Java scripts; an index completes the book. Be sure to check out the accompanying Web site for up-to-date links and information. It's also a great way to work on the exercises that require you to go to Web sites, because the text contains links to the sites.

The Little Web Book

Alfred Glossbrenner and Emily Glossbrenner

Berkeley, CA: Peachpit Press, 1996. (http://www.peachpit.com).
244p. ISBN: 0-201-88367-8. Softcover, $14.95.

This "little" book is for people who want to learn what the World Wide Web and Internet have to offer, but don't want to hear the techno-babble of some books nor wade through the hundreds and hundreds of Web sites listed in some other books. The authors are well-known computer book authors with a knack for explaining complex material in a down-to-earth manner.

The book is broken down into five main parts, along with a special "Web Browser Cookbook" section. Part One, "The Web: A World of Possibilities," begins the journey by assuming that you know basically nothing and moving on from there to explain how the Web can change your life, what it is (a little bit of history), and how to get connected, with details about buying modems, getting software, and various options to get your connection. There are some suggestions by the authors about how to start out with an online service and then move to an Internet service provider as your skills and needs grow. Included is a handy checklist of questions to consider when dealing with providers. Part Two, "The Main Internet Features," briefly explores the tools and services provided by the Internet: electronic mail, newsgroups, the World Wide Web, Gopher, Telnet, FTP, and more. Part Three, "Hands-on: How to Really Use the Internet," explores these tools in more detail. It's not a real hands-on approach in the sense that you follow directions and go online, but the information is very practical, with concrete examples and illustrations. "How and Where to Find Things on the Internet" (Part Four) explores search tools. This includes not only the Web but also Veronica, Gopher, and Jughead and even newsgroups and some free resource lists. Part Five, "The World Wide Web in Your Life," explores a number of resources found on the Internet, arranged by subject content. Included are art, books and authors, computer help, education, free software, games, government and politics, home and garden, humor, jobs, medicine, movies and television, personal finance, science, sports, and travel. Whew! Remember that the sites listed here are ones the authors feel are worthy of visiting, based on their own exploration and personal use. Each site has a very detailed description and review to describe what it is about. "The Web Browser Cookbook" details essential browser features, along with how to get a browser ready plus "driving a browser," which covers bookmarks, links, and saving a Web page. The authors offer some helpful tips for mail and newsgroups, including using Netscape for mail, multiple sessions, and more. There's even a little bit about helper applications and Java. An appendix lists the authors' preferences for software to go into an Internet toolkit.

Actually, the name *The Little Web and Internet Book* would probably be more appropriate for this book, as it does cover more than the Web. If you like your reading light, and want to learn the basics and get started with the Web, this is a good beginning source.

NetResearch: Finding Information Online

Daniel J. Barrett

Sebastopol, CA: O'Reilly & Associates, 1997. (**http://www.ora.com**). 240p. ISBN: 1-56592-245-X. Softcover, $24.95.

If you're looking for a book filled with Web sites to get started exploring the Web, this book is not for you. But if you want to learn how to find all those neat Web sites for yourself, plus a lot more, then pick up a copy of *NetResearch*.

This book has a lot of very useful information in it. The chapters on how to get started, basic Web searching, and how to find people, places, and things are very easy to follow, with clear and practical examples and exercises. Some good quizzes at the ends of chapters help you to test your knowledge. Appendices A and B provide the necessary list of some sites to explore plus answers to quizzes. Though not geared specifically to K-12 educators, *NetResearch* is a worthy investment for any teachers who want to acquire the necessary strategies and techniques to use the Internet in their classroom as well as to teach it to their students. *(Courtesy of Multimedia Schools Magazine, Information Today, Inc., Medford, NJ).*

Netscape Communicator 4 for Dummies

Paul Hoffman

Indianapolis, IN: IDG Books Worldwide, 1997.
(**http://www.idgbooks.com**). 360p. (...for Dummies series).
ISBN: 0-7645-0053-8. Softcover, $19.99.

If you pick up this book expecting to learn all about Netscape Communicator, you'll be sorely disappointed. Of the 20 chapters, only 3 cover Netscape. The rest cover general information about the World Wide Web, along with Web sites. Paul Hoffman has authored a number of computer books, and he's not trying to mislead anyone. He states in the preface that this is a book mostly about the World Wide Web in general and somewhat about the product Netscape. Too bad the title doesn't reflect this, because it is rather misleading.

Following the basic genre of the Dummies series, this guide takes a light-hearted and humorous approach to the subject matter. The book targets an audience of beginners or intermediate Web users who want to learn to use the Internet and World Wide Web. It also assumes that you might be interested in creating some Web pages at some point, and does *not* assume that you already have an Internet account or access to the World Wide Web. To begin with, the book introduces you to Netscape: that it is the name of a company as well as a product used to browse the Web. It's easy to forget that some people don't know what "a Netscape" is.

The instructions for obtaining a copy of Netscape version 4 are probably out-of-date, as this was written in 1997 before Netscape (the corporation) and its Web site underwent big changes. Keep this in mind when you want to obtain a copy of Netscape.

The material in this guide is divided into six parts that cover the following areas: Part One, "Wild, Wild Web"; Part Two, "How You See What You Get"; Part Three, "Who's Webbing Now?"; Part Four, "Your Name in Lights"; Part Five, "The Web in the Future"; and Part Six, "The Part of Tens." The Netscape Communicator material is covered mostly in Part Two.

There are not a whole lot of detailed step-by-step directions for using Netscape, compared to other books with similar titles (minus the "for Dummies"). Essentially, you can learn how to browse, move around, enter Web addresses, save files, open a file on your hard disk, and open multiple windows in Netscape. Other Netscape components, such as the electronic mail component called Messenger and Collabra, the news reader, are also discussed. Customizing Netscape is also covered in this chapter. In a later chapter, Composer is briefly mentioned, with a few pages of instructions on the basics. After this, the rest of the material covers general Web information not necessarily related to Netscape Communicator. Other chapters contain topics such as finding resources with search tools; some list important and useful Web sites that try to organize the material on the Web. A chapter on HTML provides the basics behind creating Web pages. You'll need additional material if you are seriously interested in authoring Web pages, either through HTML or using Communicator.

As stated previously, this book is more about the World Wide Web than about Netscape Communicator as the title implies. If you want an in-depth guide to the Communicator software, this book won't do it for you. Try one of the other titles out there that really do cover Netscape in depth.

Netscape Official Guide to Internet Research

Tara Calishain

Research Triangle Park, NC: Ventana Communications Group, 1997. (http://www.coppersky.com/ongir/). 450p. ISBN: 1-56604-604-1. Softcover, $29.99.

Here's another book directed at locating information on the Web. Although this book is not aimed at the K-12 community exclusively, it is a very useful source for anyone wishing to expand their capabilities of researching topics on the Internet. The title is a bit misleading, in that "research" does not really mean scholarly information, but simply locating many kinds of information.

Twenty-one chapters cover such topics as "The Internet Research Overview"; technical issues such as configuring Netscape; using plug-ins and helper applications; plus help with mailing lists, newsgroups, and other Internet tools such as Gopher, Telnet, and, of course, the World Wide Web.

The really helpful chapters are those that break down areas of the Internet to research, including domestic government information, international resources, business and professional resources, and (of particular interest to educators) resources for student research.

To get off to a good start in using the Internet to do research, read Chapter 10, "Friendly Suggestions for Internet Research." It provides suggestions for getting the most out of your time searching the 'Net. In fact, it's a great way to teach students how to get started doing research on the Internet. Very practical and helpful.

"Searching on the World Wide Web" focuses on search engines, with examples from the most popular ones such as InfoSeek, Lycos, and AltaVista. Each description includes hot tips and facts on simple and advanced searches plus the scope of the search engine. Chapter 13, "Resources for Student Research," is not a comprehensive listing of subjects or Web sites. Rather, it intends to introduce the reader to reference tools such as Research-IT or the Virtual Reference Desk as means for locating more information and sites on the Web, rather than merely listing pages and pages of sites.

Overall, this guide has a lot to offer. Teachers and students can learn some tricks of the trade in getting starting locating resources. The style is easy to read and the author covers the essentials necessary to make good headway in your mining of the Internet. *(Courtesy of Multimedia Schools Magazine, Information Today, Inc., Medford, NJ)*. **Note:** A second edition is out, but I was unable to get a copy in time to include it in this book.

Researching on the Internet

Robin Rowland and Dave Kinnaman

Rocklin, CA: Prima Publishing, 1995. (**http://www.primapub.com**).
384p. ISBN: 0-7615-0063-4. Softcover, $29.95.

Anyone who has attempted to find something specific on the Internet knows that it can be a daunting task. With so much information available, even with capable search tools, it can take a long time to get what you want. Still, the Internet is one of the most important research tools today. With its 24 hours/365 days of service, there is nothing like it. That's not to say the Internet is a panacea for all research needs, but it is definitely an important resource. Today, more and more students, teachers, librarians, businesspeople, and families can make use of the Internet's vast resources with a computer and modem. Being an effective searcher, however, may require some time spent learning about searching effectively. Anyone who knows they are going to be using the Internet for research will appreciate this guide to almost every aspect of successful Internet searching.

Fifteen chapters cover a wide range of topics: getting started; choosing an access method; getting ready for research; the various Internet research tools; how to focus your goals; libraries on the Internet; using e-mail to interview people; and, of course, chapters that provide specific resources. There is something for everyone. If you already have a connection and know something about the Internet, then skip the introductory material and move on to the meat of getting started with research. For librarians who know about search strategies but need some more help with the specific search tools on the Internet, there is a chapter that deals with these details.

What sets this book apart from some other "researching the Internet" books is the amount of time devoted to getting ready to research. Let's face it, surfing the Web is not researching. A search is only going to be as effective and successful as the time spent developing a search strategy or plan before you hit those first keys and type in some words. There are very specific tips and suggestions for planning an effective search. Examples illustrate how to use Boolean and proximity operators to narrow a search or broaden it as necessary. Answers to the question of whether to work online or offline will depend on the access method and cost for being online. After preparing a plan and finding some information, it's necessary to seriously evaluate the material found. The Internet is not a refereed journal or professionally prepared database. There is an evaluation checklist to help sort through some of the main points to address when searching.

One drawback to the book is its older date of 1995. In Chapter 4, "Internet Research Tools," it's more obvious that some of the information is dated or even out-of-date. Unfortunately, the Web and its tools have undergone a lot of change since this title appeared. Some of the e-mail and Web software has changed or is no longer used anymore, and tools like Jughead, Veronica, and Gopher are not used nearly as much today. There is a chapter full of details on using FTP. Today, it's possible to use the World Wide Web to FTP software or files using a browser like Netscape or Internet Explorer. The one chapter that probably dates the book even more is "Researching on the World Wide Web," which is only a small chapter compared to one on FTP and even Gopher. Today the Web has taken over as the most important resource for researching the Internet. You'll probably notice that some of the browsers and sites no longer exist.

The standard "history of the Internet" chapter is done somewhat differently in this guide. Most noticeably, it's not first, but is presented later in the book. The idea is to absorb the feel of the Internet by using it for a while, then go back and look at what makes it the incredible tool it has become. To do this, the authors highlight some of the original Net creators and users, such as Michael Hart, the Project Gutenberg creator; William Connelly, a librarian who created an online Holocaust memorial museum; and others. Along with a description of their work is a "Tips for Researchers" section that includes their personal thoughts on researching on the Internet. Knowing how to send e-mail, reply properly, participate in mailing lists and newsgroups, and generally be a good Internet user are covered in a chapter on netiquette. Some excellent suggestions, as well as sources for more information, are included in this chapter.

Researching on the Internet does give you very practical material with specific examples of projects that made use of the Internet. At the time this book was written, it was a very vital resource. Today, because of the dated material, it is not as unique. There are newer books out today that will offer more current information when it comes to search tools, browsers, and even resources. The most helpful material is the search strategy and research suggestions and tips found in the earlier chapters. The writing style is easy to read and the technical information is explained in plain English. Screen shots help illustrate Web sites as well as directions for downloading or installing software.

Researching on the World Wide Web: Spend More Time Learning, Not Searching

Cynthia N. James-Catalano

Rocklin, CA: Prima Publishing, 1996. (**http://www.primapublishing.com**). 357p. ISBN: 0-7615-0686-1. Softcover, $24.99. (Includes CD-ROM).

Although this book has a 1996 date, the concepts and information presented are still very useful. It's not meant to be a book of 500 Web sites, but a reference guide to explain how to do research on the World Wide Web. Sometimes those new to electronic research, especially on the Internet, do not even understand the differences between using an index tool or a search engine.

The author's approach is informative and very conversational, which makes reading the material easy for anyone. The book does assume some Internet experience; that is, that you know the basics of surfing the 'Net before beginning. The material is divided into three parts. Part One is "Research Tools," Part Two is "Search Strategies," and Part Three is "Appendices."

Part One covers all the different types of research tools, as well as a basic introduction to the Web; it explains how the Web works, what home pages are, links, sites, and all the basics encountered when navigating the Web. But there is no tutorial or step-by-step directions for using a browser. These are skills you'll need to acquire elsewhere before you begin to learn to do research.

There's no doubt the Web has changed how people do research. It's opened up a whole new set of possibilities for obtaining information. But the author also recognizes that there are times the Web is not the most suitable tool for finding what you need, and offers examples. When you need a word spelled, or a quick definition, there are probably print tools (such as dictionaries or encyclopedias) that will answer your question faster. Another example does show the datedness of some of the material. The author mentions that finding tax forms is not a good choice for the Web. Maybe when this book was written that was the case, but not today. They are available in PDF formats that can be downloaded and printed very easily. And many of the more obscure forms are now available as well.

There are separate chapters on indexes and search engines, which cover how they work and offer examples of each type. Surprisingly, with this older date, the most important search tools are still covered. Besides search engines, online libraries are invaluable tools for research. If you aren't sure what these are, this chapter spells it out and explains when you might find one a handy tool.

Often background material is necessary for a good research project. Using LISTSERVs and newsgroups might not be the first thing that comes to mind for this, but they are often excellent tools for contacting experts or locating discussions on research topics.

In Part Two, the author explores all about search strategies, starting with "Where Do You Begin?," which is a good question. The material covered here is applicable to almost any research project. Knowing what you want and where to look for it—no matter whether you are using print indices, a professionally developed electronic resource, or the Internet—is important. Using the Web for research entails a bit more work on the researcher's part. Knowing what tool to use is the first step. Being aware of when to start over, after following some results in a search that seem to lead nowhere, is also important. Finally, using the Web means spending some time evaluating what you find, as information on the

Internet is not necessarily peer-reviewed. It's important to ascertain the quality of the information. The rest of Part Two contains chapters on search strategies for searching the following areas: business, education, genealogy, government information, the Internet, medical information, music, news, reference and literature, and science.

Several helpful appendices round out the book. Appendix A is "How to Cite Internet Sites," focusing on tips for Internet citation elements and giving examples. Appendix B is "Cyberlibrarian FAQs," offering questions and answers about access, some more general Internet facts, and lots of other interesting questions. The final appendix is "Experts on the Web," which is a good resource giving specific addresses of experts in various fields of study. A glossary is also included. The CD that accompanies the book provides an encyclopedia for the World Wide Web. It offers more than 500 in-depth definitions, plus cross-linked terms, references to print sources, tutorials, and step-by-step directions to Web activities.

For anyone who needs to do research on the Web, having a guide like this can prepare you with the kind of information to make your research successful and effective.

Sams Teach Yourself the Internet: Quick Steps for Fast Results

Galen Grimes

Indianapolis, IN: Sams Publishing, 1998.
(http://www.samspublishing.com). 185p. ISBN: 0-672-31320-0.
Softcover, $12.99.

Ten minutes may be a slight exaggeration unless you've taken a speed-reading course and have a photographic memory. Although it is a quick read, you might want to set aside more time to cover these 23 chapters. The book covers basically all you need to know and a little bit more about the Internet and its tools. Though the introduction states that the book is for anyone "using a Windows or Mac platform," there is a definite Microsoft Windows flavor to it, with a lot of material about Internet Explorer, ActiveX, and other Windows-based Microsoft products. For example, in the chapter on hardware and software, it states, "While it is possible to access the World Wide Web with any computer that will run Windows 3.1…"; there is no mention of Macintosh as a possibility. Beginning with an overview of the Internet, necessary equipment, and how to get connected, the book assumes that you are accessing the 'Net through a service provider, not a local area network or online service. Brief descriptions of Internet tools, such as Gopher, chat, FTP, e-mail, Usenet news, and the World

Wide Web, precede a discussion of Internet Explorer as a browser. Several of Internet Explorer's interesting features are covered, such as how to subscribe to a Web site and then select and set up a schedule to download those pages regularly. This feature allows offline reading of Web pages and can be a help if you are paying for service by the hour. ActiveX Controls, which enhance Internet Explorer's capabilities, are explained in a separate chapter. Instructions are given for downloading ActiveX from the Microsoft Web site.

Netscape Navigator, still the most popular Web browser (at this writing), receives attention in a chapter that has details on downloading the software, installing it, and then using it to browse the Web. Setting bookmarks, as well as using Netscape's plug-ins such as Live Audio and QuickTime, are also covered. There are directions for accessing the site and downloading the software. Subsequent chapters devote pages to search engines, e-mail, Usenet news, Internet Relay Chat, Internet telephones, and push technology.

The language is friendly and the material easy to follow. The book does give you enough to get started. It offers tips and shortcuts along with some cautions and pitfalls to avoid along the way. The screen shots illustrate various points being made. If you are a Windows user, this book will appeal to you more than if you use other platforms.

Search Engines for the World Wide Web

Alfred Glossbrenner and Emily Glossbrenner

Berkeley, CA: Peachpit Press, 1998. (**http://www.peachpit.com**). 228p. (Visual Quickstart Guide series). ISBN: 0-201-69642-8. Softcover, $16.95.

Are you one of the growing number of people who are tired of surfing aimlessly on the Internet, trying to find what you want? Maybe you like to surf sometimes but other times you want to get on and off quickly with the information you need. Today it's easier to do that. There are many excellent search tools to choose from. But how do you know which one(s) are best for you? This guide is an excellent resource for anyone who needs answers to these questions. Another of the successful Visual Quickstart Guides from Peachpit Press, this book will demystify the process of searching on the Internet and open your eyes to the possibilities.

Search Engines for the World Wide Web is organized into three main parts. Part One, "Getting Comfortable with Search Basics," offers several chapters on how search engines work, creating an effective search strategy by choosing the best words or phrases, and the basics of search tools. There is an excellent chapter that describes Boolean operators, proximity operators, and how these are interpreted on the Web. An especially helpful section focuses on the difference in searching with keywords in a professionally prepared database or online catalog, as opposed to searching on the World Wide Web. Once you understand some of the key differences, you'll be able to create more effective searches. Did you ever stop to think about how to choose the most effective words? For example, the authors illustrate what would happen if someone typed in "tigers" expecting to find out about the animal. You'd also get any sports team named "Tigers" as well. Choosing very explicit keywords is extremely important. Using "Siberian Tiger" or "Bengal Tiger," rather than the much more general word "tiger," will get better results.

Part Two, "Using the Leading Search Engines," provides six chapters with detailed information about AltaVista, Excite, HotBot, Infoseek, Lycos, and Yahoo, the most important search engines out there today. Each chapter zeroes in on the main features, basic search techniques, advanced searching, and lots of helpful information to make you a better and more effective searcher. It's not necessary to read all the chapters. Choose two search tools you know you want to use. Go right to those chapters and skip the others. There are all kinds of useful tips provided for each search engine.

Sometimes the broad search engines may not be the best tool for locating a specific piece of information you need. Part Three, "Using Specialized Search Engines," has chapters on how to search for newsgroups, mailing lists, subject guides, people, directories, and everything from authors to zip codes.

Appendix A is a quick reference to the search engines. It has the most important commands and basic information for each search engine in a chart format. Appendix B contains Internet domain and country codes. Appendix C lists newsgroup hierarchies, and the final appendix is a searcher's toolkit full of essential ones for Windows users.

The Glossbrenners' book is a valuable tool. With a succinct writing style and many graphics, it's appropriate for any beginner or anyone who just wants to learn more about search engines. The handy charts and search engines quick reference are handy to keep by your computer. More and more books are being written about searching on the Web. This is one of the best.

Searching and Researching on the Internet & World Wide Web

Ernest Ackermann and Karen Hartman

Wilsonville, OR: Franklin, Beedle & Associates, 1998.
(http://www.fbeedle.com). 477p. ISBN: 1-887902-26-0.
Softcover, $29.95. (Includes CD and floppy disk).

Written as a textbook for college-level courses teaching the Internet or for anyone who wants to teach themselves how to search successfully on the Internet, this guide can also be used by pre-service and in-service teachers or librarians. Actually, it's a great source for anyone who wants to learn to "search smart" on the Internet and World Wide Web. The author assumes that you have knowledge of computers, the ability to use applications, and access to the Internet, so that you can follow and work through the exercises provided in the book.

Essentially, the text covers creating successful search strategies; understanding Boolean logic and proximity operators; evaluating information; and citing resources found on the Internet. Step-by-step instructions take you through the material, along with appropriate exercises afterward to test your understanding of the facts learned. The platform for the exercises and sample screen shots is Windows. Netscape Navigator 4.0 is the browser used throughout.

The book is organized into 14 chapters, with an introduction to the Internet and Web and material on how to use a Web browser, as well as an introduction to research skills and the various tools used on the World Wide Web. Subject directories and virtual libraries, as well as search strategies and tools such as meta-search engines, specialized databases, and other resources like FTP, white pages services, address locators, and e-mail, are all covered. There are important chapters that teach how to evaluate information and cite what you find, followed by sample research projects that allow you to "put it all together."

This is a very good textbook. The material is written in an easy-to-read style. The information is detailed and well organized. The accompanying CD has Netscape Navigator 4 on it, to make it easy to work along with the exercises. The floppy disk contains HTML pages for the exercises and projects in the chapters with embedded links. The platform is Windows.

Searching Smart on the World Wide Web

Cheryl Gould

San Carlos, CA: Library Solutions Press, 1998.
(http://www.library-solutions.com). 100p. ISBN: 1-882208-28-5.
Softcover, $40.00. (Includes floppy disk).

Teachers realize the importance of the Internet in their classrooms. Finding relevant sites to add to their curricula is important. Teachers are also busy people, and let's face it, searching the vast World Wide Web can be a frustrating experience for even the best surfers. Sometimes you need a little help to learn the skills to search effectively. Here's a book that will guide you through all the techniques, skills, and practices necessary to become an efficient and smart searcher.

Written as a tutorial or workbook, it includes lessons on the World Wide Web as an information resource, Web construction, building blocks of search tools, types of search tools and how they work, and setting bookmarks, plus assessing your search results and searching smarter. The material is presented in a series of lessons. Information about the topic is followed by self-paced exercises to test what you've learned. The material does not cover searching on Gopher, FTP, or Telnet, just the World Wide Web. You will need a connection to the Internet to complete the exercises and view the examples. There is some overlap in some of the lessons, especially on search engines and directories, but each one offers something useful so you won't waste your time if you go through all the chapters. The accompanying floppy disk provides a file of Netscape bookmarks and a folder containing Internet Explorer favorites that go along with the chapter on bookmarks.

Teachers who want to become more effective and successful searchers will find this valuable tool an excellent resource to teach themselves, as well as for instructing their students in how to "search smart" on the Web.

Teach Yourself Netscape Navigator Visually

Ruth Maran

Indianapolis, IN: IDG Books Worldwide, 1997.
(http://www.idgbooks.com). 320p. (IDG's 3-D Visual series).
ISBN: 0-7645-6028-X. Softcover, $29.99.

This book is by the same author who wrote *Teach Yourself the Internet and World Wide Web Visually*, as well as many other computer-related titles. It offers the same simple visual approach to teaching the use of Netscape Navigator. The illustrations are in full color and, along with the straightforward approach used in the text, work well to create a very easy way to learn. Rather than just talking about what to do, the visual approach can give you a sense of actually using the program.

The book discusses topics such as how to install and set up Netscape Communicator; the characteristics of the Netscape Professional version; basics about Web addresses and how to enter them; hypertext; bookmarks; how to browse all kinds of pages that present sound, animation, and movies; plus Communicator's e-mail component.

For anyone who likes a visual approach to learning, this guide will be a good investment. Keep in mind, however, that versions of Netscape have most probably changed, so that the screen illustrations may not be exactly the same. Make sure to get the latest version of the book.

Teach Yourself the Internet and World Wide Web Visually

Ruth Maran

Indianapolis, IN: IDG Books Worldwide, 1997.
(**http://www.idgbooks.com/**). 303p. (IDG's 3-D Visual series).
ISBN: 0-7645-6020-4. Softcover, $29.99.

With more than 300 pages full of color screen shots to illustrate the Internet and World Wide Web, this visually oriented guide's intent is to teach anyone all about the Internet/Web in a simple, straightforward manner. As each new point is presented, the drawings help to explain the content graphically. The concept seems to fit with the graphical nature of the World Wide Web and Internet. It is intended for beginners through intermediates. Along with the illustrations are easy-to-read instructions and concise information.

The 16 chapters present a pretty comprehensive look at the Internet and World Wide Web, covering such basics as connecting; using Internet tools such as FTP, Telnet, and Gopher; the Web and its features; electronic mail and mailing lists; newsgroups; and searching for information, plus a lot more. The illustrations are very colorful and often take up more of the page than the text—but sometimes it really is easier just to read the text to get the meaning. Other times, especially if you are really new to all this stuff, the visual cues can be very helpful. For example, when discussing modems, the illustration helps to see what one might look like. Sometimes, however, the graphics seem a bit superfluous, as they don't really help you to "see" the idea any better. The chapters on connecting go into a lot of detail about connection terms, modem choices and possibilities, and service providers. There is even a service provider listing accompanying this section. The chapters on the kind of information available on the Internet cover all types of possibilities and give a beginner a good idea of what's out there and in what format. The World Wide Web receives its own chapter and covers Netscape; Internet Explorer; Lynx; Web page characteristics; how to surf securely and safely; plug-ins and helper applications, such as Shockwave, Java, ActiveX; and more. Obviously, this set of chapters has a particular appeal for a visual approach, especially for topics like hypertext or home pages. It is also helpful when explaining the concept of Java and Java applets. Illustrating how a search engine works is very appealing presented this way. When referring to robots, the concept makes more sense when viewed visually. There are additional chapters on games, and one that introduces the concept of intranets, a popular form of network access. The glossary is even illustrated. Can you image the ones for "flame wars" and "flaming"? Many of the terms in the glossary were new to me, including "puppy," "warez," and more.

The visual approach taken by this book will not necessarily appeal to all beginners to the Internet. If you don't need a lot of visual cues to learn, then you probably won't want to buy this book. On the other hand, if you like to visualize things to learn them, you'll be well on your way by reading this book.

10 Minute Guide to the Internet and the World Wide Web, 2d Edition

Galen Grimes

Indianapolis, IN: Que, 1996. (http://www.mcp.com/publishers/que/). 208p. (Ten Minute Guide to . . .). ISBN: 0-7897-0909-0. Softcover, $14.99.

Busy? But you know you need to get started using the Internet? Here's a guide with 23 mini-lessons that take about 10 minutes each to go through. You won't learn the history or in-depth information, but the chapters take you from hardware and software selections and choosing an Internet service provider through learning to browse with Netscape or Internet Explorer, setting bookmarks, and using search engines to locate information, plus lessons on chat, newsgroups, e-mail, and the lesser-used tools such as Gopher, Archie, and Veronica. As well, there are chapters on accessing the Internet through online services such as America Online, CompuServe, Prodigy, and Microsoft, and the advantages and disadvantages of using them. Several lessons provide detailed instructions for configuring your software for Windows, Macintosh, and UNIX platforms.

Read it cover-to-cover or select the chapters you want. Either way, it's a handy little guide to keep next to your computer. When you have a few spare minutes, crank up your computer, choose one of the lessons, and off you go!

The language is easy to understand. No real frills, but the screen shots help illustrate Web sites or points being taught. Not geared to educators; nevertheless, if all you want is a quick read on the Internet and Web, this is a good little source to have.

Web Search Strategies

Bryan Pfaffenberger

New York: MIS Press, 1996. (http://www.mispress.com). 427p. ISBN: 1-55828-470-2. Softcover, $29.95.

The 1996 date makes this book somewhat outdated in parts. But there aren't very many books that cover this topic as comprehensively. The book still contains a lot of useful information about strategies for searching the Web. Just keep in mind that information about search engines has undoubtedly changed.

This guide is more appropriate for an intermediate or advanced Internet user, especially one who is serious about learning how to search using power search techniques. It's not a book for the casual "type-in-a-few-words" kind of searcher. Librarians, teachers, students, businesspeople, or anyone who wants to know how to search effectively will benefit from reading it.

Pfaffenberger is the author of numerous Internet books, including *The World Wide Web Bible*. He has created a seven-step strategy for locating information on the Internet and World Wide Web. His approach is quite comprehensive and allows you to learn strategies to be able to locate just about any document you are interested in on any topic. The book is divided into 7 parts (the seven-step strategy) and contains 28 chapters. Basically, the seven steps include: Know What You're Up Against; Find Something That's Relevant; Learn the Techniques of Deep Searching; Perform a Deep Search; Explore Specialized Search Resources; Keep Up with the News; and Give Something Back.

Beginning with the presumption that the Web is a difficult place to find information, the author surveys why that's the case and helps you see what you have to understand to be successful in searching. This introductory section explores some basics about hypertext, which is the essential component of Web pages. Pfaffenberger believes that you need a lot of help to find the information you're looking for and that's what his book is all about—providing the strategies to educate surfers about searching successfully. After a brief survey of Web tools, starting point tools as well as search engines and subject directories are discussed, with illustrations of those in each category. There is a lot of information here. Spiders, subject directories, distributed subject trees, and so on are some of the tools you'll learn about. Most people don't have a clue as to the distinction between search tools. If you are serious about learning, then this section will provide an understanding of the various structures important when preparing a search strategy.

Getting down to the nitty gritty happens in Chapter 3, with an introduction to "deep searching." Here's where Boolean operators come into play. Understanding how to use them is crucial to a successful "deep" search. InfoSeek, Open Text, Lycos, Inktomi, Yahoo, and TradeWave Galaxy are featured. Some of these have changed names or no longer exist. Inktomi now powers many search sites; HotBot, as one of them, is now one of the most popular search tools at this writing. Excite NetSearch is now Excite.

Along with details on the various engines, specialized search sources are also included. Here's where some valuable information lies. At times you may need a specialized resource to locate a very specific type of information. Web-based reference sources for locating general-interest as well as special-interest topics reveal all kinds of possibilities. Topics may include colleges and universities, book publishers, literacy, maps, measurements, movies, religion, and lots more. Among other specialized search sources are news, weather, businesses, government, databases, Internet resources, software, people, and careers. The final step is to give back by publishing your own "trailblazer" page or hotlist page.

If you decide to buy this book, be aware that a lot of material has changed, particularly Web sites and descriptions of what a Web site contains. For example, the Weather Channel Web site is an excellent source for current weather today, but back in 1996 it wasn't as supercharged as it is today, so the description is not really up-to-date. Other search engine books have been published since this one and contain more current descriptions of the search engines and tools. You may want to look at some of them if your real interest lies in keeping current.

Chapter 2://Internet Books for Educators and Librarians

Introduction

Among the many Internet books published today are a group written expressly for educators and librarians. These titles focus on the K-12 environment and consider issues of importance to teachers, librarians, and administrators. Many are written by educators or librarians. Included in most of these books are issues of funding, how to get started learning about the Internet, how to connect, how to choose a service provider, and why it's important to use the Internet in the classroom. In some cases, the book also presents ideas for projects and includes Web sites to visit or for use in the curriculum. Occasionally, the books contain projects, lesson plans, and Web sites, but if it is included in this chapter, the focus is on the Internet and its tools, not the curriculum. The books explain how to use the many tools and resources, such as e-mail, the World Wide Web, Gopher, Telnet, and FTP.

Some titles include all of the Internet resources; others may be much more focused and discuss one aspect or a type of software or only one issue, such as funding. Formats can include tutorials with hands-on instruction activities or guides with step-by-step instructions.

America Online for Teachers

Bard Williams

Foster City, CA: IDG Books Worldwide, 1996. (**http://www.idgbooks.com**). 384p. (...for Dummies series). ISBN: 1-56884-697-5. Softcover, $24.99. (Includes CD-ROM).

Another in the series of Dummies books, this one targets teachers who want to learn all about accessing the Internet through the commercial service America Online. Because it's geared to teachers, the examples and activities focus on education-related materials. The book comes with a CD that includes America Online software and system requirements, as well as instructions on how to install America Online and create network preferences. It's for both Macintosh and Windows users.

The book is divided into five parts. The author intends the book to be used as either a tutorial that can be followed chapter-by-chapter or as a reference source where you use specific chapters as you need them.

Part One, "AOL Primer," covers a little of the history of America Online. Reading this gives you a perspective on how AOL fits into the world of online services. The authors offer information on how AOL compares to Internet service providers, the pricing structure of AOL, and its advantages. Part Two, "AOL Educator's Tour," explains how AOL is set up, how the software works, and basics about the interface when you sign on. This is a good chapter to read to understand how America Online is organized and works and why it can be a good choice for educators. There are a lot of details on getting up and running, good places to begin exploring, and how to navigate using AOL's menus and toolbars. In this section, there are some tutorials that take you through some of the shortcuts for storing "favorite places" that you visit, as well as other specialized AOL features. The authors are high on America Online and their enthusiasm shows in their descriptions throughout the book.

Part Three is "AOL in Your Classroom," which discusses some of the considerations necessary for bringing the Internet into a classroom: how it changes your teaching from being a "sage on the stage" and can "build a community of learners" with you as the "guide on the side." Educators can learn some tips about how to teach students to be good "netizens," the ethics of telecommunications, and what is expected from them in the classroom. There's a good section on how to manage AOL in a classroom, with specifics on managing students, content, and instruction. Finally, the financial aspect of bringing AOL into your class is discussed, with suggestions for funding opportunities and how to explore ways to make it available at your school. "Marketing 101 for Teachers" offers tips on how teachers can make the most of their skills to get the word out and obtain support from the community.

Part Four, "Online Projects by the Tens," presents chapters on how to be successful with online projects, along with many ideas for using America Online in the classroom. Included are 10 online projects for elementary classrooms, middle schools, and high schools, and for K-12 classes in general. Each lesson has a set of goals, objectives, and step-by-step directions to implement them. Part Five is the appendices, which include a glossary, AOL keywords, and troubleshooting tips. "About the America Online CD" is also included.

Educators using America Online will find this guide a useful tool to have on hand. It's a good resource for learning about the service as well as for online projects, tips, and suggestions for creating a successful Internet experience in your classroom.

Best Bet Internet: Reference and Research
When You Don't Have Time to Mess Around

Shirley Duglin Kennedy

Chicago, IL: American Library Association, 1998.
(http://www.ala.org/editions). 194p. ISBN: 0-8389-0712-1.
Softcover, $35.00.

Today it's often frustrating for busy librarians who want to locate a specific piece of information—only to find it seems to take forever to do so. For any librarian who feels this way, or perhaps if you're just starting out and want to get a good foundation on effective reference using the Internet, here's a book written by a librarian who has been there, seen that, and come up with a tool to help. After reading this book, frustrated librarians will have the ammunition to search the Internet effectively and successfully.

The 12 chapters are presented by type of resource and include indexes, subject trees and resource catalogs, virtual libraries and newsrooms, major Web search engines, all-in-one pages, e-mail databases, mailing lists and newsgroups, Gopher, Telnet, and finding help and software. Each chapter describes the type of resource under discussion and then lists several excellent examples of sites to use. Many are ones you will recognize right away, whereas others will be completely new to you.

Terminology used by the author may be slightly different (or perhaps more detailed is a better way to say it) than in other search guides. But whether you call them *parallel search engines* or *meta-search engines* or *mega-search engines* isn't really important. If you can understand how they work, that's what counts. The real substance of the book is the number of resources you can learn about to help you choose just the right one for your reference need.

The descriptions are excellent, giving you a real idea of how the sites work. You'll learn what's good and not so good about search tools. Of course, the Web is the featured player, but space is also given to the oldies, such as Gopher, Telnet, and FTP, in a chapter titled "Intelligent Life Outside the Web." There are wonderful technical support resources on the Internet, which are examined in the chapter titled "Computers and Computing." With more than 500 sites listed, it's impossible to remember them all, but having a handy resource like this guide will give you a beginning point. And you'll have this as a reference tool for the future.

Knowing how to use the Internet is one skill. Knowing how to locate pertinent information in a timely manner on the Internet is a different set of skills. Thousands of hits for a topic are not always a good thing—not when all you really want is just that one site with exactly the information you need.

To be a successful searcher, it's important to understand why it's hard to find information. *Best Bet* offers a look at some of the reasons, including lack of authority control, lack of quality control, ephemeral nature of resources, and technical instability and limitation. After becoming aware of pitfalls, getting started is the next step. Having some good starting places makes searching easier. Therefore, in two chapters, the author covers  "Starting Points," with examples of indices, resource catalogs, and subject trees. You don't have to remember which is a subject tree or subject directory or resource catalog to use them, but it's helpful to understand the two ways to locate information (browsing versus searching). There are several "old-timers," such as BUBL and Galaxy. Yahoo is included as well. A definition of subject trees helps you understand what they are and descriptions of the chosen subject trees let you compare what they do. Examples are The Argus Clearinghouse and the WWW Virtual Library.

After reading this section, you'll have an understanding of how they operate and differ from the other subject directories. Essentially, these sites are collections of pathfinders put together by experts in the subject area. Most contain resources in a particular subject.

The book explores "Selective Subject Catalogs" integrated with many search engines, such as Excite, Lycos, WebCrawler Select, and Point Top 5% Reviews. These sites select the "best" of certain subject areas to offer. They often have reviews or ratings attached to them. There are some good suggestions for well-known sites, as well as lesser-known ones that provide a certain feature or quality useful to individuals. Here are such sites as "Nerd World Media," "WebDictionary," and "PC Magazine's Top 100 Web Sites." There are subject-specific sites for research in areas such as business and government as well. Some of the more important Web sites associated with these topics are described.

The ways librarians and journalists have contributed to reference sources on the Internet are covered in a chapter that describes virtual reference desks. These have been around since Gopher and illustrate how librarians can use their expertise to create meaningful Web sites. For example, one of the first is "Librarians' Index to the Internet," created by the Berkeley Public Library in California. INFOMINE illustrates the best of the virtual libraries in an academic setting, with more than 10,000 links to scholarly resources. Of course, the Internet Public Library has established itself as the foremost such site for the Internet and is well known by most librarians who use the Internet. This chapter is a gold mine of information about many little-known sites that offer a great deal in the way of reference tools.

Best Bet contains descriptions and reviews of hundreds of sites that can be used as reference tools by librarians. By dividing the material into types of catalogs, the author helps you learn the features and differences in various search tools. Knowing a bit about how they work will help you make an effective decision as to which tool to use for your purposes.

Bread & Butter of the Internet: A Primer and Presentation Packet for Educators

Virtual Dave Lankes

Syracuse, NY: ERIC Clearinghouse on Information and
Technology, 1996. (**http://www.askeric.org/ithome**). 133p.
ISBN: 0-937597-41-4. Spiral notebook, $20.00.

The target audience for this "primer" is the classroom teacher and library media specialist new to the Internet. The author's goal is to provide a way for teachers to gain enough confidence so that they want to learn more. The primer constitutes the first half of the book; the second half is a set of presentations that can be used as overheads or handouts.

Bread & Butter is a bit dated, but even so there's material worth reading. The introductory chapters about networks cover more technical information than many similar books, but the author feels it's important to understand the basics and that this understanding will make teachers more effective in using the Internet. The examples and explanations are very easy to understand.

Like many Internet books, this one covers Gopher, e-mail, the Web, and other tools. The author, "Virtual Dave" as he is often known, emphasizes the role that library media specialists should play in setting up the Internet in schools. He firmly believes that a close relationship among parents, educators, and the community is important for a successful plan to emerge. *(Courtesy of Multimedia Schools Magazine, Information Today, Inc., Medford, NJ).*

Building a Web-Based Education System

Colin McCormack and David Jones

New York: John Wiley & Sons, 1998. (**http://www.wiley.com/compbooks**). 451p. ISBN 0-471-19162-0. Softcover, $49.99. (Includes CD-ROM).

Have you been thinking about getting involved with distance learning, or perhaps just learning more about what's involved with a Web-based instructional course? This practical, step-by-step book takes you through the whole process. Organized much like any design process, the chapters cover analysis, planning and design, implementation, testing and evaluation, and maintenance. The authors state that the target audience is any educator who wants to understand what's necessary to implement a Web-based instructional class; the ultimate goal of the book is to provide a combination of theoretical information, possibilities for using the Web, and some nuts and bolts about networks, hardware, and software. It is hoped that this book will serve as a resource with enough material that, after reading the chapters and doing the exercises, you will be able to have a good foundation for building your own Web-based education system. Because this book is really about creating an entire course online, college faculty are probably more likely to find the material relevant than most in the K-12 community.

The "Analysis" chapter looks at some very good questions to consider when deciding whether to implement an online system. Administrative procedures, Internet access policies, and workload considerations, as well as colleagues and superiors, can all affect an online course. This chapter is full of things to think about. The "Planning and Design" section begins the first real steps to implementing a site and is therefore very important to the success of a project. Here, lists of goals as well as potential problems or concerns to think about are discussed. Both administrative and Web design questions are presented. Case studies help illustrate the topics in a concrete way. "Content Development" is the next chapter, which looks at how to select and organize material for your Web site. The question of browser characteristics in handling various multimedia components is reviewed. This is really a chapter of "possibilities" for content, including kinds of file formats; creating video, sound, and animation; all about links and viewing tools; and helper applications, as well as more technical considerations, such as getting your material distributed as well as using files offline with CD-ROMs and floppy disks. Take a deep breath, because there is a lot of information contained in this chapter.

The chapter on "Distributing Information" helps you understand how to use the Web as a distribution environment, with an examination of the components involved, what you can and cannot do, materials needed, and some troubleshooting help. The process for creating an information distribution system is done step-by-step, from defining what you want to designing access to the distribution methods. "Enabling Communication" discusses the importance of the electronic communication component to a Web-based education system. Theoretical aspects of interaction and computer-mediated communication are both discussed. A section on advantages of electronic communication in various models gives you an overview of the choices. This material, which includes how to choose the tool for communication along with examples of agents available, presents a lot to think about. Chats, MOOs, and MUDs also receive attention. So many possibilities may seem overwhelming to a beginner, so a nice set of charts helps illustrate them in an easy-to-read manner.

"Online Student Assessment" discusses why assessment is necessary and why online assessments offer some new possibilities. Success factors and forms of assessment are covered. Screen shots and charts illustrate the various topics under discussion. It's necessary to understand some of the technical workings of some programs, such as Java and Cookies, to get the most out of this information. "Class Management" is a component of any class and an online course is no exception. After a description of what is meant by the phrase, the authors go through what is necessary before, during, and after a class and why the Web is a useful tool for class management activities. There are samples of the components for class photos, attendance, and records. "A Comparison of Web Classroom Builders" is a very useful chapter because it offers some choices for tools to help create your Web course. WebCT, a formerly free software program now available commercially, is described in detail for creating an online course. Webfuse and TopClass are also compared as creation tools. The final chapter is "Setting Up and Maintaining a Web-Based Education System," which covers setting up components of the system as well as what is necessary to maintain the system once up and running. This is mostly technical in content about Web servers, file servers, etc.

This is a very comprehensive book on creating a Web course. Not only does it have a lot of detailed information on theories and background information, but it also has practical, step-by-step directions for working through the whole process. This is where you can actually begin to see how to do it, not just why.

If you are serious about getting up and running with an online course, and have the Web basics down, this is a tool that can take you through the entire process from analysis through evaluation and maintenance. Don't expect to be an expert with one reading. You will probably find that this is a book you have to study, not just read over once. Make use of the case studies and samples, examples, charts, and diagrams that accompany the written material. Don't forget to examine the CD-ROM for some of the software and samples, but make use of the Web site too; this site not only allows you to update information from the book, but serves as a forum for ideas, concerns, and questions from you as a reader of the book.

Design Tools for the Internet-Supported Classroom

Judi Harris

Alexandria, VA: ASCD (Association for Supervision and Curriculum Development), 1998. (**http://www.ascd.org**). 81p. ISBN: 0-87120-294-8. Softcover, (member) $16.95, (nonmember) $20.95.

Judi Harris is a noted educator and writer known for her Internet book, *The Way of the Ferret*. Now she has written a guide for educators, administrators, and parents or anyone who offers staff development and needs a resource tool or wants to get a better grasp of how they can work with educators in the role of trainer. What are the possibilities for staff development? Who learns first and who is usually the last to take up a new technology?

Harris's guide is not a hands-on, "how to use the Internet" type of work. If you are looking for such a tutorial, this book is not for you.

Harris calls on research to help develop her ideas and cites researchers in describing how teachers learn to accept innovations in the classroom. In Chapter 2, "What Research Reveals About Teachers and Innovations," she describes the varying groups of people who adopt innovation (innovators, early adopters, early majority, late majority, and laggards) and then suggests how to work with them successfully. Harris also points out that offering workshops rather than requiring them usually works better.

Instruction generally falls into eight styles of learning: independent learning, large groups, one-on-one, large group demonstration with independent practice, large group demonstration with assisted practice, hands-on lab with intensive schedule, hands-on lab with paced schedule, and hands-on lab paced schedule with scheduled activities. Each of these has its own merits and should be considered in relation to the needs of the trainees.

Chapter 3, "Eighteen Activity Structures for Telecomputing Projects," introduces three general activities: interpersonal exchange, information collection and analysis, and problem solving. Harris presents examples of each and then describes projects that use them. Among the examples are key-pals, global classrooms, electronic appearances, telementoring, question-and-answer activities, impersonations, information searches, parallel problem solving, and telepresent problem solving. Among activities in the interpersonal exchange category are "Ask Dr. Math," which uses e-mail for questions about math problems; and an information exchange about place names that uses e-mail to elicit responses from all around the country about names of cities that capture a certain chosen theme. Among the information collection activities are publishing online and virtual field trips that include such places as the Mayan civilization and NASA. Problem-solving activities might include using information online to solve problems or Internet Relay Chat to hold real-time sessions to discuss various topics.

Teachers have the responsibility to facilitate and instruct students on acquiring knowledge using the Internet. Using search tools often allows students to locate information, but unless they understand what the need is for the search and how the information will be used, they are not going to use the search tool as effectively. The author gives five purposes for searching: to practice information-seeking skills, to learn about a topic or answer a question, to review different perspectives on an issue, to solve a real problem, or to publish information. The final chapter devotes itself to the eight objectives in designing an Internet project. These will be very helpful to teachers ready to begin their own efforts to incorporate the Internet into the classroom. Among the objectives are: choose curriculum-related goals, choose the activity's structure, explore examples of other online projects, determine the details, invite telecollaborators, form the telecollaborative group, communicate, and create closure.

The issue of the Internet in the classroom has spawned all kinds of written materials. Educators can find guides to using the Internet's tools, learn to send and receive e-mail, search the World Wide Web, and much more. Tutorials and step-by-step directions provide practical information. This guide, in contrast, is based on theory and research. Throughout the book, Harris uses "telecomputing" rather "Internet," and yet the Internet is obviously the main "telecomputing tool" and perhaps the only one used in the book. This is not a bedside table book to pick up and read for a few minutes at night. You may find that it's necessary to study the material and to read it several times to digest exactly what the point is. This may be due to the language, which tends to be a bit stilted at times. For example "…powerful educational applications of new technological tools with unique media attributes cannot be conceived until potential adopters are aware of the full range of those attributes."

The title itself may be a bit misleading, in that it implies a more practical kind of material. "Design tools" sound like they might be very specific types of software or applications that would be used in the Internet classroom. In reality, the design tools are much more involved and not so easily identified. However, if you need a theoretical and research-oriented approach to teach others how to use the Internet or "telecomputing activities," then read (and study) this book for lots of ideas. Just plan on taking notes as you read about tools, until you understand all that they can do. A glossary is included.

Educator's Brief Guide to the Internet and World Wide Web

Eugene F. Provenzo, Jr.

Larchmont, NY: Eye on Education, 1998.
(http://www.eyeoneducation.com/). 196p. ISBN: 1-883001-43-9.
Softcover, $35.95.

The aim of this brief guide is to present practical material concerning technical issues related to the Internet, as well as to provide resources for Internet sites of interest to educators. For a "brief" guide, this book contains quite a bit of information. Beginning with an introduction to networks, it moves from the simple to the more complicated aspects of various types of networks. Whenever the author has points to emphasize or particular definitions to highlight, he puts them in a box so it's easy to spot the most important facts. The topic of connecting to the Internet is covered with information from equipment to online services to service providers, so educators learn what's involved in getting an Internet connection. In each of these introductory chapters, besides presenting general facts, the author includes specific education-related information, such as how a school can find ways to afford to connect to the Internet or specific education-related sites.

The World Wide Web is a very important education tool. Provenzo focuses on how it is integrated into the curriculum today and some of the issues teachers face in deciding about using it in their classrooms. There is also an historical perspective of technology issues in general and the problems educators and administrators face in making technology available in the classroom. To illustrate a powerful application of the Internet, virtual field trips are discussed, along with potential Web sites that create an interactive learning environment. A list of online resources, plus references to researchers, provides educators with further reading opportunities.

The book also includes some practical information and provides actual models of Internet integration into a classroom, especially alongside an already existing curriculum. Teachers are encouraged to think in terms of what works for them. Suggested projects include researching a contemporary problem, penpals, researching a favorite topic, newspapers, visits to a town or country, and more. Each topic contains relevant subject areas as well.

A step-by-step process uses seven points to create a model lesson plan including the title, purpose, competencies to be met, theme, materials, design/procedure, and evaluation. A sample lesson plan shows how the model works.

Other topics covered present material on electronic mail, MUDs/MOOs, acceptable use policies, the multicultural aspect of the Internet, and creating Web pages. Learning how to create a Web site is the topic of Chapter 10, with basic information about how to get started with HTML. Chapter 11 lists fun Web sites for students. There are appendices for acceptable use forms, policies, an index to the boxed definitions, and an extensive bibliography.

This guide is more than just an Internet tutorial or resource guide. For a combination of issues and helpful knowledge, this book is a good tool to have on hand. It combines the practical information to use the Internet with the issues faced by educators and administrators in bringing the Internet into the classroom.

Educator's Guide to the Internet: A Handbook with Resources and Activities

Catherine Anderson and Christine Freeman, eds.

Reading, MA: Addison-Wesley/Innovative Learning
Publications, 1997. (http://www2.awl.com/corp/). 236p.
ISBN: 0-201-49609-7. Softcover, $16.95.

This third-edition handbook provides a user-friendly introduction to the Internet for K-12 teachers, especially anyone who's a bit apprehensive about computers. The intent of the eight chapters is to help teachers learn and make use of the Internet in an "easy and painless" manner. The book begins with an introductory chapter that explains all about what the Internet can do and what equipment is needed to get started. The rest of the chapters cover popular Internet tools, including e-mail, LISTSERVs, Telnet, FTP, Gopher, and the World Wide Web. A final chapter covers model lesson plans.

Each chapter follows a similar organization. The tool is introduced; a "Getting Started" section explains what the tool can do, and has corresponding "Confidence Builders," a step-by-step tutorial on how to master the tool's features. The authors suggest reading each chapter completely before attempting the online activities that accompany the material. The online lessons often use screen shots to illustrate features. At the end of the core material for each chapter is an "Odds & Ends" section where various hints and suggestions may be found. Frequently asked questions may be included as well. When applicable, Internet sites provide a starting point for exploring what has been learned.

Further chapters reemphasize the reasons for using the Internet in the classroom. The wide variety of lesson plans gives the beginning "surfer" an easy way to get started. Each lesson consists of objectives, materials, descriptions, and extensions for the activities.

Appendices feature a list of subject resources, a glossary of Internet terms, and frequently asked questions. A bibliography is also included.

This straightforward guide is written in a nonintimidating style and should provide educators with a tool to learn the basics and feel comfortable getting their feet wet as they begin to surf the 'Net on their own.

Educator's Guide to WebWhacker

Tim McLain, senior ed.

Lancaster, PA: Classroom Connect, 1997. (**http://www.classroom.net**).
159p. ISBN: 0932577-39-3. Softcover, $44.95. (Includes CD-ROM).

Many schools still don't have an Internet connection, or at best the connection is slow and there are not enough workstations connected. So how does a teacher bring the Internet into a classroom under these circumstances? WebWhacker is a software product that allows you to "whack" partial or full Web sites and download them to a floppy disk, hard disk, or Zip drive. Then you can "surf the Web" and never be bumped off or have to worry about slow connections, as all the files are on your hard drive.

Educator's Guide is a tutorial and guide prepared by Classroom Connect to help teachers get the most out of this software. It has step-by-step directions for installing and learning to use the software. A frequently asked questions section provides a look at the more advanced features of the program. Along with WebWhacker are chapters about other software, including GrabNet, WebSeeker, and Surf 'n' Print. All of these tools can make organizing information, searching for information, and creating class handouts less tedious for busy teachers. The CD-ROM that accompanies the book includes the software so that you can try it out for yourself.

Sometimes it's nice to read how others have used a product successfully. A section of case studies examines why teachers chose to use it and how they incorporate it into their existing curricula, along with specific projects and lessons. For example, one teacher uses it to create presentations with "whacked" sites rather than rely on a bad or nonexistent connection at a meeting or conference. Web-Whacker can be very handy for this type of situation. An appendix presents installation instructions for each software package, as well as some troubleshooting tips.

Essentially, this book is a guide to using WebWhacker, from installation to getting started "whacking" and building your desired set of Web sites. The $44.95 price is rather hefty. If you already have WebWhacker, then the accompanying manual should be all you need to get familiar with the product. If you would rather try the software out first, then perhaps $44.95 is a reasonable deal for the book and CD-ROM.

Educator's Information Highway

Lillian Biermann Wehmeyer

Lancaster, PA: Technomic Publishing, 1966.
(http://www.techpub.com). 307p. ISBN: 1-56676-294-4.
Three-ring binder, $29.00 ($19.95 for two updates).

This notebook is written for teachers, staff, and administrators as well as graduate students of education, to help locate information about education. The title suggests another "how to integrate the Internet into the classroom" guide. However, this book is different and perhaps the choice of the words "information highway" is what makes the title somewhat ambiguous. *Educator's Information Highway* is an in-depth, step-by-step guide to locating all kinds of research in the area of education, including print, online services, and, of course, the Internet. Not only does it offer resource lists and sites of interest, but it also provides instruction for developing effective research strategies for searching the tools; ways to find citations for media, software, etc.; using ERIC and others; a tutorial on Boolean operators; plus more.

Recognizing that online resources change rapidly, a subscription to this work contains supplements every six months. With 20 to 25 pages of new information, it is easier to keep up-to-date. The binder format makes it easy to replace outdated pages.

The book consists of four parts: "Preparation," "The Highway," "Byways," and "Resource Lists." "Preparation" is an introduction to libraries, information online, and basics about some of the technical aspects of computer searching. "The Highway" describes searches, finding citations, retrieving resources, and actually writing the report. "Byways" gets into the Internet's tools and also discusses descriptors, terms, critiquing research, and more. "Resource Lists" covers abstract journals, software, the Internet, writing guides, commercial services, and more. If you want a comprehensive reference tool for how to locate, use, and write about education, this book is for you. *(Courtesy of Multimedia Schools Magazine, Information Today, Inc., Medford, NJ).*

Educator's Internet Funding Guide

David G. Bauer

Lancaster, PA: Classroom Connect/Prentice-Hall, 1997.
(**http://www.classroom.net/**) (**http://www.prenhall.com**). 434p.
ISBN: 0-13-569492-2. Softcover, $39.95. (Includes CD-ROM).

This guide from Classroom Connect focuses on learning how to locate funding information on the Internet. The book is intended for teachers, principals, parents, school board members, school technology personnel, or anyone who seeks information on funding for getting started using the Internet in schools.

Along with funding information found on the Internet, the author provides tips on the basics of fund raising and grant seeking. Many chapters provide worksheets with sample letters to use in the search for funding sources.

Topics covered include corporate support for Internet access; federal and state opportunities; fund raising for technology; effective fund-raising strategies; foundation grants; and individual and organizational donors.

Appendices include "Net Basics," "Internet Resources for Funding and Grant Seekers," "An A to Z List of Grantmakers and Their Addresses," plus a list of foundation centers and more. A CD-ROM accompanying the book contains all the worksheets and letters, plus an extensive list of grant makers in the form of a searchable database. A Web page with links will also help you get started.

This very complete guide is for anyone who wants an in-depth look at fund-raising sources on the Internet or help getting their school connected and bringing technology into their schools. *(Courtesy of Multimedia Schools Magazine, Information Today, Inc., Medford, NJ).*

Evaluating Internet Web Sites: An Educator's Guide

Kathleen Schrock

Manhattan, KS: The MASTER Teacher, 1997.
(**http://www.masterteacher.com**). 32p. ISBN: 0-914607-48-0.
Softcover, $9.95.

More and more educators are using the Internet as a tool for learning in their classrooms. Students are searching the Web, involved in all kinds of classroom projects. Classes are putting Web pages up on the Internet every day. Finding resources on the Internet is a challenge in itself, but knowing which ones are worthwhile or quality sites is even more difficult. This is the challenge that educators face when they open their classrooms to the world.

Kathleen Schrock is an educator and well-known Internet expert. She created "Kathy Schrock's Guide for Educators," a Web site for teachers that annotates more than a thousand links for their professional growth and curriculum needs. Now she has written a booklet for teachers to help them learn how to effectively evaluate Web sites. As more and more teachers learn the ways to look at Web sites and make decisions on the effectiveness of those sites, they will be able to teach their students the same skills. Beginning in the early grades, to help students learn how to look critically at what they find on the Internet, will increase their information-gathering skills for the rest of their school lives.

The book begins with an introduction on how to look at Web sites with open eyes, that is, to think about why you use the Internet and how it fits into your classroom. Why should you choose the Internet as a resource for your curriculum? Once you have answered that question, it's time to evaluate. The "Web Site Rating Form" can be used as a checklist to evaluate Web pages. It contains four parts: technical and design features, navigation, authorship and authority, and content. Each part is broken down into questions to ask yourself. For example, "Does the Web page extend beyond the side edges of the monitor?" How many would think of that as something important to look for? This checklist can help you know what to look for when evaluating sites. The next few pages break down each question in detail, to help you understand what makes a good Web site. Following this checklist are three evaluation worksheets designed for use by elementary, middle, and secondary school students. These allow students at any level to learn what to look for as they locate resources in their classrooms. Most questions require only a yes/no answer. The last section provides students with the opportunity to express their opinions about the Web site. "The Lesson Plan Instructions" provide educators with the means to teach others how to evaluate Web sites. Accompanied by a set of transparency masters, they have everything necessary to teach other educators, students, or administrators all about what makes a good Web site. There is a short glossary and reference section as well.

Being confident in knowing how to choose quality Web sites is an important part of using the Internet. With this carefully prepared booklet, educators and students will be equipped to do just that.

Frameworks for Teachers

Terri L. Robinett

Rancho Mirage, CA: NetQuest Consulting, 1997.
(**http://home.earthlink.net/~netquestcons/**). 132 p.
ISBN: 0-9660226-0-2. Spiral notebook, $29.95.

This spiral-bound notebook is a teach-yourself manual that can help educators learn to use the Internet in their classrooms. There is nothing to indicate what computer platform this book was aimed at, but if you are using a Macintosh, the screen shots for things like printing will look different. The author seems to assume that everyone is using Windows. Because this is a beginner's book, it might have been a good idea to mention this in the introduction.

The step-by-step lessons are meant to be used alongside your computer. Produced in a landscape format, the book has a paper stand to prop it up so that you can read the directions as you are working at your computer. Updates to the lessons are provided at a Web site produced by the book's publishers.

Part One focuses on how to access the Internet, with topics that include browsing with Netscape Navigator and its many features. Here's where you will also learn about searching for information and electronic mail.

If you are somewhat familiar with the Internet's workings, you can skip Part One and go to the Internet resources in Part Two. Mini-quizzes interspersed throughout let you see how you are progressing with the lessons.

Lessons include the World Wide Web, Netscape, bookmarks, searching for Web sites, and using newsgroups and e-mail. In Part Two you will find many Web resources, arranged by subject. Part Three focuses on student activities, with suggested lesson plans. A glossary and index are included.

A couple of conventions are irritating. There is inconsistency in capitalizing the word "Web": sometimes it is capitalized, but other times it is not. And there is no mention of why certain words appear in quotes; for example, phrases like "Information Super Highway" or "Web" or "browsers" are placed in quotes throughout the chapters. Words that can be found in the glossary have an asterisk next to them in the text. All of these special styles seem distracting when reading the lessons.

No doubt you can learn the basics of the Internet, and the material is self-paced, but at $30.00 this guide is a little pricey for what you get. If you want a workbook format that you can prop up next to your computer, then you may want to invest in this title. Otherwise, there are other guides that cover more ground and cost less.

High Wired: On the Design, Use and Theory of Educational MOOs

Cynthia Haynes and Jan Rune Holmevik, eds.

Ann Arbor, MI: University of Michigan Press, 1998.
(http://www.press.umich.edu/bookhome/highmoo/). 342p.
ISBN: 0472-06665-X. Softcover, $18.95.

Many of the older Internet tools, such as Gopher, FTP, and Telnet, are commonly used by educators today. And, of course, the World Wide Web is now the tool *du jour*, capturing everyone's attention with its dramatic visual impact. Two tools that have been around for quite a while but have received less attention in most Internet guidebooks are MUDs and MOOs. A MOO is a virtual educational community; the acronym stands for Multiple-user, Object-Oriented environment.

High Wired is a collection of essays written by scholars, contributing their expertise in the creation and use of educational MOOs and MUDs to help answer questions about using them in an educational setting. The book is divided into three main parts, organized in a practical way to take you from an entry level of understanding all the way to a more theoretical exploration of the MOO community. Along the way the book covers some of the technical information about how MOOs work and reviews case studies of their implementation. Experts in the field contribute essays on setting up MOOs/MUDs.

High Wired is designed to have something for everyone interested in learning about MOOs/MUDs. It can be a reference tool or a guide or even a textbook, depending on individual needs. An appendix titled "MOO Central" is an excellent source for obtaining links to existing MOOs around the world. Among the subject areas are general, university, online writing centers (OWLs), foreign language, K-12, professional, experimental and programming, and more. Brief descriptions help you to understand more about the individual sites.

For those new to MOOs, this text is an excellent tool to learn all about them. The foreword by Sherry Turkle is filled with introductory information that provides good background on MOOs. Although each chapter is self-contained, the information seems to build so that you do not feel overwhelmed. There is a lot of excellent information on designing and using MOOs here. For educators interested in taking a class into "MOOland," all kinds of help can be found, not only for learning how they work, but also for learning how to go about creating one of your own—as long as you remember that MOOs are more complicated than just "gophering" or "surfing the Net." This book is a wonderful tool; using it along with the links to further information, interested educators will be "MOOing" before they know it.

Internet Access Cookbook: A Librarian's Guide to Commonsense Low-Cost Connections

Karen G. Schneider

New York: Neal-Schuman, 1996. (http://www.Neal-Schuman.com/).
332p. ISBN: 1-55570-235-X. Softcover, $35.00.

The first step to using the Internet effectively is buying the appropriate hardware and software, gaining access, and then learning how to connect. Karen Schneider knows this from the many training sessions she's held and from the questions she's received over and over again. The result is *The Internet Access Cookbook*, a primer for librarians who want to get connected but aren't quite sure how to go about it. The author presents her information almost as if providing a recipe, and perhaps she is—a recipe for successful Internet access. In any recipe, you must have all the ingredients to make it work. The same goes for using the Internet.

Gearing her book to the librarian on a budget (and who isn't?) as well as those with little extra time, Schneider recognizes the need to get the most for the money and to do it in a way that is both economical and effective. Be aware that this book is dated as far as technology recommendations. As fast as the computer world changes, it is almost impossible to keep up with new equipment in a book. This may be a bit of a letdown for the complete novice who really needs to know what model computer to buy, but the author provides a complete chapter on tips and suggestions for learning how to buy your first computer or upgrading the one you have. Armed with this knowledge, a fledgling computer buyer will be educated enough to know where to look, what to look for, and what questions to ask.

This "cookbook" can be used as a reference tool (just skip over the sections you don't need) or it can be read cover-to-cover. Written in a practical, jargon-free language (as much as possible when describing technical things), Internet access is broken down into 12 chapters, beginning with an overview of the Internet. This is about the only similarity to other Internet books, as the rest of the material is all about how to get set up, find an Internet account, and purchase equipment (such as the right computer, modem, and software). In other words, it's all about access, which includes SLPP/PPP, commercial services, and Free-Nets. After completing it, librarians should be more educated buyers.

Practical advice based on experience, along with charts, diagrams, and illustrations, helps you visualize some of the technical information. Appendices include an Internet service providers list, a list of Free-Nets, mail-order sources, and a glossary.

There are not many books with this same focus and even fewer that narrow the scope to libraries. Therefore, this book, though somewhat dated in technology recommendations, is still a valuable tool for anyone ready to step onto the Information Superhighway on-ramp.

Internet Adventures: Integrating the Internet into the Curriculum, Version 2.0

Cynthia B. Leshin

Needham Heights, MA: Allyn & Bacon, 1998. (http://www.abacon.com). 314p. ISBN: 0-205-27883-3. Softcover, $24.95.

Leshin's book reads like a travel guide, with chapter titles such as "Tourist Information Center," "Touring with Browsers," "Visiting Virtual Communities," "The Internet Landscape," and "Expedition Experience." Much like beginning a trip, the "Tourist Information Center" provides background information necessary to have a successful road trip. In this case the background is about the Internet's history, with a timeline of important dates and events and a comparison between the World Wide Web and the Internet. It then discusses how to get connected and introduces URLs and the standards used by the Web.

Beginning the journey means knowing how to use Web browsers. Guided tours of both Netscape and Internet Explorer, as well as a discussion about the browser wars, help get you started. Some hands-on, step-by-step directions help you learn the features and understand how browsers operate, with information on navigating frames, multimedia environments, and helper applications. Once on the road, visiting virtual communities is next. Here you'll take some "guided tours" on how to use, send, receive, read, and reply to e-mail, plus learn about mailing lists and newsgroups. Chats, Free-Nets, MOOs, MUDs, and Internet phone are also stops along the way. A practical section called "Expedition Experience" provides resources for teachers to locate mailing lists and newsgroups of interest. Gopher, file transfer, and Telnet are presented along the road trip, with specific steps to learn how to locate education-related material.

Perhaps one of the most useful stops is the chapter on Internet research, where browsing skills can be put to work in a practical way. After explaining the basics of search directories and search engines, and giving examples and tips for several, the author presents seven steps for researching information on the Internet. The material is very practical, with step-by-step directions and screen shots to provide a comfortable environment for exploring and learning. Once all the basics are covered, "Internet-Based Learning Expeditions" provide real projects and thematic units for teachers. Each one demonstrates the active learning approach created by applying the Internet in the classroom. Examples of the units covered include oceans, ancient civilizations, and the rain forest. The lessons include an introduction to the subject and objectives to be covered; the really helpful part is the various "connections" made to other subject areas. In the Oceans unit, there are connections to social studies, math, science, language arts, and the fine arts. There are numerous Web addresses, along with exercise suggestions. The lessons are an excellent use of the Internet and show connections among various subject areas to enhance the learning process.

Clear, nontechnical language, lots of white space and bolding, plus illustrations and screen shots make this guide a valuable learning tool for anyone interested in making a successful road trip on the Internet. It will be a great time saver for busy teachers who want to make the most of their time yet want to get going with the Internet.

The Internet and the School Library Media Specialist: Transforming Traditional Services

Randall MacDonald

Westport, CT: Greenwood Press, 1997. (**http://www.greenwood.com/**).
ISBN: 0-313-30028-3. 224p. Hardcover, $39.95.

This author takes a more academic viewpoint in his look at the Internet and school library media specialists. The audience is novice Internet users. Because of this, he covers general topics such as the "Internet and Education," "Why Explore the Internet?," "Establishing Internet Access," and "Internet Tools" in more depth and detail than other introductory Internet texts.

The book breaks down into four main parts, including "What Is the Internet?," which explores the Internet and its relationship to education. Part Two, "The Internet and the School Library Media Specialist," covers why librarians should explore the 'Net; "Connecting to the Internet" provides information on how to obtain access, tools, how to learn from colleagues, and the World Wide Web. Part Four, "Incorporating the Internet into the Media Center Program," has chapters that deal with planning and evaluation, transforming services, and acceptable use, as well as safety issues.

There are several appendices including one that offers an essay by Ester Grasian, who probes the issue of evaluating Web sites. Her checklist is a valuable tool for procedures to use and questions everyone should ask when locating information on the Web. An acceptable use policy, a list of World Wide Web sites, and a glossary and bibliography complete this work. *(Courtesy of Multimedia Schools Magazine, Information Today, Inc., Medford, NJ).*

Internet Communication in Six Classrooms: Conversations Across Time, Space and Culture

Ruth Garner and Mark G. Gillingham

Mahwah, NJ: Lawrence Erlbaum Associates, 1996.
(http://www.erlbaum.com). 167p. ISBN: 0-80582-275-5.
Softcover, $16.50.

This is not a typical "what educators are doing with the Internet" book. It is, however, as the title implies, about the ability to communicate in classrooms using the Internet and thus allow "conversations across time, space, and culture." This scholarly yet practical book includes six case studies of teachers and their classrooms, providing a look at how the Internet has brought them a means of communication with the world they hadn't previously imagined. Many of the settings are in rural areas, with less than adequate funding and often a new or nearly new teacher in charge. It's amazing to see how these professionals have brought a sense of world culture into their classrooms through e-mail. Students can learn about others in far-off lands, learn about customs and cultures, and make new friends. This is especially well illustrated in a chapter that follows Alaskan elementary school class members as they use e-mail to correspond with and ask questions of a class from Illinois.

Each case study begins with a description of the geographical region. These well-written, descriptive narratives give you a real sense of where the students come from. Next comes a brief introduction to life in the classroom. Here the author presents a bit about the teachers, their experiences, and the classes they teach. The rest of the chapter documents how students use the Internet as a communication tool. Examples of e-mail messages, along with analyses of what is going on in the communication process and the writing, help readers see how electronic correspondence teaches skills to students. Along the way, citations and references make the connection between the scholarly world and what's going on in the classroom.

The book is successful in a number of ways. First, it is able to present the cultural environment of each class and capture its personality, to illustrate how communication can flow across "time, space, and culture." Second, it teaches you how to make effective use of a network on a variety of levels to further communication and writing skills in the classroom. Finally, it demonstrates vividly the ability of teachers to come up with new and innovative ideas, often under some very daunting circumstances, to enhance the learning experience for their students. This book is a great example of how computers can bring together rather than isolate students.

For educators who want to see some real success stories from "extraordinary" teachers in "ordinary" settings, and might need some inspiration to get started, this book will provide it. Even with the references and theories discussed along the way, it's still a quick read. Share it with your teacher friends.

Internet for Active Learners: Curriculum-Based Strategies for K-12

Pam Berger

Chicago, IL: American Library Association, 1998. (**http://www.ala.org**). 189p. ISBN: 0-8389-3487-0. Softcover, $30.00.

The student of the future will have a different learning environment. In her opening chapter, Pam Berger describes what it might be like for "Socrates," a 21st-century student. Incorporating technology into the curriculum is more important than ever, and the Internet is the leading tool for curriculum support.

Librarians are key ingredients, especially school media specialists, and have the daunting task of providing instruction to students in information literacy. Today there are many publications dealing with connecting schools to the Internet or integrating it into the curriculum. The public is very interested in what's happening and how their children are being taught. Today, the integration of technology, especially the Internet, into the curriculum allows for creative student learning. It also breaks down walls and opens the whole world to classrooms.

From the ICONnect publication series, this book has a great deal to offer educators and librarians, both for those new to the Internet and those with a lot of experience. In eight chapters and four appendices, the book covers an introduction to the Internet, a look at the future for students, Internet tools, evaluating Web sites, integrating the Internet into your classroom activities, resources for active learning, developing a library home page, and teaching the Internet.

An electronic online extension of the book includes various cybertours to learn how to use the Internet effectively and foster active learning. Check out the list in one of the early sections of the book. Throughout the chapters, relevant cybertours are always highlighted.

Helpful "Tips" are presented in the margins and provide Web sites to illustrate the information discussed. Screen shots are very helpful when needed to illustrate Web sites or some of the step-by-step directions for certain tutorials. There are also "Advanced Strategies" for anyone who wants to expand upon the material covered. Anytime there is a useful connection to an ICONnect site, an icon gives you the information.

There are many K-12 Internet books out there today. It's not that this book has a lot of information not found in others, but the way the material is organized and presented makes it a very effective guide. It's important to provide theory and research about the Internet at times. But it's also essential to give educators the practical help that allows them to get started using the Internet. This book does both in a very readable style. One of its really excellent qualities is the way the author has interjected Web sites and addresses for just about any piece of information under discussion. It's a great way to provide many more resources to readers when they are ready to move on to more advanced ideas, or just continue with more of the practical information provided. Busy educators don't have the time to surf and find all of these valuable Web sites. With *Internet for Active Learners* in hand, teachers will just need to mark the places they want to refer to. For example, when discussing the history of the Internet and the popularity of the Web, the author puts in several Web addresses for finding statistics on the Internet. What a great resource for anyone who has to be the advocate and moving force to get a school up and running with the Internet! It's also a valuable tool for a presentation or paper.

The book's material is very relevant, in part because the Internet tools chapter focuses on the Web and e-mail, not Telnet or Gopher and other older Internet tools. Also, the discussion of Web browsers targets the top two, Netscape Navigator and Internet Explorer. Here are specifics about each one, along with several exercises for setting bookmarks, saving files, and more. The basics are targeted here. It's not comprehensive, but further resources are provided. The chapter on evaluating Web sites is a gem. It is packed full of ideas, concepts, and practical information. The main questions that should be asked are broken down with examples of Web sites to illustrate the concepts. There are examples of evaluation forms that can be used in schools by students for practice.

What exactly does integrating the Internet into the curriculum allow you to do? One main idea is that it lets you focus on student learning and permits a collaborative and active learning environment. The author presents many excellent strategies and examples of telecollaborative projects to incorporate into the classroom. Specific projects are described and detailed as illustrations of what can be done. Examples include "The JASON Project," "I'EARN" (International Education and Resource Network), "The Global Schoolhouse," and more. Besides formal projects, the Internet offers many resources to change a passive learning environment into an active one. This topic receives attention in a section that focuses on Internet resources supporting student learning and examines the unique features and how they can impact teaching and learning. For instance, the author suggests using Pointcast to bring specialized and individually chosen news resources to your desktop. Another interesting Web site is one called InvestSmart, which provides students with an exercise teaching how to invest and handle money wisely. Along with the nicely detailed descriptions of the sites are screen shots and addresses to access them. Busy educators will find these a gold mine of information.

Other types of Internet uses could be full-text databases, online magazines, and digital libraries. As the Web continues to grow in popularity as a communication tool, the importance of having a library Web site is even more crucial. "Developing a Library Home Page" takes you through the considerations for getting started creating one. Tips on planning ahead, determining goals, and deciding on content, along with suggestions for content, provide an excellent reference for budding Web page creators. There is also a chapter that focuses on how to offer Internet workshops for teachers and parents. Examples of online courses available to teachers and librarians who may be assuming a new role as instructor are very helpful. An excellent section of online resources provides further information.

The four appendices include "Developing Active Learners," "Reference Sources," "Parent Resources on the Internet," and "Resources for Developing Library Home Pages." For educators and librarians charged with developing technology in the curriculum, this is an excellent and well-written source with plenty of practical information and a world of resources. It packs a lot in its 189 pages.

Internet for Educators, 2d Edition

Randall James Ryder and Tom Hughes

Upper Saddle River, NJ: Prentice-Hall, Inc. (http://www.prenhall.com). 198p. ISBN: 0-13-699075-4. Spiral notebook, $22.00.

When learning is active and involved, students learn more. That's the premise of this book. It's geared to pre-service and in-service teachers ready to learn how to incorporate the Internet and its tools into the curriculum. The book is divided into four chapters. "Getting Started on the Internet" is an overview, along with the types of resources available, how to navigate it using links, connecting from home and/or school, and choosing an Internet service provider. Netiquette issues and safety concerns are covered as well. Software considerations for accessing the Internet are also discussed, with material on Telnet, e-mail, and the World Wide Web. Chapter 2, "Communicating and Exploring for Information on the Internet," goes into more detail about e-mail, using discussion lists, and Usenet newsgroups, along with how to receive files from the

Internet. There's a chapter on search engines and a special section for educators on special resources in education. Chapter 3, "Internet Resources: Evaluating and Instructing," brings up the issue of evaluation of Internet resources, an important component in successfully using the World Wide Web for information. It's got some very practical guidelines and activities for practice in evaluating information. Teachers will find this section particularly helpful. The authors have produced some strategies that will help students "filter information" as they use the Internet for locating resources. The goal is to provide teachers with the means to teach students how to effectively evaluate what they find on the Internet, by providing them with a framework and plan.

Chapter 4, "Creating Information on the Internet," explains the basics of HTML for creating Web pages. A brief tutorial follows an explanation of HTML, along with examples of specific software tools for the various platforms.

Each chapter provides activities at the end so you can practice the material learned. There are helpful references and a summary of the chapter. Appendices include acceptable use policies from several school districts. Appendix B is a list of Internet sites especially for educators, and Appendix C lists national service providers and ISDN information. Appendix D has a checklist for evaluating resources on the Internet.

The accompanying Web site makes this book especially appealing to any educator who wants a practical and thorough look at how the Internet can be used successfully in the classroom.

The Internet for Newbies: An Easy Access Guide

Constance D. Williams

Englewood, CO: Teacher Ideas Press, 1996. (**http://www.lu.com**).
144p. ISBN: 1-56308-483-X. K-12. Softcover, $20.00.

Geared to educators, librarians, and other information professionals, this book concentrates on the basics of the Internet and its tools for "newbies," not to be confused with "dummies." You will not find any really technical information here, nor will you read an in-depth history of the Internet. What you will find is an easy-to-read, very practical guide to getting comfortable with the Internet. Beginning with a description of the Internet environment, addresses, and getting connected, the author moves on to the major Internet tools, such as e-mail, mail lists, newsgroups, and the World Wide Web. All are discussed in detail, with good examples and pointers to places to obtain more information. Less time is devoted to Telnet, Gopher, and FTP. The chapter called "Finding Information on the Web" explores examples of search engines and subject directories such as Yahoo and AltaVista. This section is particularly helpful for newcomers wishing to get an idea of how search engines operate.

There have been a flood of books on the Internet for educators and librarians recently. *Internet for Newbies* promises to offer a more concise and simple approach and does just that. If you are looking for a well-written, practical guide to the Internet, I recommend this one. It has everything you need to get started exploring the 'Net. *(Courtesy of Multimedia Schools Magazine, Information Today, Inc., Medford, NJ).*

The Internet for Teachers, 2d Edition
Bard Williams

Foster City, CA: IDG Books Worldwide, 1996.
(**http://www.idgbooks.com**). 406p. (...for Dummies series).
ISBN: 0-7645-0058-9. Softcover, $24.99. (Includes CD-ROM).

The Dummies series of books is known for its straightforward approach to subject matter, and this book, written for busy teachers and students who are just beginning with the Internet, is no exception. The author has written other computer-related books and has more than a dozen years' experience teaching, as well as a doctorate in education.

Though geared to the new user who may need to read the book cover-to-cover, this book can also be used as a reference tool. Those with some experience can jump into the chapter needed and move around as necessary to brush up on skills and increase knowledge.

The book has six parts and includes a CD that contains software for connecting, plus other demo applications for products such as Claris Emailer, HomePage, CU-SeeMe, Eudora, and more.

Beginning with the mandatory introductory chapter, "Log On: The Internet in Education," the author covers the basics behind the Internet, its history, and its effectiveness as an education tool, focusing on electronic communication, file exchange, discussion groups, live conferencing, and knowledge navigation as highlights. The chapter called "Why Use the Internet in Schools?" offers great ammunition for teachers who have to impress their administrators with reasons why they need an Internet account.

The nuts and bolts of hardware, software, and connection possibilities are the focus of Part Two, "Getting Wired." A helpful "Internet Information Checklist" allows teachers to keep up with important information such as passwords, broadcast address, dial-up number, domain server, and other facts in one handy place. Figuring out what type of connection is needed—direct or dial-up—can be a difficult question to answer. A very helpful section presents material all about dial-up and direct connections, what they mean, and how to decide what is best given your circumstances. Determining which Internet service provider is best can also be tricky. Williams separates the online service options from the private Internet service providers with the appropriate questions to ask and the answers needed when making a decision. With sections on Prodigy, CompuServe, and America Online, educators can make their own comparisons.

Knowing what's available once you have established a connection is next. Here's a chapter with a brief look at some of the free Internet tools available to educators, such as e-mail, Gopher, Veronica, Web browsers, Telnet, and Usenet.

Part Three, "Internet Resource Roundup," is the heart of the book, with chapters that present fuller details of all the Internet tools. Each one receives careful attention and gives step-by-step directions for use. Included are electronic mail, discussion lists, newsgroups, Gopher, Telnet, FTP, the World Wide Web, Internet Relay Chat, MUDs, MOOs, and more.

In Part Four, "The Net Meets the Classroom," Williams focuses on the practical uses of the Internet for the classroom, with tips about planning online lessons, how to determine whether it's appropriate to use the Internet, how to cite electronic media, special needs students, staff development, and evaluation. "CyberJourneys" include brief descriptions for projects that will help new teachers see the possibilities for lesson plans and expeditions on the 'Net. The projects are divided by grade levels.

In Part Five, "The Part of Tens: The Internet Educator," specific mailing lists, newsgroups, Gophers, Telnet, and Web sites are listed. The author has selected the 10 best in each of these categories, with addresses and descriptions.

Today there are many Internet books for educators out there. If you want a well-written guide with lots of good sound information, along with some well-placed humor, then pick up this Dummies guide and plunge into the world of the Internet in education. Appendices include a troubleshooting guide, glossary, and list of international schools on the Web, plus information about the accompanying CD.

Internet for Teachers and Parents

Paul Gardner

Westminster, CA: Teacher Created Materials, 1996.
(http://www.teachercreated.com). 256p. ISBN: 1-55734-668-2.
Softcover, $19.95.

The 1996 date makes this book somewhat dated, but much of the material is still valuable, and the practical, easy-to-use format makes it appealing as a resource for families and schools. The book is for educators or parents who want to use the Internet. The author's goal is to provide a reference tool that can be used by beginners who have little knowledge, and by the more experienced Internet user as well. For those new to the Internet, reading this cover-to-cover is the best option. Anyone who feels grounded in the basics can just use the lesson plans or the Web addresses to get going exploring.

The book has eight parts, consisting of "What Is the Internet?," "Netiquette and Nethics," "Safe Surfing," "Connecting to the Internet," "Internet Tools," "Integrating the Internet into the Curriculum," "Lesson Plans," and "Internet Resources." In fact, the first five sections only take about 59 pages of the 256 total. They cover the basics, such as explaining what the Internet is, the benefits for educators of using it in their classrooms, how to connect and choose equipment, how to choose a service provider, electronic mail, mailing lists, newsgroups, Gopher, and the World Wide Web. There are a lot of screen shots and figures along the way to help illustrate the fundamentals covered. The style of writing is easy to read and very user-friendly. Specific education mailing lists and newsgroups are listed in the newsgroups and e-mail sections.

The heart of the book begins with the section called "Integrating the Internet into the Curriculum," where the author focuses on the educational uses of the Internet for teachers and parents. For those just beginning, check out the list of possible uses for the Internet. These include research, class projects, virtual field trips, publishing on the Internet, and Internet-related lesson plans. The "Lesson Plans" offer some dandy suggestions for using the Internet in the classroom. Each lesson contains the grade level, content area, skills and concepts applied, hardware and software, other needed materials, a summary of the objective, what to do before the lesson begins, the procedure, and extension activities. There are also worksheets that accompany the lesson. For example, the book review lesson contains a form students may use to write their reviews. In the weather lesson, there is a task sheet offering step-by-step directions to work through the assignment and a handy map of the United States that lets students answer questions about what they observed. Lessons for many subject content areas focus on citizenship, poetry, geography, social studies, language arts, and literature. Lesson titles include "Let's Take a Virtual Tour," "Are All Schools the Same?," "How's the Weather?," "Shakespeare," "Drawing the Line," and more.

What makes these lessons valuable is the amount of information presented for each one. The directions are very specific, the objectives are clear, and the materials needed are stated right up front. The task sheets and worksheets are very helpful and show how to use the material effectively. It also helps because busy teachers have them right at their fingertips. Remember that some of the addresses have probably changed and might not be available. Make sure to check out each Web site before beginning a lesson. If the site isn't there, you can probably find a similar one to accomplish the objectives.

The "Internet Resources" portion provides many Internet sites for teachers and parents. Dewey Web at the University of Michigan; Web66, a popular K-12 site especially for finding schools on the Web; and the United States Department of Education, containing an abundance of links to USDE reports and publications, represent some of the sites. Each entry lists the name, URL, description of the site, and what to do there.

This book is a handy resource for both parents and teachers—but with the 1996 date, keep your eyes open for a later edition if possible.

The Internet for Teachers and School Library Media Specialists: Today's Applications, Tomorrow's Prospects

Edward J. Valauskas and Monica Ertel

New York: Neal-Schuman, 1996. (http://www.Neal-Schuman.com/). 231p. ISBN: 1-55570-239-2. Softcover, $24.95.

Many of the titles available today tell educators how to use the Internet, with sites listed and details on Internet tools. The *Internet for Teachers* separates itself from the usual format with a collection of success stories written by teachers, media specialists, and school administrators who were involved in bringing the Internet into their schools and classrooms. Their stories offer real-life examples of successful ideas for teaching with the Internet. The book's goal is to inspire others who wish to make the connection. Specific lesson plans and projects are part of each chapter.

The book is divided into four main parts. Part One, "Developing Visions, Creating Infrastructures"; Part Two, "Building Models"; Part Three, "Integrating the Internet with the Curriculum"; and Part Four, "Publishing on the Web," which puts it all together. Each chapter begins with an overview of the school environment, including name, number of teachers, number of students, and grades. Additional information includes goals, results of the programs, budget information, and curriculum information. Photos and illustrations enhance the text nicely. A couple of helpful appendices include a list of Internet sites found in the book and a bibliography of materials for additional information. The entire book was put together using the Internet. If you'd like to read why your school should be connected, or borrow some ideas from successful schools already on the 'Net, this is the book for you. *(Courtesy of Multimedia Schools Magazine, Information Today, Inc., Medford, NJ).*

The Internet Roadmap for Educators

Arlington, VA: Educational Research Service, 1996.
(**http://www.ers.org**). 91p. Softcover, $10.00.

When you are taking a trip, you need a map to guide you to your destination. The same thing applies to a journey on the Internet. Here's a "roadmap" for educators who want to get on the Information Superhighway and learn how to navigate successfully and safely. In eight sections, this guide covers reasons to get started on the Internet, Internet resources, how to get where you want to go, and help with possible obstacles on the way. *Roadmap* updates and combines two previous publications, *The Internet Handbook for School Users* and *The Internet Manual for Classroom Use*.

Geared especially to the educator, Chapter 1 helps establish the reasons why integrating the Internet into a classroom can provide so many opportunities for creative learning and successful experiences for students. Actual projects and descriptions from students illustrate the issues. Selected Web sites, mailing lists, and Usenet newsgroups are featured in Chapter 2. When you are just beginning, it's always nice to have a frame of reference, so the chapter on collaborative projects can help teachers see exactly how to apply their new skills. Teachers will also learn how to connect and use special Internet tools (such as e-mail, newsgroups, mailing lists, the Web, FTP, and more) to make their trips more successful. Safety issues, acceptable use policies, and a bit about HTML can also be found. A glossary is included.

This is not an in-depth guide that will teach you everything you need to know, but if you want to have a handy guide to get started, at $10.00 this is a bargain.

K-12 Resources on the Internet: An Instructional Guide, 2d Edition

Gail Junion-Metz

Berkeley, CA: Library Solutions Press, 1997.
(**http://www.library-solutions.com**). 237p. ISBN: 1-882208-22-6.
Softcover, $54.00. (Includes floppy disk).

Taken from an actual workshop, this is one of the Internet Workshop series from Library Solutions Press. Designed for teachers and librarians, this self-paced workbook is meant to be almost as good as attending a workshop in person. To compensate for the missing interactive discussion found at workshops, it's possible to e-mail questions to the author. Featuring three modules, this updated second edition has made some changes. Gone are sections on Veronica, Jughead, and WAIS—replaced with a module on search engines. A Web site now updates any link changes found in the exercises. The acceptable use policy section is now more extensive, as the issues of copyright and safety loom large on the Internet scene.

There are many other education and the Internet books out now. Junion-Metz, a veteran Internet trainer, has taught the Internet for a number of years. Her book incorporates the topics of education and the Internet, along with basic instruction on how to use Internet tools with K-12 resources.

Geared to be used as a learning tool or as a source to teach others all about the Internet's vast resources, the workbook contains three modules. Module One is "Learning the Internet," Module Two is "Teaching the Internet," and Module Three is "Acquiring the Internet." It seems impossible not to include an introduction to the Internet in almost any book out now, and this one is no exception. But it's a friendly and a rather short one that includes some tips on what you can do with the Internet and a few highlights from Internet history. Rather than putting the "glossary" at the end, it's right up front: "The Jargon (Made Understandable)" lists various terms and phrases useful to a beginner. Beginning with Internet tools such as electronic mail, LISTSERVs, and newsgroups, and moving to finding e-mail addresses, Telnet, and Internet Relay Chat, there are also sections on Gopher and, of course, the World Wide Web, a "power cruiser." Most of the material here is basic and introductory. What makes it different from many other books is the ability to practice with exercises. After each topic, Junion-Metz presents a page full of exercises. For the Web, there are navigation exercises and bookmark exercises. An online connection is necessary to follow along with and complete the exercises. For those who want to know more about searching, a nicely organized section on search engines contains a list of directories, search engines, and meta-search engines, along with links to reviews. The Web search exercises suggest cruising around and finding a subject of your determination to get the feel of how search tools work. Want to find a good K-12 mailing list to join? There are many covering all kinds of K-12 subject areas. Recommended Web sites are also listed in alphabetical order.

Module Two shows how to use the Internet as a teaching tool for everyday skills. It can be used as a tool for anyone who wants to formulate a school district Internet training plan or just a basic curriculum plan for teaching in the classroom. The idea is to teach what you normally would and then begin to locate resources online for your specific subject areas. Junion-Metz has some good ideas for creating projects and ways to use the Internet in the classroom. Class communication, mentors, and even what she calls "impersonation" are all ways to incorporate Internet resources. This section is great for new teachers or teachers who haven't ventured very far out on the Information Superhighway. For those who need a checklist of necessary skills to teach, there are the author's pre-Internet skills, quick-start skills, add-on skills, and power-user skills. To help teachers learn more, teacher and librarian resources follow, with brief descriptions. These range from subject-specific topics, such as disabilities, to all kinds of projects.

In the resource directory, Web sites as well as videos, books, and magazines help educators see what's out there. Some of the books are a bit dated, but newer editions may now be available. Module Three, "Acquiring the Internet," focuses on basic reasons to get involved using the Internet. This is a good chapter for anyone who has to convince an administrator of the need to get a school connected to the Internet. Hurdles as well as benefits are offered from the perspectives of students, administrators, and teachers.

Need a technology plan? There's a good section with ideas on creating a plan, options for equipment, connecting to the Internet, safety issues, and more. A special resources directory for planners and implementers highlights LISTSERVs, grant sources, schools and districts, and libraries on the 'Net. Appendices include "Comparing Gopher and the World Wide Web" and "Acceptable Use Policies."

This guide is a comprehensive resource for teachers and librarians who want to learn for themselves or teach others about the Internet. The combination of general information about the Internet, teaching strategies, and specific Internet resources brings everything together in this one volume.

Learning Online: An Educator's Easy Guide to the Internet

Amy Wolgemuth

Palatine, IL: IRI Skylight Training and Publishing, 1996. (**http://www.iriskylight.com**). 224p. ISBN: 1-57517-009-4. Softcover, $25.95.

Learning Online is a fun, easy-to-read book with plenty of practical information and some cute cartoons thrown in. Educators can learn how to connect to the Internet as well as find examples, resources, tips, and FAQs. The book is designed for new users, but more experienced ones will also find the information helpful. The first of the three main sections is Section One, "Getting Started," with options for getting connected, along with issues and concerns related to the Internet. Section Two, "The Global Classroom," presents a detailed section on communication tools, including electronic mail, mailing lists, and newsgroups. The third section, "The Virtual Classroom" explores how to access the vast array of Internet resources, including FTP, Gopher, Telnet, and the World Wide Web.

Each section follows a similar format: "What Is It?," "How Do I Use It?," "What Now?," "Key Resources," "Hints," "Did You Know?," and "Examples." The format works well, taking the reader from basic knowledge through resources to hints for effective use, followed by screen prints that help illustrate the application. As the title suggests, this is an "easy" guide to help you get started learning about the Internet and its global resources. *(Courtesy of Multimedia Schools Magazine, Information Today, Inc., Medford, NJ).*

Making the Link: Professional Development on the Internet

Ron Ostrow

Portsmouth, NH: Heinemann, 1998. (http://www.heinemann.com). 192p. ISBN: 0-325-00077-8. Softcover, $24.00.

Keeping up with new developments and learning about all the technology that's happening today can be an overwhelming prospect. In the past educators might attend workshops or conferences a couple of times a year to extend their professional knowledge—but whether the particular workshop met their needs was often debatable. Ron Ostrow's book, *Making the Link*, looks at how the Internet has become a valuable tool for teachers' professional development.

As most Internet books do, this one begins with an introduction to the Internet, electronic mail, Web browsers, and search engines. These topics are covered only to provide a framework for understanding the link between them and professional development, however.

Next, it's important to have a plan of action to make the most of the Internet. Several chapters address the issue of how to create one, with suggestions for goals, questions to ask, and a handy summary form to record a timeline, comments, and intended goals. Today, teachers have access to a wonderful "virtual professional community" on the Internet. Ostrow explains the importance of such groups and why they offer educators such a valuable means for communication and collaboration. Using mailing lists and newsgroups, teachers can form support groups and find help for almost any type of educational problem today. There are tips on the technical aspects of mailing lists, their advantages and disadvantages, and examples of how they serve as virtual professional communities. Internet Relay Chat and teleconferencing are other forms of virtual communities discussed.

Searching for information is also a way to increase professional development using the Internet. Ostrow presents chapters dealing with searching databases, finding other types of information, and devising a good search strategy to put everything together. Again, practical information along with Web addresses for search tools and Web sites provide teachers with important resources. There are step-by-step directions for finding Internet resource sites and bibliographic resources, and using meta-search engines. A look ahead to the future concludes that no one really knows how much more the Internet will impact our lives in the coming years. But for today, it offers educators a powerful means to grow and develop their teaching skills continuously and effectively online with colleagues from all over the world.

The "Further Readings" appendix provides resources by using Yahoo's subject category lists. Each chapter breaks down the references and includes the appropriate path on Yahoo for further information.

This is like most introductory Internet books in the sense that it describes and talks about the Internet, what it is, its tools and resources. Many books do this. But what's different here is the focus on professional development. The chapters target how the Internet can provide teachers with an invaluable tool for extending their own learning. Practical suggestions and tips, combined with the philosophy behind teacher professional development, make this an informative resource for any educators who want to learn how to make the Internet a tool for their professional development.

Neal-Schuman Complete Internet Companion for Librarians

Allen C. Benson

New York: Neal-Schuman, 1997. (http://www.Neal-Schuman.com/).
513p. ISBN: 1-55570-317-8. Softcover, $65.00.

Sometimes you read a title with "complete" in it and after looking at the book you wonder how they arrived at that concept. Not here: "complete" is the right word for this work. The author's goal was to include "everything" and it's apparent he was serious about doing just that. It has everything a librarian would ever need to know to use the Internet successfully. The book is geared to all librarians, so the focus is definitely on the library environment, especially for examples and resources. But there is still an awful lot of just very interesting and useful information for anyone who seeks to build their repository of knowledge.

Part One, "Essential Background," begins with an introduction of the Internet, covering its history as well as its future. In this section are basic concepts, such as Web addressing, copyright issues, and a description of the librarian's role in this vast environment of networked information. This is the type of information that's missing from many Internet books not directed at librarians, and it offers a view of the many possibilities for librarians—as navigators, publishers, intermediaries, and more. In "For Further Study," found at the end of each section, are resources to continue the topic. These are often Web sites and it's obvious the author has chosen quality resources to recommend. For anyone who needs to justify getting involved with the Internet today, this is a nice resource for answering those often-asked questions about why the library should connect.

Part Two, "What You Need to Get Ready," describes what is needed to get up and going, including a basic vocabulary of terms and concepts. Hardware and other computer-related topics are discussed in a wide range of material, including technical as well as practical topics. The chapter on choosing hardware is very detailed, with discussion of computer options, serial cables and plugs, and much more. Software topics include sections on Web browsers, helper applications, how to download browser software, virus protection, and more.

Part Three, "Tools and Resources," begins with a look at the UNIX platform and continues with a very expansive guide to all the various Internet tools, such as Gopher, FTP, Telnet, online library catalogs, and more. The author intends for this part to include information on the services provided by these tools, not their technical workings. Following these introductory descriptions is a very helpful chapter on integrating these tools into the already existing reference service. From problems encountered to various approaches to locating information on the Internet, this is a chapter any new librarian or anyone who wants to refresh their library knowledge will appreciate. With all areas of library work covered, from cataloging, serials, and children's services to reference and special collections, there's something for everyone. It's a gold mine of information and resources.

Part Four, "Communications Systems," covers electronic mail, Usenet news, and mailing lists—and how to use them—with examples for each system. Part Five, "Your Library as a Publisher," explores how to adopt the Internet as a source for publishing efforts. HTML for authoring pages, how to set up a default home page, how to use files without going online, and enhancing Web pages with graphics and sound are several of the topics covered.

One topic not often discussed in Internet guides is the creation of portable documents using Adobe Acrobat. For librarians interested in exploring this publishing option, a nice tutorial takes you through some basics. Digital and online libraries also offer great publishing possibilities for disseminating information, and a nice description of these tools helps explain how they work.

Finally, there is a very thorough set of appendices containing a glossary, library discussion list, schools of library and information science, job hunting resources, file types, and software that creates them. The software appendix is especially informative for those working with designing Web pages who might not be sure of all that's available. Network organizations and where to get assistance, plus what's new, complete the appendices.

This guide is a complete resource. It's well written and organized with just the right amount of illustrations or screen shots to highlight points. The combination of information and resources is well balanced. The only drawback is the size of the book. You can't use it propped up next to your computer very easily. At $65.00 the book is not cheap; however, when you consider the amount of information it contains, it's worth the investment.

NetLearning: Why Teachers Use the Internet

Ferdi Serim and Melissa Koch

Sebastopol, CA: Songline Guides/O'Reilly, 1996. (http://www.ora.com). 292p. ISBN: 1-56592-201-8. Softcover, $24.95. (Includes CD-ROM).

NetLearning is a teacher's guide to the Internet, using real-life stories from educators' experiences to illustrate the power of the Internet. The introduction suggests how the Internet can help teachers, students, and the community. Directed at beginners as well as those already connected, this guide can be used as a reference source or as a guidebook for the "newbie." As it focuses on educational benefits, it uses experiences of educators to show how to take advantage of the Internet's potential in the classroom. Chapters contain a nice combination of facts supported by teachers' experiences. For example, a chapter on connecting to the Internet follows several examples of schools and their solutions for connecting.

"The Basic Internet Training" chapter covers e-mail and the Web in depth, with shorter paragraphs about other Internet tools such as Telnet and FTP.

Based on the GNN Internet service, the accompanying CD-ROM provides readers with tools to get started using the Internet. There is a good mix of experiential information and basic facts about the Internet, plus an appendix of sites for educators. If you need to be convinced or to convince someone that the Internet is a powerful ally in the classroom, here's the resource you've been looking for. *(Courtesy of Multimedia Schools Magazine, Information Today, Inc., Medford, NJ)*.

Online! A Reference Guide to Using Internet Resources, 2d Edition

Andrew Harnack and Eugene Kleppinger

New York: St. Martin's Press, 1998.
(http://www.smpcollege.com/online-4styles~help). 224p.
ISBN: 0 312 17904 9. Spiral notebook, $13.33.

Perhaps this might be a little bulky for carrying in your pocket; nevertheless, this spiral-bound little gem packs a lot between its covers. Well-organized and easy-to-read, this reference tool is aimed at students in need of a reference guide to the Internet. Believing that an understanding of the language of the Internet is essential, the book begins with a glossary of functional terms. Protocols and other terms used throughout the book are featured. Terms mentioned in the glossary are highlighted in yellow.

A section on connecting to the Internet covers both direct and indirect access, with tips for accessing the World Wide Web, getting e-mail, using LISTSERVs, newsgroups, real-time communication, and more. An especially helpful section covers "Choosing and Evaluating Internet Sources," with a focus on locating sites for writing, identifying relevant sources, and evaluating the reliability of what you find. There is also a good section on how to refine a search to locate more precise information.

Because this book targets a student audience, four chapters cover citation of electronic resources for MLA style, APA style, Chicago style, and CBE style. Knowing how to be polite on the Internet and observe Netiquette rules, as well as how to make sites appropriate and successful, is also covered. A nicely organized chapter on Web publishing highlights basic HTML, effective design of Web pages, and resources to follow up on your newly acquired knowledge; it rounds out the material nicely. An appendix of Internet resources by subject completes the book.

This book seems particularly useful for students or for faculty who want to teach students about the Internet and its resources. It's easy to carry around and the user-friendly language plus its academic approach will make it appealing to the education community.

The Online Classroom: Teaching with the Internet, 3d Edition

Eileen Giuffre Cotton

Bloomington, IN: ERIC/EDINFO Press, 1998.
(http://www.indiana.edu/~eric_rec/bks/alpha.html).
262p. ISBN: 1-883790-29-8. Softcover, $26.95.

Divided into two parts, "Learning" and "Lessons," this guide presents the tools and resources classroom teachers need to successfully integrate the Internet into their curriculum. The author's organization seems unique. She begins with the easiest ways to use the Internet, progressing to more challenging topics as the basics are mastered.

"Learning" introduces the World Wide Web first: browsers and how to work with them, as well as details of navigating with Netscape and using the toolbar, buttons, and directory buttons. Step-by-step directions provide a nice tutorial style for learning—but remember, the version of Netscape may be different. Discussion of common error messages encountered helps prepare you for those times when things don't go the way you expect. There is a section on Telnet and Gopher, but the author suggests you skip over this if the Web is your main tool for using the Internet. She introduces "A Wealth of Web Sites" in one chapter and focuses on what are called "mega-sites." These are places with lots of links to many different sites and are a good way to cut down on the time spent locating sources. The sites are listed by curriculum areas and screen shots illustrate many of the Web sites.

After introducing basics and indicating the kinds of resources available, the guide turns to some "rules of the road," including censorship, acceptable use policies, safety issues, classroom management concerns, and lesson planning. Reproducible forms for these policies make it easy to implement them in a classroom. Other chapters introduce search engines and directories, explaining the basics of each type with examples and tips from the author on what to look for. A nice feature is some pros and cons of several search engines.

Web design is introduced with a description of the basics of HTML, a little about design issues, and some material on how to create pages with editors, plus resources to locate them. There is not enough to make anyone an expert, but the material does provide help to get started. A particularly useful section offers information that targets teachers creating a home page for their classes, with specific objectives and ways to involve the class in the process. An evaluation rubric provides a way to evaluate the final product.

Part Two, "Lessons," focuses on practical uses of the Web and electronic mail as tools. The author shares ideas for how to achieve success, along with lessons on Netiquette, available K-12 lists, and the basics of subscribing to a newsgroup or LISTSERV. There are lessons for key-pals, containing supplies, goals, rationale, and objectives, plus procedures and evaluation. Black-line masters will help busy teachers be able to use these plans with little time required. Detailed plans make these lessons very useful. The grade levels assigned to the projects make deciding what's appropriate for a class easy.

The Online Classroom is a guide that will help teachers see how the Internet can be incorporated into the curriculum and used to create lessons for almost any subject area. The combination of lesson plans, resources, and guided tutorials makes this a valuable tool for any busy teacher wishing to get up to speed on the Internet.

School Libraries and the Electronic Community: The Internet Connection

Laurel A. Clyde

Lanham, MD: Scarecrow Press, 1997. (http://www.scarecrowpress.com).
350pp. ISBN: 0-8108-3197-7. Softcover, $24.95.

This scholarly work by Clyde, a professor in the faculty of social science at the University of Iceland, is the result of a grant for a research study conducted in 1993. The study investigated school library use of the Internet, its resources, and its services. There are eight chapters, including "The Internet," "Internet Resources and Services," "LM_NET on the Internet," "The Research Project," "The Users of LM_NET," "The Internet in School Libraries," "Barriers," and "Issues and Developments."

The book is described as "an essential guide" that can help school librarians use the Internet effectively and use its tools to avoid "junk" on the Internet. Yes, it does have an introductory chapter on the Internet; in fact, it is more detailed than many other books. Yes, it has a chapter on Internet tools, including Telnet, Gopher, FTP, the Web, electronic mail, and many more, but it's difficult to see this as a "guide" that school librarians would pick up to learn how to use these tools. Other Internet books do a more thorough job and are written with that goal in mind. This is a scholarly, academic book that presents research about how school libraries use the Internet. There are extensive references after each chapter, with many tables and charts to illustrate the research presented.

The bulk of the material centers on the research project survey and results. The research is described in detail. The LISTSERV LM_NET, an important resource for school librarians, also receives in-depth coverage. It was a major component in conducting the research and receiving results. The author describes how it serves the school library community, as well as how to join, access, and use it.

One particularly useful chapter is "The Internet in School Libraries." Here is where the author summarizes results of the "respondents' use of the Internet" questionnaire. Several tables illustrate the results. Uses of the Internet include contact with people outside the school; getting information about resources; discussing professional interests; having fun; finding answers to reference questions; expanding students' awareness of the world; developing students' information and inquiry skills; and playing Internet games.

The chapter on "Issues and Development" discusses important aspects of Internet use that have come up as more and more schools become connected. Censorship, equity of access, network etiquette, information skills, gender issues, and future developments are some of the topics discussed. Appendices include a glossary and "Some Useful Journals and Newsletters." An extensive bibliography and index complete the book.

This is a well-written, research-oriented book that can help librarians learn about the uses of the Internet and what others are doing. For anyone who wants a well-researched look at school libraries and the Internet (perhaps to be able to present documented facts to an administrator for arguing about getting a library up and running on the Internet) this book has the necessary information. What it's *not* is a step-by step guide with exercises or lots of screen shots to teach how to use the Internet in a classroom. Check some of the other titles available if you want that type of resource.

The Teacher's Complete and Easy Guide to the Internet
Ann Heide and Linda Stilborne

Toronto, Ontario, Canada: Trifolium Books, 1996.
(http://www.ingenia.comm/trifolium/). 336p.
ISBN: 1-895579-85-6. Softcover, $24.95.

Winner of the Small Press Book Award for 1997, this Canadian title targets teachers who are new to the Internet, especially ones who are reluctant to jump onto the Information Superhighway. The authors, both teachers, present eight chapters full of information that should make any reluctant teacher appreciate all the Internet has to offer. It begins with some tips for success that offer teachers ways to successfully master the material and become comfortable with the Internet. The introductory chapter follows with facts about the Internet, the role of technology in education, e-mail as a communication tool, and the benefits of using online sources for enhancing the learning experience. A detailed chapter on options for connecting to the Internet highlights online services, a LAN connection, and SLP/PPP connection. Software and modem requirements are also covered. The charts and diagrams are especially helpful for understanding some of the technical discussion. The authors provide a checklist for connectivity to help you know when you are ready to go online and start surfing. Educators will really appreciate the chapter titled "Bringing the Internet into the Classroom," because it's chock-full of ideas for getting started with the Internet along with reasons why they work. The step-by-step guidelines will help teachers see how the process begins and works. At the end of each chapter is a "Project Ideas" section with learning outcomes, appropriate age levels, and the project suggestions. Sample rubrics (charts for recording outcomes) help make the education and learning connection very real.

Subsequent chapters focus on electronic mail, the World Wide Web, Gopher, and other Internet tools. All contain plenty of background information, examples, online resources, and sample projects. The final chapter touches on how to bring the Internet into school systems, focusing on implementation plans, training issues, and resources online.

This book is a thoroughly researched guide to the Internet for educators. The combination of easy-to-read writing style, activity sheets, illustrations and graphics, a few cute cartoons, and the abundant information makes this a winner for any educators who want to jump-start their Internet education. Includes an extensive glossary, appendices with sample acceptable use policies, and a huge list of links to hundreds of education Web sites.

A Teacher's Guide to the Information Highway

William Wresch

Upper Saddle River, NJ: Prentice-Hall, 1997. (http://www.prenhall.com). 202p. ISBN: 0-13-621558-0. Softcover, $20.00.

Written to help busy teachers learn what others are doing with the Internet in their classrooms, this guide is based on a PBS television show. It was written to expand on the material in the 28-minute TV presentation. Unfortunately, a lot of the material sounds out of date. Most citations are to books or articles with dates of 1994 or 1995. Of course, the lag time for books to be published is well known, but here the discrepancy seems more noticeable.

The book divides its 16 chapters into topics covering getting connected; e-mail; Internet tools, such as Gopher and the World Wide Web; and uses of the Internet in classrooms and how it helps foster collaborative learning. There are several chapters highlighting curriculum resources in the sciences, social sciences, and humanities, as well as a discussion of who's connected and who isn't, plus how school libraries fit into the picture. There is a chapter on training resources for teachers, along with one that covers district planning and acceptable use policies.

The book emphasizes how things can be used rather than the technology itself. The author wishes to present practical illustrations of how the various Internet tools can help teachers in the classroom. The chapters present the material, then offer several ideas for projects, followed by specific examples of projects and suggested readings. It's the readings, as well as the emphasis on Gopher, that point out the datedness of the material. The illustration of using Gopher to access information about Harvard University seems particularly inappropriate today, given Harvard's presence on the World Wide Web. The author states that

Gopher lives on in academic circles, but today many universities have done away with their Gopher sites, choosing instead to focus on the Web as the means for distributing information. The idea that Gopher is a better learning environment because it is more "staid" just doesn't ring true anymore.

The discussion of search engines, which uses Yahoo as an example, shows a certain lack of attention to detail. Yahoo is really a subject directory. Even if this book is intended to be an introductory guide, it's a good idea to pay attention to detail, and so it's especially noticeable when a name is misspelled. Throughout the book, *AltaVista* is always spelled as if it were two separate words (Alta Vista) instead of the correct one-word spelling (AltaVista).

The interpretation of Yahoo's search results for the keyword *NASA* is not really accurate. The author says a search of *NASA* brought up "362 Web sites," but the 362 represents not just Web sites but categories as well. Perhaps these are minor details to some, but they seem to indicate a less than thorough knowledge of the subject.

Even though there is a Web site that lists links to interesting sites for children and teachers, there is nothing to indicate how often it is updated. There are some useful sections on collaborative learning and tips on using it with technology. But for the most part, there are many other guides for educators that do a better job, are written in a more interesting style, have fewer typos, and are more current.

A Teacher's Project Guide to the Internet

Kevin R. Crotchett

Portsmouth, NH: Heinemann, 1997. (**http://www.heinemann.com**).
174p. ISBN: 0-435-07104-1. Softcover, $26.50. (Includes floppy disk).

The author, a teacher himself, intends this book for other teachers who wish to begin using the Internet in their classrooms. Its step-by-step approach is meant to encourage beginning teachers. Each of the book's seven chapters describes an Internet tool, such as email, Usenet, or the Web, along with a history of the tool and resources illustrating its use in the class. The author's writing style makes the material easy to digest, and the mix of practical illustrations of projects with the author's personal experiences help make it a useful Internet guide. Appendices include lists of newsgroups, LISTSERVs, Web sites, Gopher, FTP, and basic HTML tags. The floppy disk that comes with the book contains software for access to sites listed when used with a browser. *(Courtesy of Multimedia Schools Magazine, Information Today, Inc., Medford, NJ).*

Using the Internet in Secondary Schools

Eta De Cicco, Mike Farmer, and James Hargrave

London: Kogan Page, 1998. (http://www.kogan-page.co.uk/).
154p. ISBN: 0-7479-2522-9. Softcover, no price listed.

Teachers worldwide are having to make the same decisions: how to use the Internet effectively in their classrooms. This British publication is mainly for educators in England and Wales, and does speak to their national curriculum, but it also has universal information for any educators who want to know more about the Internet as a tool for learning and communication. Unlike many other Internet books, this one does not teach about the technical aspects of the Internet, nor does it teach how to get connected or choose a service provider. Educators needing that type of information should check out some of the other books first and then come back to this one. This book focuses on secondary schools in England and in particular addresses the key stages of the National Curriculum of Wales and England.

Part One contains chapters giving "Tips on Using the Web," including ones on searching, designing Web pages, and useful Internet tools. Each chapter explains the information in the form of tips. Hardware (both PC, Macintosh, and a lesser-known system called Acorn, used in England), Web addresses, when to use Web sites in the United States, how to enter addresses, and tips for those times you encounter the dreaded error messages are all covered.

Screen shots show a European Yahoo rather than the customary American version. There is a small paragraph mentioning unsuitable material on the Internet, and the material on searching the Web focuses on the concept of having effective search strategies. Boolean operators are explained and examples shown. There are also sections on other common search features, such as wildcards and field searching. In "Tools of the Trade," search engines and subject directories are highlighted. Some examples may look a bit different, because they are not as well known in the United States. There is also a special "UK-Based Search Engines" section. One especially helpful set of tips is a "searching wish list" that offers suggestions for what search tool to use based on the type of query. For example, if "[y]ou want a small number of hits with excellent summaries and then be able to order them so that the ones most useful to you are displayed first," then use either Excite or AltaVista. "To search an event by its date," use HotBot. "To see a site just for young people with its own search engine," use Yahooligans.

The chapter on Web pages for schools seeks to get educators started in understanding what's involved in creating Web pages, but it does not intend to create Web authors. It's not an HTML primer. There are useful tips on what can be done before actually composing any HTML documents, such as planning for your audience, thinking about why a Web page is necessary, and planning exactly what goals there are for publishing on the Web.

Reasons to have a Web site might include marketing the school, publishing material, displaying students' work, and allowing students to do a lot of the work themselves. Many practical aspects of Web creation are covered, such as how to create graphics; what kind of software to use to write Web pages; and what equipment to use, such as a scanner or digital camera. There are design issues, such as who owns the page, the title and contact details, page size, and more, that many people don't take into consideration before they begin creating Web pages.

There's not as much detail in this chapter as some other books that are just for creating or designing Web pages. But the material provides food for thought for educators who are serious about creating a Web site. Just plan to use another HTML book when it comes down to the actual creation of a Web page.

Part Two consists of a single chapter called "Curriculum Activities." The British focus is most obvious here because the lessons address the National Curriculum in England. Activities are arranged by subjects, including science, math, English, geography, history, design and technology, modern languages, music, art, and religious education. For each activity, there are teacher notes identifying the National Curriculum Key Stage and the objectives of the activity. There are step-by-step directions for students to complete the exercises. The activities are not presented as reproducible worksheets as other books have chosen to do.

Much of the information contained in this book is useful. It's well-organized and written in an easy-to-read style. For anyone interested in the British perspective on the Internet as a teaching tool, this book provides all the necessary facts. If you are an American educator, there really isn't anything here that you can't find in one of the many Internet books published in the United States.

Web-Based Instruction

Badrul H. Khan, ed.

Englewood Cliffs, NJ: Educational Technology Publications, 1997.
482p. ISBN: 0-87778-296-2 (hardcover); 0-87778-297-0 (softcover).
Hardcover, $89.95; softcover, $59.95.

As the World Wide Web continues to grow, it is emerging as an important tool for instruction. This compilation from more than 100 experts worldwide contains 59 chapters in 5 parts. The author put together the book after posting a message via e-mail to find out more about Web-based instruction. He discovered a need for a compilation of the worldwide information available and began to assemble it into this book.

The author's goal is to offer readers online sources, case studies, and other references related to Web-based instruction; in particular, design, creation, delivery, control, and evaluation. This scholarly work presents a wealth of information on the issues surrounding Web-based instruction. There is an introduction to the concept of Web-based instruction, to offer a foundation in the concept, with articles about its evolution and relation to distance learning.

Suggested readings enhance the information provided, and e-mail addresses and URLs are given for each chapter's author. The charts, diagrams, and tables found throughout the book help illustrate the more complicated theories and learning modules discussed. This book is not a hands-on guide or tutorial. It's a scholarly compilation of information across a broad range of often complex topics.

The five parts consist of "Introduction to Web-Based Instruction," "Web-Based Learning Environments and Critical Issues," "Designing Web-Based Instruction," "Delivering Web-Based Instruction," and "Case Studies of Web-Based Courses." The case studies are a nice way to assimilate all the previous information and demonstrate how various Web courses make use of the various components of Web-based instruction. URLs provide a way to check out the sites.

Much of the material is theoretical and covers pedagogical issues relating to use of the Web in teaching. As a source for studying the issues related to Web-based instruction, this is a valuable book. It is more of a text than a casual read, however. For those who want a theoretical background in why and how the Web can be incorporated into teaching, this book provides a wealth of information.

Web-Teaching: A Guide to Designing Interactive Teaching for the World Wide Web

David W. Brooks

New York: Plenum, 1997. (http://www.plenum.com/). 233p.
ISBN: 0-306-45552-8. Softcover, $25.00.

This book is written to help teachers deal with the many kinds of software, hardware, and networks that are part of the expanding World Wide Web and learn how to make use of them for instruction. The main subject area focuses on science education and the targeted audience is K-12 teachers, college professors, graduate students, and adult education students, as well as the business community.

The author intends to offer concrete ideas of what is happening today with the Web and to provide effective strategies for teachers who are thinking of adding their courses to the Web. A second goal is to "get teachers to favor one kind of instructional strategy over another," according to the author. Besides Web-related information, the guide includes discussions of learning theories and how to use an interactive learning approach.

In the chapter titled "Research on Teaching Web Issues," the author points out the lack of solid research to consult for proof that teaching with the Web is effective or better than traditional teaching. Here Brooks discusses interactive teaching and active learning, and how the Web can be a tool to promote them in the classroom. Multimedia is discussed with a look back at how it has evolved as a teaching tool throughout the years. Other Web issues include electronic communication, the Web as an instructional delivery system, ways for teachers to begin thinking about multimedia creation, hardware/software issues, and the question of replacing teachers with computers.

To help see what components of a course are appropriate for Web-based instruction today, there is a comparison of an old course and how it was redesigned for today's environment. An informative chapter on Web-ready materials, with some technical information on how a browser determines what to do with a file or plug-in and what is needed to accomplish your goal, helps illustrate possibilities.

A whole chapter is devoted to images: how to save them in the correct format, all about GIFs and the software to manipulate a file for maximum usage, how to get the pictures, and more. Just keep in mind some of these procedures require more than a little skill and superficial knowledge to be successful. Still, it's nice to know what is possible.

Besides the Web, television production, movies, and desktop editing are all part of Web teaching and are covered as well. There are many illustrations and examples of the ideas discussed. But remember, this is a text about science education, so the models are in the areas of science and mathematics.

Brooks's work is more than "this is how you use the Web in the class." It has research principles alongside suggestions for using the Web. Cooperative learning is discussed, with a section on supporting discussion on the Web using e-mail, LISTSERVs, and newsgroups. Sample screen shots illustrate the points at times. Forms as a tool for interactive learning are a focus in one chapter, with examples of how they can be used for exams. Lots of details about buttons and their functions for forms are part of this section. The author is very good about telling you when something may be more difficult for a beginner.

A glossary and software list (with URLs when available) and an index complete this text. For teachers who want a background on what's possible with Web-teaching, rather than just how to use the Web, this guide has a broad spectrum of information. There are more technical concepts in this book than some others geared to educators, and more theory and research than other more down-to-earth guides. But if a combination of theory and practical use to learn about Web teaching is important to you, then you'll want to pick up a copy of this book.

Wired for Learning

Jane Lasarenko

Indianapolis, IN: Que, 1997. (http://www.mcp.com). 278p.
ISBN: 0-7897-1045-5. Softcover, $24.95.

Everyone is aware that big changes have occurred in education, especially as they relate to technology and teaching. Lasarenko believes that teachers owe it to themselves to learn the new technology and writes about how the Internet can help achieve many of the goals of education. The Internet brings the world into the classroom, fosters learning by doing, and facilitates collaborative learning and interactive learning. These are all points made in the introduction to the book.

In eight chapters, the book seeks to show how this can be accomplished by learning the tools provided by Internet access. The book targets both beginners and experienced users. However, for those who are really experienced, there probably isn't much that can be learned from this book except to see the author's way of using the tools in her teaching. The book is "loosely arranged" into technologies from the simpler to the more complex. For beginners, reading it cover-to-cover is the best idea. Those with some experience can skip around until they find the appropriate chapter. Maybe you know all about e-mail, but very little about chat and MOOs....

After an introductory chapter on the Internet, others cover Telnet, Gopher, FTP, e-mail, LISTSERVs, chat, MOOs, the World Wide Web, HTML, and more. There doesn't seem to be a chapter on newsgroups, which are mentioned in most Internet books. There is a separate chapter just on LISTSERVs, and the one on MOOs is very detailed. The World Wide Web chapter covers basics about navigation and searching as well as a brief introduction to HTML. Don't expect to be able to put together a state-of-the art Web page after this; the material just provides a taste of what HTML does. A strength of the book lies in the way the author always relates the educational advantages to the tool under discussion. If it's the Web, delivery of information is enhanced as well as collaborative learning; e-mail helps students become better writers and provides shy children with the ability to "speak out." Each chapter presents projects that allow transfer of the information learned. Each lesson indicates the subject area, grade level, description, objective, and preparation required, plus the step-by-step procedures to implement the lesson.

Appendices include a glossary, LISTSERVs and newsgroups, education resources on the Web, and links to other projects of interest.

World Wide Web for Teachers: An Interactive Guide
Ralph Cafolla, Dan Kauffman, and Richard Knee

Needham Heights, MA: Allyn & Bacon, 1997. (http://www.abacon.com). 231p. ISBN: 0-205-19814-7. Softcover, $29.95.

Designed for teachers, education majors, and students, this interactive tutorial offers hundreds of Web sites, tools, and lots of practical information in six chapters devoted to preparing them to become confident users of the Web. The approach is definitely nontechnical, with user-friendly language, lots of step-by-step directions, and accompanying lessons to make sure the material is understood. The authors suggest using the tutorial when seated at a computer to obtain the maximum benefit. Those who already have a little bit of knowledge can go ahead and select appropriate chapters to begin.

Chapter 1, "The Internet and World Wide Web," introduces the basic concepts of the Web, why it's important, and how to connect, plus suggestions for software and hardware to use. Chapter 2, "The Netscape Interface," is an in-depth look at the browser with all its buttons, menus, and displays. Screen shots help illustrate these features. After learning the basics, it's time to take the first tour. Chapter 3, "Interactive World Wide Web Tours," offers four tours consisting of "Setting a Home Page," "Kid's Tour of the White House," "A Tour of Web66," and "Yahoo—Looking for Stuff." The chapter begins with some commonly found error messages to help assure that it's not uncommon to run across them when navigating the Web.

Chapter 4, "Using Search Engines," teaches about the search tools for locating information on the Web. The authors have selected about 13 search tools, including the most prominent (AltaVista, Yahoo, WebCrawler, InfoSeek), and provided brief descriptions of each. At the end of the chapter is a little quiz to check out what was learned.

Chapter 5, "Using Bookmark Files," is a rather detailed look at how bookmarks can help organize sites and provide a means of categorizing sites. It's much more than just a look at how to set a bookmark. There are also 100 pages of educational Web sites arranged by subject. A glossary covers common Internet terms and an appendix lists colleges in the United States.

The interactive nature of this guide makes it a fine tool for beginners to get started learning how to navigate and locate education-related information on the World Wide Web.

Chapter 3://Internet Books for Parents, Children, and Students

Introduction

More and more children are Internet users. One survey estimates that 10 million are online either from school or home. As more and more schools are connected and teachers introduce the Internet as a curriculum resource, parents will need to be aware of what it offers both positively and negatively.

Today this is easier than ever. There are a number of good Internet books geared specifically to the family. In this section of the book I have included books written for students or children and families. Some may be guides to Web sites focusing on those for children. Other titles are actually children's books, written for the child, explaining what the Internet or World Wide Web is. Others have a theme of safety on the Internet, exposing the dangers of children connecting. The audience may be students (meaning in an educational setting) or a book may focus on the home and family.

Researching on the Web is a topic that has received much attention. These books seek to help guide students in learning how to make the most of the Internet and its resources. The majority of the books included have a K-12 focus, but a few may reach beyond, into college, as well. As more children and young adults connect, more books are being written for this audience. If a book included parents and teachers but the emphasis was on a school setting, I put the book in the educators or curriculum chapters.

Casting Your Net: A Student's Guide to Research on the Internet

H. Eric Branscomb

Needham Heights, MA: Allyn & Bacon, 1998. (**http://www.abacon.com/**). 188p. ISBN: 0-205-26692-4. Softcover, $15.96.

Casting Your Net is different from most other Internet books. It focuses on how to conduct academic research on the Internet, evaluate research results, and apply Internet materials in your writing rather than on all the Internet tools and how to use them in the classroom. The approach and writing are more scholarly and the focus emphasizes skills needed for constructing searches in order to be a more effective searcher.

Beginning with a chapter on "Academic Research and the Internet," the author cautions about the difference between "research" found on the Internet and through other databases and stresses that the student as researcher must take the responsibility for reviewing what is found. "Boolean Logic" is a short chapter to get students up to speed with the syntax necessary to search effectively, regardless of whether it's the Internet or a CD-ROM database. Exercises at the end of a chapter provide a means to check what was learned. The chapter on search engines and searching the Internet reemphasizes the material learned previously, along with other methods of refining a search.

Electronic mail, and in particular LISTSERVs, receives attention as a tool for locating information. The World Wide Web is analyzed for its research potential, with descriptions of several major search engines and directories, such as Yahoo, AltaVista, InfoSeek, and others. Use the handy chart that highlights major pros and cons of each to decide which will work best for you. Other Internet tools, such as Gopher, Veronica, and WAIS, are covered along with commercial online services. A chapter on "Specialized Internet Resources" highlights less discussed super-sites and commercial online search services, such as DIALOG, Lexis-Nexis, and others.

After covering how to locate and evaluate information, Branscomb moves on to the writing of the paper. Here he follows the evaluation of sources used for a paper on endangered species to show how the process should work.

Appendices include one for "A Critical Look at a Usenet Thread" and another on "Documenting Sources on the Internet"; there is a glossary of useful terms.

For faculty who want a good source for teaching the Internet as a research tool, this guide provides a well-organized and balanced presentation of the information necessary for students to understand how to search effectively, make the most of the resources they find, and write an effective paper. The exercises at the end of each chapter make it possible to evaluate progress along the way.

Child Safety on the Internet

Vince Distefano and the Staff of Classroom Connect

Upper Saddle River, NJ: Prentice-Hall, 1997. (http://www.prenhall.com). 296p. ISBN: 0-13569-468-X. Softcover, $34.95. (Includes CD-ROM).

Parents are concerned about the safety of the Internet. This guide from the publishers of Classroom Connect will help to educate parents about safety issues and ensure that visiting the Internet is safe. Besides discussing dangers and the "dark side" of the Internet, the authors offer common-sense ways to protect children online. Suggestions for family guidelines and acceptable use policies contain practical strategies for parents. The CD included contains a trial version of CyberPatrol, software to help control children's access to the Internet. The book also contains resource lists that provide access to more information about organizations and associations.

For parents who want to be armed with information to help guide their children's Internet exploration, this is a complete source. Practical and well written, it does not contain many illustrations or photos, just text and an occasional screen print. Appendices. Glossary. Index. *(Courtesy of Multimedia Schools Magazine, Information Today, Inc., Medford, NJ).*

Childproof Internet: A Parent's Guide to Safe and Secure Online Access

Matt Carlson

New York: MIS Press, 1996. (http://www.mispress.com). 262p. ISBN: 1-55828-499-0. Softcover, $19.95.

There are several books out on safety and the Internet. Some, like *Danger Zones*, approach it from a "what's dangerous" view and give plenty of examples of what's bad about the Internet. In contrast, the author of this book is a professor at Emory University and an associate of Safety Net Services, a firm that conducts seminars for parents and educators on the issues of safety and the Internet. His approach is to examine ways to make it safe for children to use the Internet and focus on what parents can do to make surfing the 'Net safe. His goal is to supply information that will help parents lose their fear of technology and step up to the challenge of becoming involved with their children's use of the Internet. It's all about parent involvement, according to Carlson. To be involved, parents have to know something about the Internet, how to access it, what's on it, and ways to supervise their children's access.

It's all here in a well-written, positive approach to the Internet. The author assumes that his audience consists of parents who have very little computer literacy. That's not to say that technical material isn't covered, because it is, much more than in some other books. There are sections on how information is sent via the Internet (packets, ITP/TP, etc.), and all about modems and computer hardware choices, but it's in a nontechnical style, making it easier to understand. One of the most helpful sections describes how parents can work out agreements with children concerning how they will use the Internet, when they can access it, the kinds of sites they are permitted to visit, and more.

For parents to be effective supervisors of their children's use of the Internet, they need to get into a comfort zone themselves for using the Internet. This book is a great starting place to do that. There are activities to practice skills learned, along with step-by-step directions.

Appendix A is a very handy resource containing a "Safety Net Checklist" for equipment, service providers, agreements, and more. Appendix B is a map of Safety Net's home page for additional resources. Appendix D offers a starting point for kid-safe Web sites, Appendix E is a glossary of terms, and Appendix F is a very complete look at the issue of government censorship versus parental monitoring, with information from the findings of fact from months of testimony and investigation by the government.

All in all, this book provides the necessary information to make parents aware of the issues related to Internet safety, yet still provides a positive outlook on the benefits of the Internet for children.

Children and the Internet: A Zen Guide for Parents and Educators

Brendan Kehoe and Victoria Mixon

Upper Saddle River, NJ: Prentice-Hall, 1997. (**http://www.prenhall.com**). 215p. ISBN: 0-13-244674-X. Softcover, $24.95. (Includes CD-ROM).

Brendan Kehoe, the author of the very popular *Zen and the Art of the Internet*, has co-written a volume for parents and educators who want to provide a safe yet exciting journey on the Internet for children. Topics include safety, acceptable use policies, curriculum uses, and, of course, places to get started exploring. The basics of Internet tools, like e-mail, newsgroups, file transfer, and more, are also covered.

The authors devote a chapter to "The Role of the Internet in K-12 Education," focusing on the shift in teaching models, problems of introducing computers, training teachers to use technology, and integrating the 'Net into the curriculum. Another chapter offers case studies to illustrate how schools have successfully integrated the Internet into their classrooms. Several appendices include lists of Web sites mentioned in the book, acceptable use policies, and sites that can help teachers apply for grants. A glossary and bibliography are also included.

The accompanying CD-ROM provides a trial copy of CyberPatrol, software that parents or educators can use to prohibit access to questionable areas of the Internet.

The book is very readable, with type that is slightly larger (and easier on the eyes) than many other books. The style is almost conversational, making any "technical" information easy to understand. Cartoons are interspersed throughout and an occasional screen print helps illustrate points. *(Courtesy of Multimedia Schools Magazine, Information Today, Inc., Medford, NJ).*

The College Board Internet Guide for College-Bound Students

Kenneth E. Hartman

New York: College Board, 1996. (http://www.collegeboard.com).
208p. ISBN: 0-87447-548-1. Softcover, $14.95.

This step-by-step guide is geared to the college-bound student who would like to use a computer to obtain information about scholarships or colleges, contact faculty or other students, or just locate useful information concerning colleges.

In a basic Internet information chapter, the author takes the time to explain how to navigate the Internet, and includes e-mail and the World Wide Web as well as chat rooms.

Beginning with Chapter 3, the book goes back to its focus and explores how students can find college-related information. Helpful sections provide facts about how students use the Internet, considerations on what to look for when checking out colleges, and a worksheet designed to help get as much as possible out of a Web site by knowing what to look for. Chapter 4 discusses e-mail; in particular, how to correspond with faculty and staff at colleges. A sample form letter makes corresponding easy by providing students with the right questions to ask. Chapter 5 looks at some personal home pages from departments, staff, and faculty, complete with lots of screen prints to illustrate the sites.

"Top College Searches on the Web" provides addresses for some of the major sites and organizations, including the College Board, College NET, and others that focus on services to college-bound students.

This book has helpful tips, checksheets, and sample letters, as well as important sites for gathering just the information you need. It is a well-organized look at college information and could be a time-saving tool for busy students who wish to use the Internet to locate college information. *(Courtesy of Multimedia Schools Magazine, Information Today, Inc., Medford, NJ).*

College Connections Web Directory 1997

Jackson Earl, Jr.

Emeryville, CA: Lycos Press, 1996. (**http://www.tenderbuttons.com/lycos/**). 400p. ISBN: 0-7897-1057-9. Softcover, $29.99. (Includes CD-ROM).

This Internet guide takes a different perspective: that of the college-bound student who wants to use the Internet to locate information about colleges and universities, as well as know how to use it once enrolled. Strictly speaking, this book is for more than the K-12 community, but it offers a great deal of helpful information for the prospective college student.

The book is divided into six parts. Part One is "Entering the Net," a guide to what's available on the World Wide Web and how to access it. Part Two, "First Campus Connections—Finding Colleges and Educational Resources on the Web," covers educational resources geared to the college-bound student, with chapters on selecting a college and preparing for college life. Part Three, "Directories of University and College Web Sites," lists hundreds of college and university home pages. There are no descriptions for any of these, just the Web address to locate the home page.

Online research tools, preparation for graduation, and graduate school possibilities, along with a resource list and selected graduate school Web sites, are covered in Part Four, "Onsite Insights—The Internet in College Life." Part Five explores "Expanding Horizons Beyond the Campus Gates," with a focus on distance learning opportunities and international education as well as lifelong learning. Finally, Part Six, "The Connected Community—Integrating the Digital and the Real Campus," explores how to access the Internet in regular life. It also gives some Web authoring guidelines and suggests how to integrate the Internet into the curriculum.

The accompanying CD-ROM provides links to an HTML version of the book, along with a Web browser and shareware.

This book is a good resource for college-bound students, guidance counselors, or teachers who would like to be able to provide a source with hundreds of resources related to higher education. It provides a look at the college selection process as well as life on campus, graduation, and selecting a graduate school, and extends the focus up through lifelong learning.

Connecting Kids and the Internet: A Handbook for Librarians, Teachers and Parents

Allen C. Benson and Lisa M. Fodemski

New York: Neal-Schuman, 1996. (http://www.Neal-Schuman.com/). 382p. ISBN: 1-55570-244-9. Softcover, $35.00.

This handbook's goal is to help teachers, librarians, and parents introduce the Internet to children. The book covers a lot of information and the format is such that the book can be used as a self-paced tutorial or as a reference tool. The author assumes no previous Internet experience. There are five sections covering "Internet Introduction," "Getting on Board: How to Connect," "Tools and Resources," "Communicating on the Internet," and "Bringing It All Together." The "Tools and Resources" section covers FTP, Archie, Gopher, Telnet, WAIS, and the World Wide Web. "Bringing It All Together" provides examples of places for children to get started, including Web sites and libraries on the Internet.

The approach taken is more academic. Topics are more extensively covered than in most books that seek to teach Internet skills to children. Mostly text, with a few illustrations or screen prints along the way, the information contained here is much more detailed and technical, although the authors are careful to use non-technical language.

This book would fit on a library shelf for the serious Internet learner who wants a lot of information and less entertainment. *(Courtesy of Multimedia Schools Magazine, Information Today, Inc., Medford, NJ).*

CyberSurfer: The Owl Internet Guide for Kids

Nyla Ahmed

New York: Firefly Books, Ltd., 1996. (http://www.firefly.com/). 72p.
ISBN: 1-895688-50-7. Softcover, $19.95. (Includes floppy disks).

This brightly illustrated guidebook makes learning about the Internet a fun and interesting exploration for children. Young-at-heart adults will also find it fun reading. The text moves right along and presents information as fun facts, with all kinds of diagrams, puzzles, and games to highlight Internet facts. The basics are well covered, including "Life Is a Highway," "Surfing the Net," "The Safety Net," and "What's Next on the Net?," among others. A floppy disk with software for a "cyber blastoff" accompanies the book. However, you will need an Internet connection and a graphical Web browser at your disposal to use the software. The "yellow pages" directory at the end of the book provides some "cool cyber stops" that will appeal to any child. Kids can take quizzes along the way to test their knowledge. Answers are written upside down on the page for handy checking.

"Good-bye Snail-mail, Hello E-mail" gives you an idea of the slant most of the chapters take. It's a light-hearted approach with a fun yet practical style. Here's a sample: "At first an e-mail address looks like a bowl of alphabet soup."

Children will find this title fun and enjoyable while learning about the Internet. Parents may want to borrow it to read as well. *(Courtesy of Multimedia Schools Magazine, Information Today, Inc., Medford, NJ)*.

Danger Zones: What Parents Should Know About the Internet

Bill Biggar and Joe Myers

Kansas City, MO: Andrews & McMeel, 1996.
(http:// www.AndrewsMcMeel.com). 144p.
ISBN: 0-8362-1317-3. Softcover, $10.95.

For parents who have heard vague things about the child abuse and pornography available on the 'Net, here's a book that will put things into perspective. Many parents would probably be surprised at how easy it is to come across pornography or sexually explicit chat room conversations on the Internet. For those with little Internet knowledge, surfing the 'Net could be an eye-opening experience.

The authors' focus is on the "danger zones" that crop up for unsuspecting kids as they chat, or send e-mail, or even just visit the World Wide Web. Although the main theme is the bad things about the Internet, the authors also offer useful information about connecting, choosing an online service, how to use the Web, newsgroups, chat rooms, and Netiquette, and provide a selection of interesting and safe Web sites for kids to visit.

Parents can learn how to protect their kids online as well as what kinds of limitations and rules should be set up beforehand. To protect children from the "danger zones," parents must be educated themselves. This book provides the ammunition necessary to make educated decisions about children's access and use of the Internet. Once armed with the necessary information on how to avoid "danger zones," pick up a more detailed Internet guide and have some fun on the Information Superhighway.

Dear Parents, How Safe Are Your Children on the Internet?

Robert Spanton

Zion, IL: Internet Unlimited, 1997. 122p.
Softcover, no price given. (Includes floppy disk).

Safety is a big concern when it comes to the Internet. Parents have read newspaper stories about some of the problems associated with permitting children access to the vast world of the Internet. The author's goal for *Dear Parents* is to help them to develop a plan for their families so that the Internet can be accessed and enjoyed safely. The purpose is to provide materials to help parents create the plan.

Beginning with a "Dear Parents" letter as the preface, the author describes how the Internet can benefit children. He also recognizes the dangers and lists the various negative aspects that might be encountered on the 'Net. He describes adult-oriented materials, fraud, hatred, cultism, violence, and abduction as examples of the darker side of the Internet. Rather than having the government control material on the Internet, the author advocates parental education as the means to making the Internet safe for children.

The book is divided into four main sections of resources: "Guidelines," "Books," "Sites," and "Software." Becoming knowledgeable in all these areas will empower parents to control their children's interaction with online resources. The first section, "Guidelines," is packed full of checklists covering topics such as how to talk to your child about the Internet, expectations of children online, observing your child online, how to handle situations when you believe your child may be downloading objectionable materials, limiting access, stopping access, and rules for online safety.

There is some duplication among the checklist items for these topics. Many suggestions for directing children's interaction with the Internet are just good child-rearing ideas. They have to do with teaching responsibility. If a child is already a responsible person, and can be trusted, then some of these rather stringent rules are probably not necessary. What a parent takes or doesn't take from this section is a personal decision. They do provide a family that is not familiar with the Internet some very good issues to think about.

"Books for Internet Parents" presents a selection of titles that can help families educate themselves. The titles are divided into "Internet Books for Children," "Books for Internet Parents," and "Internet Books for Teachers." Unfortunately, many are older at this point, but again, they provide the novice "Internet parent" with resources to get started. Today there are many, many more titles from which to choose. The entries contain only descriptive information supplied by the book cover or from the Web site. No reviews are presented.

"Sites for Internet Parents" presents Web sites in a variety of categories of interest to parents, teachers, and children. They cover homework, parenting, teaching, search engines, and home schooling. The entries contain the title and Web address, with a very brief description in a sentence or two. "Software for Parents" highlights filtering or blocking software available. The accompanying floppy disk contains links to sites in the book and text documents such as the "contract" agreement between children and their parents concerning their responsibility in using the Internet. Appendices explain how to install the files from the disk.

This book is somewhat dated as to book titles and many of the Web sites, but the checklists are a valuable source for parents who are just starting to think about the Internet as a tool for family use. There are more detailed books out now that cover this topic in more depth and are more current.

E-Mail (A True Book)

Larry Dane Brimner

New York: Children's Press, 1997.
(http://publishing.grolier.com/catalog/pub.htmls/cpindex.html).
47p. ISBN: 0-516-26168-1. Softcover, $6.95.

E-Mail is a child's book that teaches all about communicating electronically. Written in big "kid-sized" letters, with lots of illustrations and pictures, this is an appealing book to learn about a rather cut-and-dried topic. The book covers all the basics. Chapters include "Communication," "What Is E-Mail?," "How Does E-Mail Work?," "Good News and Bad News," "E-Mail Addresses," "Mailing

Lists," "Netiquette," and "Safety First." The photographs are excellent and chosen to effectively illustrate the point being taught. Illustrations and graphs are colorful and also contribute to the visual appeal of the pages. Geared to students from ages about four through eight, the language is simple but well written. The author doesn't talk down to children.

Everything is explained very logically and in a straightforward manner, too. E-mail addresses are often difficult for adults to learn, much less children. The page devoted to this is easy to understand, using the example "doglovers@ucsd.edu" with a colorfully illustrated graphic that separates the parts of the address visually. It's exactly how to teach an e-mail address to anyone, not just children. Adults intimidated by technology talk can read this with children and learn all the facts to get started with e-mail. The book contains a glossary of "Important Words" and a resource list for further information.

Everything You Need to Know (But Were Afraid to Ask Kids) About the Information Highway, 2d Edition

Dr. Merle Marsh

Palo Alto, CA: Computer Learning Foundation, 1997.
(http://www.computerlearning.org). 147p. No ISBN listed.
Softcover, $5.95.

Does your seven-year-old know more about the Internet than you do? Maybe you've wanted to get in there and surf along with your children, but just don't know how to get started. Here's a book written just for parents in situations like this. If you are completely new to the Internet or maybe have only dipped your toes in a bit, you can go one-on-one with your children after reading this slim volume. It's crammed full of information just for the parent poised to enter the on-ramp to the Information Superhighway. The Computer Learning Foundation, publisher of the book, seeks to improve education for youth and to get them ready for the workforce through the use of technology. This second edition is one way of providing information to parents to make this goal happen.

Written expressly for parents, the language is nonthreatening and nontechnical, yet the material is comprehensive enough for you to be able to grasp all you need to know to get started. The book's seven parts cover topics such as getting connected, safety issues, electronic mail, Web browsing, and Netiquette, plus more than 50 pages of projects and activities.

Sprinkled throughout are little mini-case studies revolving around families or children to illustrate a point under consideration. Tips and warnings are highlighted in special shadowed boxes for easy identification. Examples are always related to the family or child. Activities encourage parents and children to work together in building a Web page or exploring the Web sites listed. A section of help and resources, as well as a list of contacts and organizations, provides further information.

There are many books geared to the educator and general public, but if you want a guide to the Internet from a parent's perspective, take a look at this inexpensive paperback and get ready to join the crowds entering the Information Superhighway.

Exploring the Internet Using Critical Thinking Skills: A Self-Paced Workbook for Learning to Effectively Use the Internet and Evaluate Information

Debra Jones

New York: Neal-Schuman, 1998. (**http://www.Neal-Schuman.com/**). 93p. ISBN: 1-55570-319-4. Softcover, $35.00.

Created as a workbook for teaching how to use the Internet using critical thinking skills, this guide is particularly helpful to beginning students who want to get the most out of their Internet research.

The workbook's course goal is to explain how to acquire information literacy skills for lifelong learning and how to apply critical thinking to Internet navigation. The objectives of the book are for learners to identify and locate information sources on the Internet, identify and evaluate the information, apply appropriate citation styles, and understand the responsibilities that go with publishing on the World Wide Web. Students cover topics such as the basics of navigating the Web, understanding hyperlinks, addresses, using search engines and subject directories, news online, people, and using education and government sources.

The book assumes that a computer connection is in place and ready to go. There is no introductory chapter on how to buy a computer, set one up, or find a provider. There is little technology jargon. The focus of this book is the combination of learning Internet skills and the concept of thinking critically about resources found so that one can evaluate them intelligently. The approach is an integrated one, combining technical explanations with procedures only when necessary to locate information.

Each lesson contains a similar structure that uses "Concepts," the main ideas that must be understood to locate information; "Definitions," explaining any necessary terms (which may also be in the glossary); "Tools," those particular things needed to work through a practice exercise (search strategies, Web sites, etc.); and "Practice," where it's possible to use the concepts and tools introduced in a lesson. The exercises are structured to make the most of the material just learned.

Throughout the lessons—whether on using a search engine like InfoSeek or a subject directory such as Yahoo, learning Boolean logic and search strategies, or learning about newsgroups and mailing lists—the chapters emphasize evaluation of resources found and learning the steps to successful critical thinking. The goal is not to surf the Internet to find as much as you can, but rather to be able to structure your research topics, learn to create a successful strategy, select appropriate sites, and evaluate, evaluate, evaluate!

A good combination of practical Internet skills is taught, along with the theory and concepts of critical thinking that should prepare students to be successful Internet researchers. The exercises are well organized and follow through on the material taught. There are not very many similar workbooks out there that take this same focus, at least not to the depth found here. But at $35.00, it's an expensive 93 pages. It's probably just as easy to check out a good book on critical thinking, and find the other Internet information in many other books. However, if you want a well-organized guide and workbook with lessons already prepared, to teach how to use the Internet and develop critical thinking applied to it, then it may be money well spent.

The Family Internet Companion

The Staff of Classroom Connect

Upper Saddle River, NJ: Prentice-Hall, 1997. (**http://www.prenhall.com**). 330p. ISBN: 0-13-569500-7. Softcover, $34.95. (Includes CD-ROM).

There's a lot to like about this book. The approach and style of writing make it enjoyable to read. The information flows very naturally and is very readable. Learning about the Internet is fun with this guide.

Why should people use the Internet? This guide explains why and also offers a safe and easy way to learn to navigate the 'Net, along with how to use search engines and other tools to make the journey productive and safe. Included is a little about how to design a Web page, too.

The book organizes its Web sites by family member, including kids, parents, and even older members of the family. All sorts of interesting sites can be found here, ranging from entertainment to travel, money and investments, careers, sports, and much more. The chapters are nicely illustrated and the print is easy to read. Any family member who wants an immensely readable introduction to all the Internet offers will find this a valuable source. *(Courtesy of Multimedia Schools Magazine, Information Today, Inc., Medford, NJ).*

Getting Your Child Started on the Internet: A Quick Reference Guide for Parents and Kids Ages 4 to 12 to Fun, Games, and Learning on the World Wide Web

Robert S. Want and Jennifer M. Dowell

New York: WANT Publishing, 1998. (**http://www.wantpublishing.com**). 123p. ISBN: 0-942008-89-8. Spiral notebook, $15.95.

With more than 4 million children already surfing the Internet, and that number expected to quadruple by the year 2000, the Internet is obviously an influential presence. It's often difficult for parents to decide when children should be guided toward using computers or learning to use the Internet. And then there's the question of where to visit on the 'Net. With so many new Web sites appearing every day, it's often difficult for parents to know what is appropriate for their children to see.

The purpose of this workbook is to show parents and their children (ages 4 to 12) "the best of the Web." Some 100 sites have been chosen as "the most interesting and fun" for parents and children to explore together. In a brief introduction, the authors discuss guidelines from Children's Partnership on when to introduce your child to the Internet, along with tips for how to do it successfully. The guidelines offer handy tips for parents to work with their children in non-threatening and even natural situations to introduce them to the Internet.

"The Best of the Web" sites are divided into four parts according to children's ages. Part One covers ages 4 through 7; Part Two is for children aged 4 through 12; Part Three is for ages 8 through 12; and Part Four is "Exploring Further."

Other than by broad age category, the entries are not arranged in any particular order. There is a very brief description—a sentence or two—and a large illustration, usually a screen print of the home page that actually takes up most of the 8-1/2 x 11 page. Sites are labeled as noncommercial or commercial. Many are well-known places to visit, such as Mr. Roger's Neighborhood, Carlos' Coloring Book, and Winnie the Pooh and Friends. Among the kinds of sites visited are museums, coloring books, Muppets, Disney, sports, the White House, comic books, science activities, and more. In "Exploring Further," many of the Web sites contain links to other resources. For example, "Yahooligans" and "The Internet Public Library-Youth Division" are two entries.

Frankly, there's not a lot to this spiral notebook that can't be found in other, more comprehensive books for children and parents. But maybe that's a plus. If all you want is a few interesting and entertaining sites to get started exploring with your child, and don't need any kind of background help on searching or surfing, then this may be all you need. The book provides some good starting points and is easy for kids to read. The reviews are extremely brief with very short evaluative comments. But the large graphics will catch a younger child's interest and sometimes provide more information about what's contained at the site. If you want expanded coverage of Web sites and some more background on the World Wide Web, then choose one of the other titles available.

Going to the Net: A Girl's Guide to Cyberspace

Marian Salzman and Robert Pondiscio

New York: Avon Books, 1996. (http://www.avonbooks.com).
332p. ISBN: 0-380-78661-3. Softcover, $5.99.

On the cover of this paperback is the following: "Discover where to find penpals, boyfriends, shopping, bargains, fashion and beauty tips, homework help, and more!" And believe me, that's just the kind of information you'll find. This is not an educational tool for girls, but a book geared toward entertainment and leisure-time activities. Some parents may be put off by the casualness of talking about getting boyfriends on the 'Net. Many parents will find it an unacceptable practice to let young girls meet boys on the Internet, even though the authors do offer cautionary words about giving out names or personal information and are not suggesting that girls do this without parental permission. There have been plenty of warnings about the problems of chat rooms and newsgroups where children have been propositioned by adults. And this book focuses on "teens" and "tweens," which means younger girls as well.

The book is a collaborative effort, done mostly via e-mail with input from a young girl who uses the Internet. The casual style of writing reflects this. The language is full of jargon and words like "cool," "geeky," etc., which can be somewhat irritating and often seems to get in the way of the information presented. At times it was difficult to understand what the heading of the section meant. Casual writing is fine, but this style seemed too much at times.

For those who can get past the jargon or actually like it, the book does teach how to find interesting sites, information, games, and more, all related to girls and their interests. Some more serious uses of the 'Net can be found in Chapter 18, "Back to School," which covers homework help, ways to locate materials for research papers, and more. But for the most part, the emphasis is on popular, fun things girls like to do. In that respect, it's unique.

The High School Handbook and Internet Guide for College-Bound Students

Cynthia Hickman

New York: Kaplan Books/Simon & Schuster, 1997.
(http://www.kaplan.com). 282p. ISBN: 0-684-84173-8.
Softcover, $15.00.

This guide is written for beginning high school students who want to learn how to make the most of their high school years, in order to be able to have the best chance to attend their college of choice. Full of details about how to make the most of time in school, in the community, and in extracurricular activities, the author encourages students to work hard at being well-rounded, well-educated persons.

The material is divided into three parts covering "School," "Extra-curriculars," and "College." The chapters are filled with topics that range from choosing classes and getting good grades, to how to participate effectively in your community, to how to participate in sports and work during high school. There are also tips on selecting the right college, how to get through the application process, and how to finance college.

This book is not about the Internet, but it does use the Internet as a resource to provide additional information about each chapter's material. Some chapters offer extensive resources, whereas others have fewer Internet links. For example, there are five pages of online resources for a chapter on "Participating in Your Community."

The resources are divided by type of site and include educational, government, commercial, and organizations. Annotations are brief, with a sentence or two about the major focus of the site.

There are other education Internet books out there that contain similar lists of online resources found here, but they do not have the combination of an in-depth study of getting ready to go to college as well as the Internet resources. Such a combination makes this guide a valuable tool for any student looking ahead to attending college.

Appendices consist of a "High School Calendar" in the form of a timetable for setting goals and priorities to prepare for getting into college successfully. Appendix B is a directory of colleges and universities on the Internet. In today's competitive world, getting into a good college takes more than luck. This guide can help alert students to what lies ahead and help them prepare for it.

The Homeschool Guide to the Internet

Mark Dinsmore and Wendy Dinsmore

Elkton, MD: Homeschool Press, 1996. 175p.
ISBN: 1-888306-20-3. Softcover, $14.99.

Home schooling has caught on and grown greatly in the last year or two since this book was published. Though somewhat dated, there are no other books similar to it at this writing. Families today who want to home-school their children have so many more options for providing resources now. The Internet and World Wide Web have opened the doors to unlimited resources for study at home. This guide is actually a sequel to *The Homeschool Guide to the Online World*, which covers the basics of choosing an online service to access the Internet and World Wide Web. It's not necessary to read the first book to use this one, but the authors suggest that there are a number of Web sites listed in the first book which are not repeated in this guide.

The authors use a very friendly approach to teaching about the Internet. The Information Superhighway analogy is used in the three parts of the book. Part One is "Choose a Ramp, Any Ramp"; Part Two is "Excellent Internet Exits"; and Part Three is "Getting More Miles Per Hour." Essentially, the guide introduces families to the Internet and its tools, including Gopher, e-mail, Usenet news, FTP, and the Web. The authors use humor to get their material across, as you can see from chapter titles such as "Don't Wait a Minute, Mr. Postman..." and "To FTP or PPP—That Is the Question!"

"The Homeschool Resource Directory" lists more than 250 information resources directed at home-schooling families. Some are Gopher sites, mailing lists, and newsgroups. Sites are listed in alphabetical order within the subject category. The first subject is home schooling and contains a large number of sites about and for home schooling. Other topics are computing, cooking, music, education, science, social studies, history, Christian resources, and more. The entries are generally very brief, with a sentence or two describing the site, and the Web address. There are other kinds of resources listed here for entertainment, reference, and teaching, which can add to the home-schooling environment.

Appendices include an Internet service provider list by state; "Caution: Children at Play," which discusses safety issues; a "Guide to Plug-ins for the World Wide Web"; and a "Guide to Online Academies," a collection of distance learning resources. A glossary of terms encountered while surfing the 'Net is also available. No index.

Internet Family Fun: The Parent's Guide to Safe Surfing

Bonnie Bruno with Joel Comm

San Francisco, CA: No Starch Press, 1997. (http://www.nostarch.com). 184p. ISBN: 1-886411-19-0. Softcover, $14.95.

Written for today's family wishing to get started using the Internet, this friendly guide targets the complete beginner or those who have very limited computer experience. For example, there is a section on why computers are important at home, how to buy one and how to set it up, *and* a definition of a mouse! Most Internet books generally do not include such basic information. Also, not many Internet guides actually suggest using WebTV as an alternative to purchasing a computer, but this one does. The author's writing style seems almost conversational, like a good friend talking to you as you read and absorb all this new stuff.

The focus of this book is safety. So, in a chapter on access to the Internet, the emphasis is on online services. The descriptions of America Online and CompuServe are excellent, with information about the main features such as logging on, e-mail, newsgroups, and more. Enough information is provided to help families understand how online services compare to Internet service providers as an access method.

Safety issues are discussed in a chapter with tips for wary parents and information on how online services help make surfing safe. Numerous Web sites are listed at the end of the section, to help parents learn more and extend their comfort level.

The majority of the book lists and describes recommended Web sites that cover a broad range of subjects of interest to families. Examples include games and software to download, travel, weather, science, history, entertainment, and much more. The annotations are informative and the sites were obviously chosen with care. Screen shots of sites are interspersed throughout.

An interesting feature of the book is a chapter containing 21 personal home pages representing some interesting sites for families to visit. There is a brief section on creating a Web page, but not enough to make families Web designers.

This is truly a family-oriented Internet book. The author is knowledgeable and writes with a real enthusiasm about wanting to bring the Internet into the home. For parents who want a fun time learning about the Internet, this book is worth a look.

The Internet for Beginners

Philippa Wingate

Tulsa, OK: Educational Development, 1997. 48p.
ISBN: 0-7460-2689-7. Softcover, $8.95.

This beginner's guide targets children aged 9 through 12. It's fun to read and has many colorful illustrations and graphics. The idea is that children will be more inclined to learn if the subject matter is attractive and interesting. The guide covers all the essentials necessary to begin exploring the Internet via the World Wide Web; to use e-mail, newsgroups, and chat; to download files; and more. Safety issues are discussed as well.

The technical information is covered in an appealing way, with many illustrations. The language is down-to-earth and relevant to children. For example, "it is like a spider in the middle of a huge web" describes what it's like when a computer is connected to the 'Net. A description of servers and clients is also very practical: "A server computer serves a client customer, like a store owner helping a customer."

"Games on-line" tells how to get games via newsgroups as well as how to download games for use offline. A "Problems and Solutions" section deals with the reality of slow connections and high expectations. That is, what happens when it's not possible to get in, when a connection is lost, and other problems that everyone will experience some time or another. "Sites and Resources" provides the Web addresses for games and other sites mentioned throughout. A glossary of Internet terms, plus one on "net slang," helps identify the more common terms encountered when talking about the Internet.

The Internet for Kids

Charnan Kazunas and Tom Kazunas

New York: Children's Press, 1997.
(http://publishing.grolier.com/catalog/pub.htmls/cpindex.html).
48p. ISBN: 0-516-26170-3. Softcover, $6.95.

Here's another True Book about Computer Science, written for kids aged four through eight. *The Internet for Kids* tackles the Internet in a very simple yet intelligent way. Chapters include "Networks," "The Internet," "How It Works," "Internet Addresses," and "The Parts of the Internet."

Beginning with a message from Al Gore discussing the importance of computers in the lives of schools and children, there are screen shots that show the president and vice-president interacting with schoolchildren in the class. What an exciting way to introduce a child to the Internet! There are colorful photos and illustrations on most pages. When explaining "What's on the Internet," the authors choose the example of writing a paper on whales to illustrate how it's possible to find information not only in books, but also by using a computer and a connection to the Internet. Vivid screen shots from Web pages will catch children's eyes while they learn all about information sources on the Internet. Sometimes it's difficult to think of analogies to teach rather complicated concepts like a computer network. Here it's done by comparing network servers to restaurant servers. One serves up food and the other serves up information.

Newsgroups, chat, and other Internet tools are explained, along with search engines. All in all, this is a very simple yet thorough look at the Internet. Any teacher or parent of younger children should try reading this to their children, or better yet, with them…and learn all about what the Internet is and has to offer. A glossary of "Important Words," an index, and a resource list are also included.

Internet for Kids: A Beginner's Guide to Surfing the Net

Ted Pedersen and Francis Moss

New York: Price Stern Sloan, 1997. (**http://www.internet4kids.com**). 219p. ISBN: 0-8431-7937-6. Softcover, $8.95.

This beginner's Internet guide for kids presents the world of cyberspace through the view of an airplane pilot, in three sections titled "Cadet: Welcome to Cyberspace Academy," "Explorer: Living and Learning in Cyberspace," and "Commander: Welcome, Parents and Teachers." Among these three parts are ten chapters where students will learn about "Life on the Internet," "Preparing for Lift-off," "Pilot's Manual for the Internet," "Top Ten Rules for Surfing the Net," "Getting Outfitted," "Guide to the Galaxy," "Tech Talk," and a "Parent's Guide," among other topics.

Written as a pilot's manual, the writing is simple and straightforward. The introductory chapter is much more fun than most, as it uses two characters, Kate and Zach, to teach about the Internet. It follows them as they use their computers one afternoon after school.

The book follows Kate and Zach, two young Cyberspace cadets, and Cybersarge, their friend from the Academy, who guides them through their Internet learning experiences.

The language is conversational and full of "kidspeak," but it also makes reading the book more like reading a novel. As new material is presented, words in bold and sidebars indicate when a new thought or term is important.

After learning about the history of the Internet, Zach and Kate learn all about the various possibilities for the Internet. The "Lift-off" chapter explains how to get connected. E-mail and Internet addresses, along with mailing lists, Usenet, Internet Relay Chat, Web browsers, FTP, and Gopher, are covered in the "Pilot's Manual" chapter. Sections on navigating with a Web browser, using bookmarks, and other Internet tools continue the learning in the chapter called "Navigating the Internet." To graduate from the Academy, it's necessary to know certain rules of safety. In "The Top Ten Rules for Surfing the Net," safety tips are presented. "Getting Outfitted" suggests possibilities for commercial services as well as Internet service providers, with Internet addresses to locate more information.

Upon graduating, Kate and Zach can use the "Guide to the Galaxy," which lists resources to visit and explore. The "Tech Talk" chapter summarizes in one section all the technical considerations for getting up and running, including details about Internet service providers, specifics about Internet Explorer and Netscape, and Macintosh/Windows differences.

All in all, this is an entertaining and yet resourceful book that most kids will enjoy reading. Your children may be ready to help you learn about cyberspace once they have read through this practical and fun guide.

Internet for Kids (Challenging)

Sandy Spaulding

Huntington Beach, CA: Teacher Created Materials, 1997.
(**http://www.teacher-created.com**). 80p. ISBN: 1-55734-869-3.
Softcover, $9.95.

Teacher Created Materials has published a TechKNOWLEDGE series of workbooks to help teachers learn about the Internet and then integrate it into the regular teaching curriculum. The series has workbooks for primary, intermediate, and challenging. This book is one of the "challenging" workbooks. There is no grade level listed on the book. After looking at an intermediate workbook, it appears that the introductory material for each one is basically the same regardless of the level of ability.

The first part of the workbook consists of an introduction to the Internet. It's just enough to get started—no more, no less. As the introduction states, the book does not pretend to be a comprehensive work on the Internet. There are plenty of those out for educators who need more help in the basics.

Two topics—copyright concerns and making the connection—are very brief descriptions of basic issues. Beginning with electronic mail, there is more detail, such as how classes can use e-mail for collaboration and sharing information, and how teachers can use it for keeping up-to-date with other teachers, subscribing to educational mailing lists, and trading or exchanging teaching tips with other teachers. For some, mailing lists offer a way to find experts to communicate with or simply to provide a communication tool for the class. "Where Do You Find These Mailing Lists?" covers ways to locate substantive mailing lists, followed by how to subscribe and various ways classes can use mailing lists for projects or curriculum needs. Usenet news is another information/communication tool that allows students and teachers to advertise for collaborators in projects, stay current on projects and new research, or find people who know about curriculum projects of interest to the school. Material on chats, MOOs, and MUDs, as well as a bit about video on the Internet, helps teachers to see other possibilities the Internet affords. Of course, Gopher, Telnet, FTP, and the World Wide Web also have to be discussed in any book on Internet tools.

There are a few step-by-step directions when demonstrating a sample Web session or Gopher session. An acceptable use policy addresses the issue of access and safety concerns in schools. A sample permission letter is included, as is a "User Agreement and Parent Permission Form." A permission to display student work electronically is also part of a policy and a form letter to be sent to parents.

Web resources are a large part of the book as well. The first lesson is an "Online Travel Log" that allows students to choose a topic and "surf" the 'Net following project guidelines issued by the teacher. A tourist data form can be used by the student to complete information about visited sites. Other projects include "Create Class Bookmarks," where students practice setting certain bookmarks using Netscape Navigator. First they must decide if a site meets certain acceptance criteria. A worksheet gives them a place to record the information and write about the Web site. "A Scavenger Hunt" exercise lets students use clues to find certain items on the Web. A picture of a tree frog and the food guide pyramid are two scavenger hunt items in the exercise. Other subjects explore online museums, zoos and animals, book reviews, and more. A writing project as well as group projects help students work on certain skills such as collaborative learning. The variety of exercises provide a range of subject areas for teachers. Some exercises require filling in worksheets to document the Internet research or writing about information found.

The Internet affords students an opportunity to locate current facts and information not possible with textbooks. This series of workbooks allows busy teachers the opportunity to begin using the Internet with only a little background preparation, rather than having to create all the exercises and projects themselves.

Internet for Kids (Creative Kids)

Tim Haag

Huntington Beach, CA: Teacher Created Materials, 1996.
(http://www.teacher-created.com). 160p. ISBN: 1-55734-621-6.
Softcover, $12.95.

Tim Haag has written another book titled *Internet for Kids*, an intermediate workbook. This one, similarly titled, seems to be directed at a younger age group. The illustrations are cute little cartoons that seem to suit a younger audience. Actually, kids, parents, and teachers can use this book to learn how to understand and use the Internet. The material is divided into two parts, which include a basic introduction to the Internet and its tools and more than 75 Web sites to get started exploring the Internet.

Parents and teachers realize the Internet's potential. It's here and kids know about it. Sometimes the effort to get started can seem overwhelming, though. Who has time to digest the hundreds and hundreds of pages that make up some Internet books? If that idea is off-putting, this workbook may be just right. Not too much material to be overwhelming, but enough material to get up to speed and be able to surf the 'Net.

In the first section, electronic mail, file transfer protocol (FTP), Usenet newsgroups, Gopher, chat, video, and Telnet are covered. Before beginning this section, Haag offers some tips for a safe and healthy ride on the Internet. He has some good ideas for parents to make the experience of using the computer at home a family affair. For example, put the computer in a place that fosters collaboration, and give kids a chance to show off what they know. Reading this section will help the novice Internet user become aware of issues that surround the decision to get on the Information Superhighway. To cover some background of the Internet, there is a frequently asked questions section covering essentials such as "What is on the Internet?," "What is my Internet address?," "What do I need to connect?," and so forth.

The material covering the Internet tools is also presented as FAQs, with basics about each of them. How to send e-mail, shortcuts, mailing lists, and Netiquette are covered in the e-mail section. To illustrate use of e-mail and mailing lists, the KIDLINK and the LISZT Web sites are spotlighted. A few step-by-step directions help you to see what they can do. The same format is followed with the other topics. Each one has a frequently asked questions part followed by a practical example of its use. The Gopher category may be a little dated at this time. When this book was written, Gopher was more popular than it is today. Keep that in mind when reading this section of the book.

When it comes to the World Wide Web, there's a bit more detail. Netscape Navigator is highlighted. There are screen shots illustrating navigation buttons and menu bars. Again, remember the Netscape version used today is newer, so some buttons and bars will have disappeared or changed. Still, the essentials of navigating are the same. What can you do when the Web moves at a snail's pace, or you can't get to a site, or a dreaded error message appears? The author has given some thought to those "lulls" in activity and suggests some things to occupy your time while waiting. He also offers help for those rough times on the Web when things seem to be against you. It's reassuring to know those same error messages happen to lots of other people, too. Once on the Web, you'll need a little ammunition to go hunting for specific sites or resources, and search engines are the way to go. Several of the more important ones (as of the book's writing) are listed. The book's age shows here by not listing HotBot, a very popular search tool.

When you're finished learning how to use some of the Internet's vast array of tools, it's time to see what's out there. The "Web Site Reviews" takes you on a trip through cyberspace. The possibilities for fun and education are almost limitless. Most sites chosen for inclusion offer a certain entertainment as well as educational value. There are sites for sending Internet greetings or postcards, sites for the "budding artist," and those for the scientist in the family. The sites represented here show the variety of subject content found on the Web. In looking at the sites listed, it was surprising to see so many still active, though a few had new addresses. Of course, it's to be expected that sites change often. But because this book is older, there could have been many more that were inactive or had dead links.

Each site contains the Web address along with a description of the site, highlights, and a "see also" reference. The "Try this" section offers tips for getting the most out of the activity. Appendix A lists software programs that will help you with your connection to the Internet. A glossary gives you a list of important terms to know, and a bibliography gives you further resources if you wish to extend your knowledge after sitting down with this workbook.

Having a guidebook with already reviewed Web sites takes a burden off the shoulders of parents and teachers. Knowing the sites you visit are safe allows you to concentrate on the mechanics and enjoy the experience. The combination of basic material and some great Web sites to visit will allow parents and teachers and their children to get a jump-start on learning and appreciating the Internet.

Internet for Kids (Intermediate)

Tim Haag

Huntington Beach, CA: Teacher Created Materials, 1996.
(http://www.teachercreated.com). 80p. ISBN: 1-55734-859-6.
Softcover, $9.95.

Here is a quick, hands-on tour of the Internet, written by a teacher who understands the importance of including the Internet in the curriculum. This book is not a comprehensive guide to everything about the Internet—after all, it's only 80 pages. Haag realizes that the Internet is really a tool to be used along with the everyday curriculum. And his book is also a tool—a reinforcement aid to help teachers get acquainted with the Internet and some of its vast educational sources.

The book covers the basics about a number of Internet issues and tools. After finishing, teachers will see how these tools fit into the classroom's learning environment and should be ready to put them to use.

The book covers e-mail first, because it's the most popular use of the Internet. In a few pages, addresses, tips on sending and replying to messages, how to find mailing lists, and how to be a good subscriber are covered. The author's tips on classroom use of mailing lists focus on the kinds of activities teachers find most useful. Incorporating mailing lists into a class can open the world to students. A few important K-12 mailing lists, such as EDTECH, KIDLINK, and others, are listed. The same format is used for discussion of Usenet news, which also provides a number of possibilities for classroom use. Another educational tool is online chat or Internet Relay Chat, which permits actual real-time talk among students. MUDs, MOOs, and video on the Internet are other examples of communication possibilities of the Internet. Because these are somewhat more involved, it may be necessary to find a book with more detailed information for those serious about starting a MUD or MOO or getting students involved in a chat session.

Gopher and the World Wide Web are two of the more popular uses of the Internet and ones that are more commonly used by schools. The Web has overtaken Gopher as a resource, so that many Gopher sites have been turned into Web sites. But for those schools still using a connection with a nongraphical browser, Gopher provides access to some important educational information. The Web lends itself to all kinds of project possibilities. A sample project illustrates how teachers can use it to enhance their classroom resources.

The rest of the workbook uses step-by-step directions to present samples of projects. But before going into them, it gives a very nice set of guidelines from the Global SchoolNet Foundation. These will help teachers think ahead about what their goals are and how to implement a successful Internet project. With each activity comes a worksheet, along with the steps to complete the assignment and reinforce learning. Each activity contains the title, opening comments for the teacher, and things to consider or tips for teachers; then the worksheet guides students through the exercise. Some of the activities do not have a particular subject area, though others do. The subject area is always stated at the top of the page. For example, it may say "Subject Area: Various" or "Subject Area: Language Arts." The lessons cover science, math, geography, and language arts. One interesting assignment is to compare the various Internet tools such as Gopher, the World Wide Web, and FTP by using a research topic. Is the information found in a timely fashion? Is it useful? Is the tool accessible? This type of exercise will help students understand the merits of various Internet tools. A section called "Sideroads for Teachers" lists a number of Web sites teachers should visit in preparation for creating new projects, collaborations, or curriculum ideas. The glossary includes basic terms related to the Internet. A bibliography cites various books and resources that may further interest teachers.

For educators who want a guide that includes a brief introduction to the Internet along with interesting activities students can use in groups or individually, this workbook will meet those needs. It's written in a teacher-friendly manner for busy educators who want a helping hand getting started. Although the book was published in 1996, the ideas are still current, and at $9.95, the price is right.

Internet in an Hour for Students

Jennifer Frew, Don Mayo, and Kathy Berkemeyer

New York: DDC Publishing, 1998. (http://www.ddcpub.com).
216p. ISBN: 1-56243-601-5. Softcover, $10.00.

Because the Internet has so much information to offer, it's often difficult to find what you want. The DDC Publishing Company has put together a series called Internet in an Hour, which presents the basics of the Internet as well as a practical look at interesting World Wide Web sites. Each title targets a particular audience. As you can tell from this title, *Internet in an Hour for Students* targets students in both high school and college. (One of the other titles must be for sales managers, because page "V" contained the footer "Internet in an Hour for Sales People." Hmm...how did that get into a book for students?)

The book is divided into two main parts called "Internet Basics" and "Web Resources." The author assumes that certain skills are already in place. These include knowledge of Windows 95 and general computer skills such as using a mouse. The book does not cover how to get connected, but assumes that you have access to the Internet in some form or another. For best results, the book tells you the exact type of hardware you "must have" as far as computer, modem, and connection.

The "Basics" section begins with step-by-step directions for becoming familiar with Netscape 4.0 on Windows. It includes Navigator and Messenger, Netscape's browser and e-mail components. The activities include learning to navigate, use URLs, use the toolbars, read messages, delete them, and other basics about e-mail with Netscape. Microsoft's Internet Explorer and the mail component, Outlook Express, are also covered in the same manner as Netscape. There are lots of screen shots for each browser, making it possible for you to see what things look like. There are some good tips on using each browser and mail package.

Many people use America Online for Internet access, so there are several chapters devoted to how to use it; its menus and toolbars; and how to access the Internet through AOL. Again, step-by-step tutorials take you through the process, so it's a good idea to be online while following the directions. America Online also has e-mail. You'll learn how to send, receive, delete, send attachments, and more.

It's important for students to locate information for research purposes. The authors have included a chapter on search engines. Beginning with a brief description of the difference between surfing and searching, there is a section on the various types of search tools. Directories, search engines, and multi-threaded search engines (also called mega-search engines or meta-search engines) are discussed. Using the search engines effectively means learning some of the tips and techniques. Boolean operators, such as AND, OR, and NOT, are covered with examples. The + and – signs that many search engines use are also explained. AltaVista is the search engine used for demonstration purposes.

The "Web Resources" part of the book lists Web sites for various subject areas of interest to students doing research. "Finding Information" lists general sites, directories, and search engines. Other subject categories list sites for helping with homework, writing, and research. Here you'll find out about writing tools and libraries online, as well as the specialized Internet Public Library. For high school students, there is a nice section with help in finding colleges, entrance exams, college essay services, financial aid, scholarships, student loans, and study abroad. The section on getting a job includes sites for résumé information, cover letters, and sites that post job openings, as well as career counseling sites.

Finding news online is a great way for students in college to read their local newspapers or find information for current events. There are sites listed for national news media such as the *New York Times*, CNN, and more.

Appendices include ones on viruses, emoticons and abbreviations, and Netiquette. A glossary lists important terms found during your travels on the Internet.

This book is a good starter for students interested in expanding their Internet skills as they look toward college. The chapters offer basic information accompanied by screen shots that make the material easy to digest. At $10.00, the price is right. The book is small enough to sit right by the computer or take along to read during a break. *Internet in an Hour* will help students learn about helpful sites on the Web, as well as how they can use it to find information, send mail, and more.

The Internet (Kids and Computers)

Charles A. Jortberg

Edina, MN: Abdo Publishing, 1997. (**http://www.abdopub.com**). 40p.
ISBN: 1-56239-727-3. Library binding, $15.95.

Considering that this is written for kids aged 9 through 12, the writing seems a bit stilted and the topic somewhat dry. The Internet is a "hot" topic today, and yet this book is mostly about the Internet's history instead of what it is today. Do nine-year-olds really want to know about the ARPANet? Sometimes the explanations seem almost too simplistic, as if the author didn't want to use a particular word and so had to write a sentence to talk about it instead. The terms *online services* or *Internet service providers* are never actually stated when discussing how to get connected. Also, the description of the World Wide Web conveys a rather boring picture. When explaining the Web, the author says, "smaller Web sites available to users by their addresses that start with 'www'." Not all addresses begin with "www."

"Cool Internet Web Sites for Kids" highlights sites recommended for children. Some are easily recognizable, whereas others (such as "Broccoli Town") are not. Does that sound like a site kids would be excited over? Maybe "Chocolate Town" or "Beanie Baby Town," but "Broccoli Town"? Yes, it's an informative, educational site all about broccoli, but....

This is not a "fun" book. The language is serious rather than humorous. Even with color photos interspersed throughout, it's still a rather dull look at the Internet. Contains a glossary.

Internet Kids and Family Yellow Pages, 2d Edition

Jean Armour Polly

Berkeley, CA: Osborne/McGraw-Hill, 1997. (**http://www.osborne.com**). 608p. ISBN: 0-07-882340-4. Softcover, $19.99.

Written by a mother/librarian, this second edition of *Internet Kids Yellow Pages* is expanded and revised, with almost 3,400 resources. That's about twice the size of the first edition. Polly points out that sites are selected by her, as a librarian and mother, for their value to children and parents. New in this edition is a separate section for parents on how to get started using the Internet.

Given the thousands of entries, the author has included a "10 Special Don't-Miss Hotlists" section featuring the best for various subject areas, such as homework, art and music, games, reading, sports, science, and more.

Entries are arranged in alphabetical order and range from typical subjects for children to some that are more unusual, such as amusement parks, parades, and monsters. Besides entertainment, education is aptly represented with a category of "Schools and Education," as well as special sites for sciences, reference works, geography, writing, and much, much more. With in-depth annotations at times, it's easy to decide which site is the one to visit.

Along the way, "Net Files" are included. These are trivia questions that encourage children to think. Just so there's no cheating, the answers are printed upside down on the page. There is also a Web site that contains any changes to the book, so it's easy to keep current.

No history of the Internet is included, nor are there directions on how to get software or how to use the Web. But the book is an excellently organized and well-written resource for kids. The sites are safe and always appropriate for children, so just prop it up next to a computer and start surfing.

Internet Kids Yellow Pages

Jean Armour Polly

Berkeley, CA: Osborne/McGraw-Hill, 1996. (**http://www.osborne.com**). 352p. ISBN: 0-07-882197-5. Softcover, $19.95.

From the publishers of *Internet Yellow Pages* comes this kid's edition for preschool through teenagers. Selected by a librarian who is also a mother, the entries are written for children in a friendly style they will like. Topics range from typical ones seen on many Web sites for children to more unusual ones, such as amusement parks, birds, cars, Disney, monsters, parades—you get the picture.

Subjects include entertainment as well as educational ones like pollution, reference works, physics, and much more. Along the way, there are "Net Files," little facts and questions to encourage children to think. Answers are provided at the bottom of the page, usually with an Internet address for further information. (And the answers are upside down so it's harder to cheat!)

Information is arranged in an easy-to-read manner, with titles in bold and a nice paragraph about the site, followed by the Internet address. The wide range of topics will provide kids of all ages with something to interest them. *(Courtesy of Multimedia Schools Magazine, Information Today, Inc., Medford, NJ).*

Internet Without Fear: Practical Tips and Activities

Dr. Elizabeth Rhodes Offutt and Charles R. Offutt

Torrance, CA: Good Apple, 1996. (**http://www.frankschaffer.com/**).
144p. ISBN: 1-56417-853-6. Softcover, $14.99.

The purpose of this guide for elementary school teachers, grades K-6, is to provide information about the benefits of integrating the Internet into the classroom as a tool for learning. Written by teachers who understand the impact and importance of the 'Net, the practical nature of the book should encourage any teacher who is still hesitant to jump on the bandwagon.

The material is clearly written, with enough information to understand what the Internet is and how it can provide teachers, administrators, and parents with a wealth of tools and information. For those just not up to speed on the Internet, because of uncertainty about equipment or how to connect, the authors provide a "Shopping List for Internet Access," with tips on computer equipment, modems, online services, communications software, and more. An Internet glossary plus a Web glossary help define the main vocabulary terms found along the way.

Once familiar with what the Internet is, making the first connection will certainly follow. Here's where e-mail, browsing the World Wide Web, and helpful tips for searching with two of the major online services (America Online and CompuServe) are explained.

The authors provide Internet activities for teachers to help them get started integrating the Internet into their classes. The activities are arranged by subject and include the major areas taught in elementary school. Each activity includes the grade level, activity name, description, Web address, and teaching tip. E-mail lists, organizations, and associations are listed at the end for further information.

The combination of practical introductory material with the curriculum activities makes this a good resource for elementary teachers who are just waiting for some help in getting started. Learning the Internet is made painless and even fun.

Kids Do the Web

Cynthia Bix with Mary Anne Petrillo, Tom Morgan, and John Miller

San Jose, CA: Adobe Press, 1996. (http://www.adobe.com/).
207p. ISBN: 1-56830-315-7. Softcover, $25.00.

Adobe has put together a book for all children interested in learning about creating a Web site. Teachers, administrators, and parents can use this tool to learn about basic Web design and browsing. The book is basically a tour of Web sites created by kids, to demonstrate the possibilities of Web creation and to encourage children to try it. At each tour stop, special tips are offered on how the site was put together, what makes it special, and how it works. Sites are categorized as by schools, international sites, and sites for kids. Software tips provide information on how it was done. Because this book is by Adobe, you can guess that their software is what is recommended and used for creating the Web pages. Lots of illustrations, photos, and colorful pages make this a fun book for kids. *(Courtesy of Multimedia Schools Magazine, Information Today, Inc., Medford, NJ).*

Kids Guide to the Internet

Bruce Goldstone and Arthur Perley

Mahwah, NJ: Troll, 1996. (http://www.troll.com/). 128p.
ISBN: 0-8167-4131-X. Softcover, $3.95.

This little paperback serves as a "driver's manual" to the Internet, covering the basics children will need to get started using the Internet. Its style is very breezy and conversational and will appeal to children. Because it's geared to kids, the authors include "Rules for Internet Travelers," with safety tips such as never giving out personal information. Children can learn about key-pals through electronic mail, the World Wide Web, and other "cool" stuff on the 'Net. Most of the book is an introduction to the Internet rather than a resource guide to sites; however, there are sections with suggestions for getting started and a Web Wildlife chapter for exploring. MUDs and a whole chapter on the Armadillo Project show children some unique uses of the Internet. Unlike most Internet books, this is one that a child could actually carry around and read. At $3.95, it's a bargain. *(Courtesy of Multimedia Schools Magazine, Information Today, Inc., Medford, NJ).*

Kids Online: Protecting Your Children in Cyberspace

Donna Rice Hughes with Pamela T. Campbell

Grand Rapids, MI: Fleming H. Revell, 1998.
(http://www.bakerbooks.com). 269p.
ISBN: 0-8007-5672-X. Softcover, $11.95.

Donna Rice Hughes is better known for her participation in the Gary Hart scandal and subsequent loss of his political career. Now a crusader against pornography and an advocate of protecting children on the Internet, she has written a book on Internet safety along with Pamela T. Campbell, a Christian writer. Her goal is to provide parents with the information they need to protect their children in cyberspace.

There are eight chapters and nine appendices. In the chapter "Bridging the Technogeneration Gap," Hughes points out the benefits of being online, along with some of the dangers. But then, that's the perspective this book takes. Hughes states that many of the Internet books for parents and children focus too much on the benefits, with only a bit about the dangers. Hers is the opposite. To illustrate this, here are some titles of chapters: "The Serious Risks of Cyberspace," "Shedding Light on the Darkness of Pornography," "The First Line of Defense." All focus on dangers of the Internet. In fact, one chapter suggests checking out whether your school is restricting access to pornography or following safety rules. Hughes cites statistics on "pornography access" by students and offers vignettes to illustrate the risk of exposure to dangerous material. She advocates that schools and libraries adopt a policy of using filtering tools along with acceptable use policies.

The book has a great deal of advice for protecting children online. There are rules and ideas for developing a good relationship with your child, what kind of access to provide, how to talk to your child about the dangers, rules for online safety, and more. These are all good suggestions, ones any parent would want to think about.

In "Creating a Digital Toolbox," software filters and controls for limiting access are discussed, along with suggestions for deciding which works best for a particular situation. "Expanding Your Child's Safety Net" takes on the issues of Internet access in libraries and schools; offers ways to check on what they offer as far as protection; and recommends what to do if they don't provide filtering software or a controlled environment. Although Hughes is obviously against any access that is not controlled, she does present the stands of the American Library Association and the American Civil Liberties Union.

True, the Internet can be a dangerous place for children. It's important for families to know what their children are doing online and to understand the dangerous situations that might occur. Donna Hughes is an effective advocate of protecting children online. The material is easy to understand, even for the very beginner. For concerned parents who want a slant about all the bad things about the Internet, this book will provide it. For anyone who wants a more balanced look at the Internet, there are other books that combine more of the good along with the dangers.

Kids Rule the Net

Michael Wolff

New York: Wolff New Media, 1996. (http://www.ypn.com).
182p. ISBN: 1-889670-08-1. Softcover, $14.95.

Kids rule this book, too. It is written for kids by kids, with a lively flavor to it and lots of photos and graphics that give it a youthful feel. The main contents are nine chapters of kid-selected Web sites with reviews by—you guessed it—kids. Most reviewers are between the ages of 7 and 14 and come from all parts of the world.

The book begins with an introduction to the World Wide Web and Internet, but it's done differently than the tried and true "Welcome to the Internet " chapter. Frequently asked questions by kids provide some basic background information. Here's an example: "What can a kid do on the Internet?," "What's a Web Site?" And the answer is, "A Web site is kind of like a magazine, except that instead of just being able to turn pages, you can download short movies, play games...." A no-frills answer that gives a kids' view of the Web. Search engines are reviewed by an 11-year-old in Canada. In referring to AltaVista, he says it's "not exactly a well-known search engine." This rather dates the material, as AltaVista is probably still the most popular search engine. Also, comparing the lack of results from a Yahoo search to one on AltaVista shows a lack of knowledge about how subject directories and search engines work. But then, most kids probably won't even notice. Two highly recommended places to search are no longer at the Web addresses listed.

The remaining nine chapters are "World's a Zoo," "Time Machine," "Stars & Heroes," "The Laboratory," "Team Spirit," "Getting Around," "The Den," "The Dark Side," and "The Way of the Web." Topics in these chapters contain a wide array of kid-friendly material ranging from animals, ancient history highlighting myths and legends, and entertainment with television and movies to science, sports, travel, and all kinds of games. UFOs, aliens, and other strangeness are part of "The Dark Side."

Each chapter features "My Top Sites," with a picture of the writer and the sites chosen as his or her favorites. There is usually a paragraph that accompanies the chapter telling why these sites are favorites and what they are used for. The book is full of photographs illustrating the sites. Each Web site is listed in big, bold letters with a descriptive summary, the Web address in red letters, and the reviewer's name and age. Sometimes trivia notes accompany the topic under review. Additional links may also be featured.

As a book for kids, it's a great way to introduce a child to the fun aspects of the Internet in a nonthreatening way. Because there aren't many books like this (written by kids), it has a unique appeal. With luck, a newer version will appear. It does need some updating if it's going to remain effective as a learning tool. For one thing, the main Web address (www.ypn.com/) appears not to work. This was one way to get updates to the material.

The Learning Highway: Smart Students and the Net

Trevor Owen and Ron Owston

Toronto, Ontario, Canada: Key Porter Books Limited, 1998. (**http://www.keyporter.com**). 209p. ISBN: 1-55013-905-3. Softcover, $16.95.

Aimed at both undergraduate and high school students, *The Learning Highway* is designed to help them learn to use the Internet for their studies. It intends to help "bridge the gap" between secondary and undergraduate environments and to pave the way for using online resources at the college level.

Describing it as a "companion" to general Internet guides already published, the authors are careful to say that this book will not provide all the "how to log on" and "how to create Web pages" kind of material found in the more general Internet guides. They recommend using such guides along with this one to fill in any gaps about the World Wide Web and Internet.

The book is organized into four main parts. Part One, "The Internet as a Learning Highway," explores the manner in which the Internet serves as a "place of learning." One of the main ways students can benefit from the Internet as a learning tool is through "human interaction," whether it's across the city or world. Projects that incorporate the Internet allow such interaction and foster a wider spectrum of learning. The guide suggests four main areas in which it's possible to increase learning and understanding online. These are "task and purpose," "what your teachers are likely to need," "focus," and "learning is never far from home." As roles change, some teachers may be reluctant to move into the new technologies. Finding ways to introduce them to the power and potential of the Internet is demonstrated by several projects described in Chapter 3,

"Changing Roles." Be prepared: A project called Writers in Electronic Residence is used to illustrate how a poem published on the Internet by a student challenged other students and elicited discussion for several weeks. The poem, "Inborn Consent," contains language some might find offensive.

Part Two, "Tools of Learning," highlights the World Wide Web as the primary research tool. With that in mind, the next four chapters are basically a mini-tutorial of Netscape Navigator. Beginning with one on how to browse, there are screen shots and details on using the menus and buttons for navigating. Thrown in are some tips on URLs, a bit about clients and servers, and how to organize your research efforts with bookmarks. Continuing with Netscape, the rest of the chapters focus on using Netscape's mail and newsgroup components. Essentially, these follow the same format of providing step-by-step directions, this time for e-mail and newsgroups.

Part Three, "Learning Through Research," contains four chapters that introduce tools to locate resources. Beginning with subject directories, Yahoo, as the premier directory, is studied in-depth with screen shots and step-by-step directions for accessing the site. You will learn all about the structure of the directory and the organization of its categories. To demonstrate Yahoo's functionality, you can follow the process of researching two topics; "The effect of oil spills" and "Macbeth" illustrate how to effectively search Yahoo.

Next, search engines are introduced. Another mini-tutorial follows, this time using AltaVista, considered by many to be the best search engine. Simple searches, understanding results, and advanced searching are covered. Both these chapters are good starting points and provide students with basic skills to get going. A sample research example explores the same two topics used in Yahoo to compare the process and results.

It's often necessary to locate different kinds of information, so, in the final chapter of Part Two, several interesting tools are introduced: DejaNews for locating newsgroups, Liszt for finding mailing lists, SHAREWARE.COM for locating software online, and Amazon.com for finding the latest books published. York University's library catalog is demonstrated as well. Most people think of Amazon.com as a bookstore, and it is, but it's also a wonderful source for locating current books.

After you learn about the tools to use, the next chapter zeroes in on developing strategies for locating three kinds of resources—specific facts, articles, and Web sites—as well as how to evaluate what is found. There seems to be very little written about search strategies or the effect of using Boolean operators, which is rather surprising given the more serious nature of this work and the emphasis on learning and applying what you learn.

Part Four, "Learning Through Projects," details 16 Canadian projects that illustrate the kinds of learning environments that favor the Internet. "Focus on Interaction" uses the Internet for collaborative projects and communication. Examples might be penpals, "ask-an-expert," online field trips, etc. "Focus on Information" serves as a source for research projects or publishing and sharing resources on the Internet. "Focus on Task" concerns learning activities such as writing, simulations, and social issues. "Focus on Technology" includes understanding and learning about technology and its use as a tool. Each project includes a title, level, type of project, tool(s) used, and a contact person for more information. The projects are very detailed and help to demonstrate the successful use of Internet tools in Canadian schools.

The Learning Highway promotes the use of the Internet for research by students, in both secondary and postsecondary education, by emphasizing the process rather than the technology. The combination of both tools and theory makes this book a good resource for any student who wants to understand how the Internet can impact and improve research skills. Although this is a Canadian title, featuring projects and examples that come from Canada, the information is useful for any student.

Learning the Internet for Kids: A Voyage to Internet Treasures

Denise Vega

New York: DDC Publishing, 1998. (**http://www.ddcpub.com**).
349p. ISBN: 1-56243-552-3. Spiral notebook, $27.00.
(Includes CD-ROM).

Using a voyage on the sea as a way to explore and teach kids about the Internet, this workbook uses two young pirates (Larry and Carrie) and a parrot, Polly, as guides through the Internet lessons. Children in third through sixth grades are the target audience.

The book is divided into "Adventures." Within each adventure are several "quests" that help children work through learning about the Internet. To make the most of the material, it's necessary to have an Internet connection either at school or at home, as well as to know some basic computer skills such as using a Mac or Windows and how to move a mouse. For those who do not have a connection, the accompanying CD provides a simulation of the online adventures.

Throughout the book are various icons that provide hints, tips, and warnings. Look for the specially marked areas or shaded columns as you read the material.

The Adventures follow a particular format that begins with "Tools & Supplies," giving background information on the chapter's topics. New tools and language are also included in this section. Directions are given for both PC and Macintosh platforms. The "Try It!" section uses the CD to practice material covered in the chapter and generally has step-by-step directions. "Your Quest" comes at the end of the material presented and offers an opportunity for hands-on work. With step-by-step directions, all of the activities are part of the CD simulation.

"Logging Your Adventure" is a summary exercise that replays everything you've learned, just as a ship's captain does at the end of the day. It provides additional practice and a way to test what you've learned. Finally, the "Treasure Chest" contains directions on how to do some supplementary things that aren't part of the main activity. These can be done for extra practice or just for a fun time.

The lessons cover all the basics of using the Internet, in particular the World Wide Web. Netscape Communicator 4 is used as the browser. There are lots of screen shots and illustrations to enhance the material taught. When the Adventures are completed, kids will know how to use Netscape and locate resources and information for school projects or just for fun at home. They will learn about how to download files and to use FTP as well as electronic mail. There is also a unit on America Online, probably the most popular online service today.

The cast of pirates and the environment of a ship at sea make the learning fun for kids. The large type and easy-to-read writing style also contribute to the ease of use. Because it's cross-platform, if you want to use it at school on a Mac and at home on a PC, it will work fine in both environments. Young children should have mastered the basics when they dock at home after taking this cruise through the seas of the Internet and World Wide Web.

Mayfield's Quick View Guide to the Internet for Students of English

Jennifer Campbell and Michael Keene

Mountain View, CA: Mayfield Publishing, 1998.
(http://www.mayfieldpub.com). 60p. ISBN: 0-7674-0032-1.
Softcover, $7.95.

The title is rather misleading. Though apparently promising something that focuses on the special needs of students of English, there is really nothing in this booklet that makes it more informative to that particular population. Perhaps a few of the Web sites reflect English interests, but that's all there seemed to be.

Some material does reflect an educational focus. The section on finding jobs and the Internet Resources part focus on education-related material such as reference books, writing centers, sites for teachers, and books and book reviews. In another part there are sections on citing Internet sites, as well as evaluating what you find. Electronic mail, newsgroups, and a bit about real-time communication are also covered.

As a free source with other Mayfield textbooks, this little guide has a place as a mini-guide to carry with you or keep next to your computer, but as a source for English students, there's just not much to recommend it.

My First Book About the Internet

Sharon Cromwell

Mahwah, NJ: Troll, 1997. (**http://www.troll.com**). 30p.
ISBN: 0-8167-4320-7. Softcover, $2.95.

This beginner's guide for young children explores how to learn to surf the 'Net. Illustrated with colorful cartoons and written at a primary level, the material covers all the basics, including what the Internet is, and getting on the Internet. It also introduces computers and the expression *going online*. Modems, software, and service providers are worked into this section, which is illustrated with a little girl sitting at her computer connecting to the Internet while her cat sits across what looks like a mouse pad. The next couple of pages go into the specifics of a modem and online service, comparing them to a post office. How things move on the Internet discusses the way the Internet works among all kinds of computers. Safety is also part of this beginner's book. There's a really cute drawing of a little boy and his mother sitting together while he uses a laptop. The Internet "do's and don'ts" are written across a computer screen. "Signing on" breaks down the steps for getting a service, choosing a password, and signing on. E-mail is treated with a very basic explanation of sending it and what an e-mail address consists of.

Again, the large and colorful drawings help get the points across visually. Chat rooms receive attention and are explained as a connection between people who have computers and use the keyboards to talk to others. The illustration shows two different children sitting at their computers—one is from Paris (the Eiffel Tower is in the background) and the other, a little boy, lives on a farm. They are chatting by computer. "Surfing the Net" presents the concept of browsing the many words, numbers, pictures, and photos on the World Wide Web. A computer is likened to a surfboard that surfs the ocean while the computer surfs the Internet.

The Web is explained in more detail, introducing terms such as *Web site*, *home pages*, *linked*, and *icons*. URLs are explained and a suggestion is made that children may want to have an adult type in the address or URL. Home pages are also explained as the home base for a Web site. To round out the book, some fun sites are listed, including The White House, Nikolai's Web Site, and more. If you still need some help, the glossary of terms will provide reinforcement.

This is a cute little book. The Internet is here and has a lot to offer kids. The material covered is written in very simple terms and complemented by the really cute drawings, which put kids right in the picture. So, if you're looking for a new book to read to your kids at bedtime, this one will teach them something. If you're a parent new to the Internet, you may learn a few things too.

New Kids on the Net: A Tutorial for Teachers, Parents and Students

Sheryl Burgstahler

Boston, MA: Allyn & Bacon, 1997. (http://www.abacon.com).
266p. ISBN: 0-205-19872-4. Softcover, $18.95.

This hands-on tutorial uses a series of 10 lessons to cover the major Internet tools, such as e-mail, the World Wide Web, Gopher, Telnet, and newsgroups, plus material on search engines, downloading files, and more. The book targets preservice teachers, students, school administrators, parents, and anyone new to the Internet. A basic knowledge of computers is assumed by the author.

Exercises are arranged according to their importance in making use of the Internet. For example, e-mail is discussed first, after an introduction to the basics of the Internet; then the World Wide Web is covered. The language is nonintimidating and jargon-free, even when the material is a bit technical. For example, the author prefers to use the term *distribution lists* instead of mailing lists or LISTSERVs. (Unfortunately, most of the time they will be referred to as mailing lists or LISTSERVs in the real world.)

Each chapter is organized to include a set of objectives, an overview of the topic, the detailed lesson with step-by step directions, and finally references. As applicable, chapters include appropriate online examples. Screen shots are interspersed throughout to illustrate material and Internet sites. Lesson 10 puts it all together by presenting projects to try out after you finish your Internet education. A glossary of terms is included in an appendix.

This tutorial is geared to an inexperienced user, but does not seem overwhelming because of the organization and friendly language. Though they cover a lot of material, the chapters are well designed and easily navigated.

Online Kids: A Young Surfer's Guide to Cyberspace

Preson Gralla

New York: John Wiley & Sons, 1996. (http://www.wiley.com/).
288p. ISBN: 0-471-13545-3. Softcover, $14.95.

The bright, eye-catching cover will appeal to most kids. It's obvious that this book is geared to the "young cybersurfer" aged 8 through 14, with its large print, abundant white space, and casual writing style. There are a lot of "cools" and "neats" that (though sounding a bit overused to me) will probably hit the mark just fine with kids.

The book is divided into three parts. Part One, "Learning the Basics," includes seven chapters covering a definition of the Internet (or cyberspace as it's referred to here), what you can find in cyberspace, equipment needed to get online, safety issues and Netiquette, tips for browsing the World Wide Web, choosing an online service, chat, newsgroups, and e-mail. Online services are emphasized as the best access points for children. Gralla includes brief, informative descriptions of America Online, CompuServe, and the Microsoft Network.

Part Two describes recommended (or as Gralla puts it, "the best and coolest") educational sites. Subjects include reading, writing, math, science, travel, weather, and history, among others. Each entry is formatted to tell "Where to Get It," meaning through an online service or the Web; "How to Get There," which gives the log-on for an online service or the URL if on the Web; and "What It Is," which offers a brief description. "Usefulness" and "Coolness" ratings, from one to ten, are given to each site. Part Three focuses on the fun stuff found on the Web, including entertainment, sports, hobbies, and games, as well as a chapter on creating your own Web pages.

The author's writing style is casual and certainly nontechnical. Along the way, Gralla inserts dialog boxes with a cartoon character pointing to important facts he is emphasizing. Throughout the book, important terms are bolded for emphasis and headings are always large and bold. Scattered among the chapters are hands-on activities with step-by-step directions. The listing of Web sites is quite impressive and the descriptions very informative. This book should appeal to children who want to learn how to get started with the Internet at home or in school.

Parenting Online: The Best of the Net for Moms and Dads

Melissa Wolf

Brooklyn, NY: Equinox Press, 1998. (http://ralphmoss.com/index.html).
216p. ISBN: 1-881025-47-0. Softcover, $16.95.

This book is a collection of Web sites for parents who want to use the Internet as a resource to help them learn more about parenting. The author writes from the perspective of a new mother. She feels very strongly about the Internet as an important tool for information. Many topics relate directly to parenting, such as pregnancy, health, and working moms, but there are also topics such as education, discipline, home schooling, homework help, books for kids, special needs, teens, and more.

Chapters are arranged in alphabetical order by subject and begin with an introductory paragraph, followed by the site listings and annotations. Each site has a review by the author to help parents decide which ones are best for them.

As part of the preface, the author provides a few Internet terms and facts. But the complete novice who needs more than the resources will have to look at one of the other Internet guides for a more thorough discussion. This book is just what it says: a guide to what's best on the Internet for moms and dads.

Parents Guide to the Information Superhighway: Rules and Tools for Families Online

Wendy Lazarus and Laurie Lipper

Santa Monica, CA: The Children's Partnership, 1996.
28p. ISBN not listed. Booklet, $8.00.

Written in collaboration with the National PTA and the National Urban League, this publication's intent is to encourage parents to use the Internet with their children. The whole idea is to keep it simple and to provide some "rules and tools" for the journey.

The guide covers the most frequently asked questions from dozens of parents surveyed. It can be read cover-to-cover, or it's possible to flip to a specific chapter of interest.

Chapters cover children online, with basics about the Internet; the relationship of children and computers and how to determine when they are ready to use one; how to get connected, with step-by-step help in setting up; locating sites; and keeping it safe for children. The section on "Classrooms and Communities" discusses how schools can get involved with technology.

Obviously, in 28 pages, there's really not much that isn't covered elsewhere in more detailed books, but perhaps that's the strength of this little guide. Not too much information, so it's not overwhelming, and a simple writing style that is not intimidating to those parents just getting started. *(Courtesy of Multimedia Schools Magazine, Information Today, Inc., Medford, NJ).*

Parent's Guide to the Internet

Washington, DC: Department of Education, 1997.
(http://www.ed.gov/pubs/parents/internet.html). 17p.
ISBN not listed. Booklet, free.

This little booklet was prepared for parents who want to make use of the Internet as an educational tool. No technological expertise is necessary. What makes this a great tool for most parents is that it cuts out a lot of the information found in longer guides, so that parents get the essential material to learn the basics about the Internet and how to get around on it. The booklet also suggests ways that children can make use of the Internet's resources, along with tips on making their Internet surfing safe.

The language is very simple but not condescending. It explains things in a matter-of-fact way. It begins with a brief look at what the Internet is and then the benefits of being connected. Parents can use the Internet at public places such as public libraries if they don't already own a computer. But for those who want to have their own connection, the guide explains the very basics of equipment and the main choices for getting an Internet connection (online services and Internet service providers). There are some tips on considerations such as cost, troubleshooting, and the contract.

Like any well-organized trip, getting on the Information Superhighway takes some planning and some "maps" to keep from getting lost. Navigating using hyperlinks and Web addresses is covered, along with some basics about search engines. Examples of prominent tools such as Yahoo and InfoSeek are included. There's a nice example of how a child can use the Internet for a student project. Other topics covered in short paragraphs are e-mail, LISTSERVs, newsgroups, and tips on safety while interacting with others and surfing the World Wide Web.

A section of "Sites Along the Way" offers some family-friendly places for children to explore, online reference material, and sites for parents and parent groups. A glossary concludes this booklet.

For a parent or anyone with children who wants to take that first step toward gathering information about the Internet, this little guide has a very friendly and nonthreatening look to it while offering an introduction to many of the basics of the Internet. After reading this, parents will have some tools to help guide their children toward safe and productive use of the Internet. The guide is available at the U.S. Department of Education's Web site and can be reproduced to share with others.

A Parent's Guide to the Internet... And How to Protect Your Children in Cyberspace

Parry Aftab

New York: SC Press, 1997. (http://www.familyguidebook.com). 328p. ISBN: 0-9660491-0-1. Softcover, $22.95.

Parents are often way behind children in their knowledge of technology, and specifically the Internet. For those who feel hopelessly left out, don't despair. Here's a book written by someone who understands. The author is a parent and self-professed "non-geek" who has mastered the Internet and wants to help other parents keep up with their child on the Internet, or at least "level the playing field between already-savvy kids" and their "clueless" parents. The four main parts of the book address the key areas that will get parents up to speed.

Part One, "Outfitting Yourself for Cyberspace (everything you need to know to get online)," begins with an encouraging message not to be afraid. Then it moves on to a gentle introduction to the Internet, called "What's the Internet? What's the World Wide Web?," which explains the basics of each. Realizing that many parents are beginners in every respect, Aftab provides a chapter that introduces computer hardware issues and explains about the various parts of a computer. For Mac users, this information will not be as helpful, and anyone who already owns a computer can just skip this part.

Getting down to the nitty-gritty of hardware, there is a nice chart that lists key features—such as 200 MHz, Pentium, 32 MB RAM, 3.0GB HD, and 28.8 modem—and explains them in a user-friendly writing style. Along with hardware issues, there are suggestions about where to buy a computer. The author also suggests that if buying a whole computer system is not the right choice, there are alternatives, such as WebTV or Internet Box Technology. Obviously, computers are changing so rapidly that the numbers (28.8 modem, etc.) in this book will quickly be obsolete, but remember one piece of advice: buy the fastest computer affordable.

Once the computer is purchased, the next step is to get connected. This means getting service from somewhere. After succinct descriptions of the major services, another chart helps break down the pluses and minuses associated with using an online service versus an Internet service provider. It's really an individual decision based on what a family wants from the Internet.

After connecting, it's time to get out there and explore. Search engines, finding e-mail addresses, and bookmarks are all touched on. Electronic mail is explored in more detail in a subsequent chapter, highlighting differences from both online services and Internet service providers.

Part Two, "The Dark Side: Keeping Things in Perspective (everything you need to know about online risks)," presents material about the "dark" side of the Internet. This is a topic that has received much publicity in the media. The author acknowledges this fact. This section is not meant to scare parents, but it is meant to inform them about the "bad side" that does exist.

As a mother and attorney, Parry Aftab has a unique perspective about safety issues. She runs the legal bulletin boards on America Online and has appeared as an expert on Internet legal and safety issues. Her approach is honest and direct. She believes that much of the "hysteria" about the safety of the Internet can be attributed to media overreaction and to conservative groups who want to censor what's on the Internet. That is not to say that there are not real dangers on the Internet—there are, and she addresses them. In a chapter on legal issues, she explains the Communications Decency Act and why it never made it. There's also a very interesting look at what makes up a "Cyber Predator" and how to keep kids safe from pedophiles.

Parents, teachers, and anyone who wants to know how to keep their children safe can learn a great deal from chapters on cleaning up the Internet. How to get obscene sites off the Web; the hidden dangers, such as tobacco/alcohol ads, bigotry, and hate-filled sites; protecting yourself and your children from hackers; and more are all discussed. And don't forget that online addiction is a growing concern. There are tips on how to keep inappropriate mail from getting to your kids and how to get kids to share what they are doing online.

Part Three, "Making and Enforcing Your Choices as Parents," encourages parents to find the "right fit" and to find out what other parents are doing. Planning ahead and thinking about the possibilities that might occur can go a long way toward meeting the challenges that come up online. Have an acceptable use policy in place and teach kids about the potential dangers.

One way to take control of a child's Internet access is to invest in some filtering or parental control software. There are various kinds available that prohibit access either by blocking "bad" sites or by only allowing access to the "good" ones. Some of this software can also monitor offline activity as well. Then there are the rating services, such as PICS (Platform for Internet Content Selection), that rate the sites. However, Aftab points out that PICS has not caught on as rapidly as anticipated. Along with individual descriptions of the products, there are also comparisons for CyberPatrol, CyberSitter, and Surf Watch. Many online services also offer filtering software, including two named Bess and Net Shepherd.

Once she has revealed the darker side of the Internet, Aftab then concentrates on the real reason people should be out surfing the 'Net. In Part Four, "The Good Stuff...99.44 Percent Pure (enjoying your family time online)," she presents chapters that talk about all the great reasons to get involved with the Internet. From researching and writing to kid-friendly entertainment sites to shopping online or travel, there is something for every family. Parents can let their children teach them about the Internet and perhaps create a home page together. One chapter, "Special Families...Special Kids," highlights exceptional children as well as single parenting, stepparenting, parenting twins, and grandparents who are parenting again. Aftab has included recommended Web sites for families and breaks them down for kids, parents, and by subject. There is a chapter of reviews by kids from all over the country. The reviewers' ages range from 3 (yes, that's right; she dictated to her mother) to 18, and it's a great way to find out what kids themselves like.

Appendices feature frequently asked questions, a glossary for non-geeks, a directory of Web sites and products mentioned in the book, and the author's own Internet Use Policy.

A combination of excellent information, along with a lighthearted approach and sense of humor, make this an excellent source for anyone who wants to learn all the benefits of being online as well as learn how to protect their children and keep the Internet a safe place. Not just a guide to learning how to access the Internet, but one that helps to educate parents about the potential hazards, without using scare tactics or overemphasizing the "dark side." As an attorney and parent, Aftab is in a unique position to know the legal as well as family concerns. Her tips and suggestions make sense. Well-researched and organized, there is a nice balance between the good and the bad. Check it out and get started experiencing all the resources offered by the Internet—with your mind at rest.

The Research Paper and the World Wide Web

Dawn Rodrigues

Upper Saddle River, NJ: Prentice-Hall, 1997. (http://www.prenhall.com).
220p. ISBN: 0-13-461724-X. Softcover, $20.40.

The process of researching material for a paper has changed in the last few years. The Internet and World Wide Web, as well as electronic databases, provide many more choices for locating information.

Although this book is not necessarily for high school students, it contains material that can certainly help prospective college students—or anyone involved in research—learn what's available and get a head start on using technology for research. The goal of the book is to discuss the relationship between traditional print resources and electronic sources such as the World Wide Web and Internet, and to clarify how they fit together in the research process today.

The book is divided into nine chapters. The first three chapters, "The Research Process in the Information Age," "A Researcher's Introduction to the Web," and "The Basics of Web Navigation," are introductory chapters covering a general overview of the research process and writing, along with how the Internet can effectively be integrated into library research. Chapters cover various techniques for beginning the research process, along with general advice on research; a mini-guide to the Web, with all the basics about home pages, bookmarks, and hyperlinks and a bit about HTML; and how to search using various search engines and directories, such as Yahoo and AltaVista.

Chapters 4 and 5, "Finding Libraries on the Web" and "Finding Library Resources on the Web," show how to locate a library and its catalog through Gopher or the World Wide Web, as well as the kinds of resources often found on library Web pages. Step-by-step directions introduce students to ways they can access online catalogs. The example comes from Vanderbilt University, but unfortunately the directions no longer work.

To help students keep current in specific subject areas or locate relevant information, Rodrigues explains how to use subject collections out on the Web in Chapter 6, "Finding Resources in the Disciplines." Specific examples, along with their Web addresses, provide access to sites in the humanities, business, social sciences, and more.

E-mail, newsgroups, and discussion lists are featured as tools to help expand your research resources in Chapter 7, "E-mail, Mailing Lists, and Newsgroups as Research Tools." Electronic mail brings a new dimension to locating first-hand information from experts in the field. It's now possible to send mail to someone in your field and receive a quick response. Etiquette, how to create and send mail, subscribing to a mailing list, and browsing newsgroups, as well as how to use IRC and forum tools, are all included. In Chapter 8, "Organizing Research Notes and Sources," there are handy suggestions for organizing information and resources that include using bookmarks, templates, and e-mail to keep up with growing research.

There is no doubt that the Web has made its presence felt as a tool for locating information. How to cite resources in papers is a common question today. The final chapter, "Documenting Sources," presents examples from such style guides as the American Language Association and the American Psychological Association for various types of references. To keep up with and record the author, title, publication, date, and Web address, as well as when you visited the site, a handy chart is included.

In some ways, the book combines two subject areas: doing research and learning how to incorporate the World Wide Web into that process. The practically written exercises that accompany chapters and suggestions for learning more are helpful and provide a self-paced way to continue the learning process. A Web site for the book exists to provide up-to-date links for sites mentioned in the chapters. A glossary, reference list, and index complete the book.

Safe Surfing: A Family Guide to the Net

Julie McKeehan

Boston, MA: AP Professional, 1996. (http://www.apnet.com).
326p. ISBN: 0-12-484834-6. Softcover, $24.95.

Though this title is older than some others included in this book, it covers a topic that is still relevant: safety using the Internet. Some of the Web sites will undoubtedly be out-of-date, but that happens with newer books as well. There is a Web site, www.safesurf.com, that provides updated information on safety issues, a newsletter, and activities for parents and children.

Julie McKeehan is a mother, Internet user, and teacher who has written a book for parents who want to learn about the Internet. It's done in an easy-to-read, almost conversational style. The material is presented in three parts: "Figuring Out the Net," "Exploring the Net," and "Being Safe on the Net." Beginners may want to read the book straight through. If you already have a knowledge of the Internet, you can move through the material in whatever way suits you.

"Figuring Out the Net" covers the basics of the Internet. It touches on all the familiar topics, such as what it is; its history; its tools (FTP, Gopher, Web, and Telnet); how to get connected (choosing between an Internet service provider and an online service such as America Online); newsgroups; electronic mail; discussion lists; downloading files; and software. Because this is directed at parents and especially those with little Internet experience, there are quite a few details about choosing a service. Two surveys provide a way to gauge your interest and then suggest which route would be best for your needs. The advice is helpful for anyone worried about making the right choice about how to get connected. Be aware, though, that because this book is dated, specific information about the various online services may have changed. The same level of detail appears in the chapter on choosing an Internet service provider (ISP). Some hints and questions are provided that can help you when working with an ISP.

The next part, "Exploring the Net," takes you on a trip of great Web sites. Unfortunately, some of the highly recommended sites are no longer there. In some cases they don't exist or have changed locations and do not have a referral. Other times, you'll notice that the site can be located, but you'll see that the address has changed. Certainly the appearance of many of the sites has changed since the book was written. This is a problem in a book geared to Internet "newbies," because it won't be easy to use the various search tools to find where the site is or even know how to work with a Web address to see if you can find the site. Sometimes it's just the file name that has changed or the directory. Also, some very popular sites that weren't around when the book was written are omitted. For example, the Weather Channel Web site is not listed in the section on weather. Other subjects include sports, the weird and wonderful, Web sites for parents, and news sites.

Other chapters present information on locating people and finding information on the Internet and offer recommended sites such as the Internet Public Library as a good starting point. The author is concerned about safety on the 'Net, but she also wants readers to know that with the right supervision and education, the Internet is a wonderful place for children. She sets down some "Net Safety Rules" that address issues related to the ages of children allowed online and how parents should interact and be responsible in knowing what their child is doing. Children should agree to certain rules of behavior and promise not to give out personal information online. The next section offers some safe sites for children. Finally, there is discussion of security or filtering software, with specific recommendations and a chart comparing features. A glossary and index complete the book.

Julie McKeehan does an excellent job of providing just the right approach and type of information that parents need. Being able to find out what types of Web sites are available, learning about the various safety issues, and discovering ways to be good 'Net parents are all important. The only drawback is that the book is out of date in many respects as far as specific facts and Web sites go. Other books for parents and families out now are more current. If the author ever updates this book, it would be a very good choice for families that want to get up to speed about the Internet.

SafetyNet: Guiding and Guarding Your Children on the Internet

Zachary Britton

Eugene, OR: Harvest House Publishers, 1998.
(http://www.harvesthousepubl.com). 179p.
ISBN: 1-56507-844-6. Softcover, $8.99.

Protecting children from the hidden dangers of the Internet is a big issue today. Although the Internet allows children to find educational and entertaining material, it also can expose them to sexually explicit material and pornography. How can parents guide their children's Internet activities? How can parents learn enough to be effective controllers of what their children see on the Internet?

Zachary Britton is the president of an organization called KidShield.com, whose goal is to protect children online. According to the author, some families have been "destroyed by online material." He wrote the book to "enable parents to effectively guide and guard their children during their online adventures." Britton also seems to believe that the government should play a hand in controlling indecent material on the Internet, as he states, "you can become the safeguard our government and the Internet itself has failed to provide...."

The book is divided into an introduction and three parts, titled "Dangers of the Internet," "Creating a SafetyNet for Your Child," and "Resources." The introduction tells you why you need the book and contains a section called "What Is the Internet?," in which Britton discusses his definition of the Internet. After reading this book, parents will be able to provide a much safer version of the Internet. The author also urges readers to pressure the government and Internet service providers to clean up the Internet for children. In the same section, he lists four main components for the average user: e-mail, the World Wide Web, chat, and newsgroups. Someone else might decide that the Internet comprises a different set of components.

The author seems to see danger everywhere. His chapter titles illustrate how he feels: "How Accessible Is Pornography?," "Why Is the Internet a 'Pedophile's Playground,'" "Are Games More than Child's Play?," "Can the Internet Make My Child Antisocial," and "What Problems Do Adults Face on the Net?" Throughout the chapters there are boxes called "Reality Checks," which contain facts or warnings such as "Children may encounter pornography when searching for information on almost any topic." When discussing pornography, he mentions cases where children have been caught by their parents with obscene photos. Online services simplify the process of distributing pornography and pedophiles can stalk and harass children through chat rooms or even e-mail.

Games are addictive and the very violent ones can cause even more problems. Britton especially assails MUDs for their style that allows children to assume other identities and play along in their own world of reality. The Internet can be addictive to some and cause them to become antisocial and drop out of school. Adults are not immune, either. He states that the Internet is responsible for increasing marital infidelity and causing marriages to break up.

Part Two, "Creating a SafetyNet for Your Child," takes an in-depth look at how you can "child-proof" the Internet by using filtering software and establishing certain rules, as well as taking into account certain factors when selecting a service provider. The chapter on filtering software examines effective filtering components and how they work. There is a good discussion of PICS (Platform for Internet Content Selection) and how these rating systems work. In a chart there is a comparison of filtering software, which gives for each an overall family-friendly rating, the Web address, a phone number to call to order, platform, and free trial period availability. Another chart compares prices and features in an easy-to-read format. After the charts, there is an overview comparing the main filtering software programs. The chapter on Internet service providers uses the chart format to present a comparison of ISPs and their "family-friendly features." There are also suggestions for things to look for when selecting an ISP that can help protect your children, but also can save you some money.

When it comes to families and what they can do to help, there are basically seven "safety steps" outlined on house rules. Additional material covers safety at school, and there is an interesting look at Internet policies around the world. "Developing Cybersafety Worldwide" explores what other countries are doing, as well as many of the issues that make controlling content on the Internet a terribly complicated process. There is one positive look at the Internet in this book: "Safe Sites for Your Children" focuses on how to use search engines effectively and then lists various educational and safe Web sites. A brief description accompanies the name, Web address, subject area, grade level, and organization behind the site.

Part Three, "Resources," is really a set of appendices that include "PICS— Platform for Internet Content Selection," "Instructions for Using Internet Explorer," "Instructions for Using Netscape Browsers," and "Configuring AOL Parental Controls." A glossary titled "A Friendly Guide to Common Internet Terminology" helps you understand the "technobabble." A "Notes" section lists the sources for quotes used throughout the book.

This book takes direct aim at the Internet and its dangers and lets fire. Most of the book discusses the negatives of and dangers that can be found on the Internet. The author focuses on all the bad things that have happened to children who have been allowed to use the Internet without constant parental supervision. After reading this book, parents will probably never want to get involved with the Internet. Hardly any of the good things receive attention.

Site Seeing the Internet: Plain & Simple for Teachers, Parents & Kids

Gary M. Garfield and Suzanne McDonough

Winnipeg, Manitoba, Canada: Peguis Publishers, 1996.
(http://www.peguis.com/). 160p. ISBN: 1-895411-81-5.
Spiral notebook, $16.00.

This little spiral notebook spends the first part introducing parents, kids, and teachers to the workings of the Internet. Topics covered include a brief history, how to connect and costs involved, why you should get to know the Internet, and how to find information using search engines. The book's main purpose is to present a compendium of Web sites, organized by broad categories that include "Mostly Museums," "Cyber Science," "People Places and Purpose," "Lively Literature," "Math Magic," "Kids' Fun," "Cyber Smorgasbord," "Kids' Links," and "References, Resources, and Reality."

The Web sites' wide variety will appeal to parents, teachers, and children. The entries are not arranged in any apparent order, and there is no index, either. Each Web site lists the name and URL, and then a descriptive paragraph about the Web site. The language is friendly and the entries are easy to read, with plenty of white space and bolding to highlight the address. The plain and simple approach may appeal to beginners, but for those who need to learn how to navigate or use browsers, this book won't be enough. This book is good for finding out about good sites to visit as a parent or child.

A Student's Guide to the Internet: Exploring the World Wide Web, Gopherspace, Electronic Mail and More!

Elizabeth L. Marshall

Brookfield, CT: Millbrook Press, 1996. (**http://www.millbrookpress.com/**). 159p. ISBN: 1-56294-923-3. Hardcover, $23.90.

This book's 11 chapters cover all the various Internet tools for locating information, as well as areas of particular interest to students (such as publishing, using the Internet for reports, and playing it safe on the 'Net).

The book targets students who want to learn how to make the most of the Internet as a tool for gathering information. Besides its obvious entertainment value, the 'Net has become a very important tool for research and learning. The author spends Chapters 2 through 7 discussing the Internet tools used most in the classroom.

After an introductory chapter on the history of the Internet, Chapter 2, "Electronic Mail," explores the advantages of using e-mail, how it works, and Internet addressing. The intent is to make it easy to get started using e-mail but not to discuss specific programs to use. Students can take the basic information and (it is hoped) apply it to whichever mail program they use. Chapter 3, "Newsgroups and Mailing Lists," helps students learn how they can share opinions and how to make the most of newsgroups as a potential source of expert information. The author introduces basic terms, such as *threads* and *post*, to explain how newsgroups work. Mailing lists are contrasted with newsgroups to show how they differ. Examples of both serve to show how they are set up and what to look for in recognizing them. Internet Relay Chat, a source for real-time interaction, is also presented.

Chapters 4 and 5 concentrate on Gopher as a research tool. There are some step-by-step instructions for working through Gopher menus. Today, with the phenomenal growth of the Web, Gopherspace has been mostly eclipsed as far as new site creation, and many hot Gopher sites have been replaced by World Wide Web sites. Thus, it is rather unusual for a fairly current book to spend two chapters on Gopher and only one on the Web. FTP files are covered in Chapter 6. Again, many of the archives are now accessible through the Web rather than an FTP program. Chapters 8 through 10 focus on how to use the Internet as a tool for collaborative projects and publishing, as well as how to incorporate the information into reports for class projects. Students can learn some tips for focusing their topics, designing a Web page, and searching the Internet as they try out some of the sites listed in the "Resources Chapter" for beginning their Internet journeys. Chapter 11 presents safety issues in "Playing it Safe on the Internet," giving ways to keep your Internet travels free from pornography and obscene messages, and listing ways to help educate parents.

With a 1996 date, some material seems a bit out of date. For example, when mentioning browsers, Mosaic and Netscape are included, but not Internet Explorer. Instead, something called InternetWorks is listed.

This book may be most valuable to schools that are still without a full-blown Internet connection and need to use tools such as Gopher, FTP, and Telnet more than the Web. There is some valuable information here for moving through directories and menus in those programs.

Success in College Using the Internet

Jack Pejsa

New York: Houghton Mifflin, 1998. (**http://www.hmco.com**).
160p. ISBN: 0-395-83016-8. Softcover, $45.00.

Increasingly, students need to know how to use the Internet to be successful in completing research in college. That's the premise behind this guide. Though directed mostly to college students, the material can also be used by college-bound high school students who want to get a jump on using the Internet's vast resources.

Written in a nontechnical, jargon-free style, this guide is not intended to be an exhaustive work on every aspect of the Internet. It *is* intended to help students find resources to enhance their educational experiences. The author sees this book as acting rather like an "instructional guide" and "tutor." There is also a Web site for updating material from the book as it changes over time. The Web site will have an online glossary, additional readings, and extended Internet exercises.

The material moves from simple to more complex topics, to help students digest what they learn. For those with little Internet knowledge, it's best to start at the beginning and work through the chapters. They are not written in any particular order, so it's possible to jump from one to another depending on what's best and most interesting. The book can be used as a text in a classroom setting or read independently. All the basics of the Internet are covered in six chapters.

Along with the main content of each chapter, the author includes a summary of the material, followed by "Review Questions" and then "Exercises" to reinforce the main ideas. The exercises are geared more to the college student rather than K-12, but that is the focus of the book. Still, any college-bound student would benefit from learning how to use the Internet before getting to college. Also, teachers can make use of this book as well. Because it does not attempt to give step-by-step directions for specific platforms or software, the appeal is more universal.

Tech Girl's Internet Adventures

Girl Tech

Foster City, CA: IDG Books Worldwide, 1997.
(http://www.idgbooks.com/). 178p. ISBN: 0-7645-3046-1.
Softcover, $19.99. (Includes CD-ROM).

This colorful, lavishly illustrated little book is definitely aimed at youth and, in particular, girls, as the title suggests. Aimed at ages eight and up, the computer-generated author and guide is Girl Tech. Her goal is to make learning the Internet fun and exciting and to focus on "girl-friendly" sites.

Because the book is geared to children, it includes suggestions and precautions for parents and mentors to make the Internet learning experience a safe one. Safety control software is recommended before going online.

Internet basics are covered with a subject difference. Whenever possible, examples relate to the female gender. Chapters cover getting online, sites to visit and games to download, books and articles on the Internet, locating information, and a special one on keeping healthy. Subject areas for sites mentioned include entertainment, education, nutrition, and health, plus a special section on chat rooms for girls.

This book should appeal to the visually oriented teenager, with its often colorful pages and fonts, drawings, illustrations, and photos heavily interspersed throughout. It's almost like looking at one of today's modern cartoons. Don't be misled, though; the information is there and the style of writing will appeal to children. *(Courtesy of Multimedia Schools Magazine, Information Today, Inc., Medford, NJ).*

300 Incredible Things for Kids on the Internet

Ken Leebow

Marietta, GA: VIP Publishing, 1998. (**http://surf.to/300Incredible**). 128p. ISBN: 0-9658668-1-5. Softcover, $7.95.

This is a little book with a lot of Web sites for kids—300, to be exact. The author's intent is to provide children with selected sites that are interesting and of value for educational as well as fun purposes. The sites are divided into 12 chapters on topics that range from sites of interest to parents; to subject-specific ones, such as language, literature, geography, history, and politics; to reference sources in the educational genre. For entertainment, there are listings for pets, hobbies, sports, music, movies, holidays, and fun and games. Each chapter's subject contains subcategories. For example, in the chapter for parents, there are listings under "Trash on the Net," which features safety and filtering information; "Parent Time," on how to be a better parent; "Be Safe," safety tips for children and parents; and "Web Novice," for beginners to the Internet.

Interspersed throughout are some cute cartoons, but other than that there are no illustrations or photos. Each entry has a Web address and a sentence or two about the site.

This little guide is a handy reference for parents and teachers who want some "safe" sites on the Internet. For those needing more help getting started, it will be necessary to check some other titles that offer more information about the Internet and World Wide Web.

The World Wide Web

Christopher Lampton

New York: Franklin Watts, 1997. (**http://www.gi.grolier.com/**). 64p. ISBN: 0-531-20262-3. Library binding, $21.00.

You can't watch television today without seeing references to the Internet and World Wide Web. If you'd like to help your child learn all about the Web, here's a book written for children aged 9 through 12 that presents the history and use of the World Wide Web as well as how to navigate and find interesting sites.

Five chapters include "Welcome to the Web," an introductory chapter covering what the Internet is, how the Web began, a bit about HTML and Web pages, plus even a little information about computer or data files. "Getting on the Web" explores how to get connected with a modem, Internet service providers, how to get a browser, and more. "Navigating the Web" continues with facts about hyperlinks, URLs and how to interpret them, why they make links, and other protocols used in URLs. "Touring the Web" explains in basic language how to search for information using "Web indexes" such as Yahoo. Nothing very technical here, of course; just some good, practical information that explains how to locate information. "Sites on the Web" provides examples of the kinds of sites you can find, including museums, art galleries, government sites, commercial sites, and, of course, entertainment sites, which would interest children a great deal. There are many colorful illustrations and screen shots to illustrate concepts. In fact, "older children" like me could read this and learn about the World Wide Web, as well as the age group for which it was written. Who says you have to read a cut-and-dried "adult" book to learn about the Internet? Includes a glossary and index.

The World Wide Web for Kids and Parents

Viraf D. Mohta

Foster City, CA: IDG Books Worldwide, 1996.
(http://www.dummies.com). 362p. ISBN: 0-7645-0098-8.
Softcover, $24.99. (Includes CD-ROM).

Here's a book written with a kid in mind. (Parents will enjoy it, too.) It's for a first-timer or someone just looking to increase her skills and knowledge. The author's goal in writing this guide is to make it fun to learn about the Internet. His style of writing and language are full of "cool" jargon kids will relate to.

Six major sections make up the content, along with two appendices and a CD. Chapter titles are clever: "Look Out, Web! Here I Come—Via Netscape Navigator" is an example. The focus on Web sites is to show fun and cool places, but there are some educational subjects as well. An especially interesting chapter is "Welcome to Funtasia," where the reader is introduced to software, audio, video, phones on the Internet, chat, and MUDs. There are also a couple of chapters on creating your own Web site.

The author covers all the topics necessary to get up and running on the Internet, and does it in an entertaining and fun way. If you want a serious reference manual to the Internet, this isn't for you, but if you'd like to learn and be entertained at the same time, pick up a copy. *(Courtesy of Multimedia Schools Magazine, Information Today, Inc., Medford, NJ).*

Chapter 4://**Internet Books for Curriculum Development**

Introduction

The Internet has introduced a new resource for curriculum development. Lesson plans and projects can now be found on the 'Net. Today teachers can open their classrooms to the world by using the Internet.

The books in this section contain ideas and suggestions for lessons, projects for teachers to use. Some may combine a brief introduction to the Internet and its tools, but the reason they are listed here is that the majority of each book focuses on Web sites or Internet resources rather than on learning about the Internet. Many are compilations of Web sites arranged in some logical order, generally by broad subject categories. Most contain a brief description of the sites listed and the lessons are often reproducible. The value of many of these titles lies in the fact that the resources have been carefully selected by teachers and recommended as good educational tools. The main benefit from books in this section is that they provide busy teachers with the materials to get started right away. One thing to keep in mind is the reality of the World Wide Web. It changes frequently. It's a good idea to check out the Web addresses to see if they have changed. In some cases, a CD is included with the book. Also, more publishers recognize the changing URL problem and are addressing it by establishing Web sites with regular updates.

The Best of Internet Activities from Teacher Created Materials

Shari Basch

Westminster, CA: Teacher Created Materials, 1999.
(http://www.teachercreated.com). 320p. ISBN: 1-57690-449-0.
Softcover, $24.95.

Chock-full of fun activities and lessons selected from their many Internet activity workbooks, this collection from Teacher Created Materials has taken some of the best exercises in a wide variety of subject areas, as well as grade levels and exercise types, and compiled them into one resource for teachers. The lessons can be used just as they come or modified to suit individual preferences. Most activities require approximately 20 to 30 minutes for completion.

Along with the lessons are a few sections of introductory material. For beginners, there is a brief introduction to the Internet, some tips on classroom management, and benefits of using the Internet in a classroom. "Fitting It All In" offers novices ideas on ways the Internet works best in the classroom, as well as times when it might be best to use another tool. With limited time available, it's good to know how to make the most of your online experiences. There's an informative section on what teachers can do beforehand to make the online activity go smoothly and be successful.

Copyright issues and unacceptable material are also covered. Acceptable use policies and safety issues receive attention as well. If you are already familiar with the Internet, you may just want to go right to the lessons and skip the introductory material.

Something for everyone can be found among this book's variety of topics, which include electronic mail, search engines, people, history, places, science and natural phenomena, math, art, holidays, and collaborative projects.

A typical lesson includes the title of the lesson, the objective for the activity, and materials needed, along with a focus Web site that begins the lesson. Most activities also present alternative Web sites, if applicable. Occasionally a pre-Internet activity is inserted to help get students involved in the topic. Extended activities are sometimes part of the lesson, but materials needed are not listed.

Teachers will appreciate that most of the work is done except to verify the Web addresses before beginning the lesson. In some cases, answers are provided in the "Key to Selected Exercises" at the end of the lesson. Finally, "Selected Teacher Resource Sites" provides a list of favorite Web sites for curriculum projects, news sources, coloring sites, and those just for fun. There are also links to search engines and Web sites just for children.

For a variety of lesson plans using the Internet, this collection provides something for most subject areas. Busy teachers who want to get started using the Internet, but just don't have time to spend creating their own materials, will benefit from this collection of activities and lessons.

Big Basics Web Directory

Jill Byrus et al.

Indianapolis, IN: Que, 1997. (http://www.quecorp.com).
218p. ISBN: 0-7897-1422-1. Softcover, $14.99.

This guide to Web sites has more than 100 subject categories with sites hand-picked by Que's editors. Each entry has a descriptive summary of the site. The book is organized by the topics, which are generally pretty broad. If you want to go directly to a subject you are interested in, just consult the contents and go to that page. Each topic has two pages and within each topic there are five sites selected as the best on the Web. The "best of the best" is given a full page, while the other four sites are on the next page. Screen shots illustrate various parts of the best site. There are shorter descriptions of the other four sites. Topics range from alternative medicine to auto racing to car buying to weddings to yoga. Of particular interest to educators are subjects such as books, children's health, computers, education (college as well as K-12), encyclopedias and reference, finding people, government, history, kids, languages, libraries, magazines, museums, news, nutrition, parenting, politics, religion, searching the Web, software, and teaching. The K-12 sites chosen as best are Discover Learning, The Jason Project, Federal Resource Center for Special Education, AskERIC, and the Family Education Network.

For anyone who wants an idea of the wide range of possibilities for Web sites on the Internet, this will provide a good look at what's available. It's not especially geared to educators, but would be a good source for parents who want a handy guide to begin exploring. The idea that the sites have been chosen and reviewed makes them more appealing. The size of this guide may be more suitable for those who don't want to be overwhelmed by too many Web sites.

The Busy Educator's Guide to the World Wide Web

Marjan Glavac

London, Ontario, Canada: Nima Systems, 1998. (http://www.glavac.com). 178p. ISBN: 0-9683310-0-9. Softcover, $14.95.

Written by a teacher for busy teachers, this is a guide to sites that the author has selected to help teachers easily introduce the Internet into their classes. Unlike other "guides," there is no Internet history or descriptions of the World Wide Web or its tools. This is simply a curriculum guide that teachers can use in their classes.

Chapter 1, "How to Use the Internet...Real Fast," introduces top education sites to get teachers into using the Internet very quickly, with overviews of top sites for parents, educators, and students. Included are some popular and well-known sites, such as Kids Teachnet, Kidlink, Canada's SchoolNet, and more. The annotations are detailed with the author's review of their offerings. In Chapter 2, "What's Behind Those Links?," two sites are explored in-depth: the Global SchoolNet Foundation's Web site and the Digital Education Network. The reason these are featured is to allow "busy" teachers a chance to see what effectively designed education sites look like without having to go online; or, if you prefer to go online, the book can be used along with your virtual tour.

Essentially, this book contains 40 pages of screen shots with the author's comments about various layers and links to the Web site. As much as sites can change, this is a lot of material that could be totally different by the time the book is even published. Some of the screen shots with black background are not easy to read, either. Perhaps fewer pages could have done the same thing. Chapter 3 contains "Sites That Motivate, Engage and Stimulate Students (and Educators)." Recognizing that there are times when something stimulating may be needed to motivate students, the author has put together a collection of Web sites that meet this need. In an interesting organization, he includes ones that change daily, weekly, and monthly. They provide a special way to introduce something new on a regular basis. The sites incorporate projects, teacher's guides, games, pictures, words of the day, and more. Material is arranged by subject content, including art, science, social studies, language, and more. Suggestions for grade levels are included with each entry. Many sites can provide teachers with quick new ways to add fun resources to their established curriculum. The annotations are brief for the most part, but supply the necessary information to decide if you want to use them. Chapter 4, "Internet Projects That Really Work," focuses on well-established sites and those with telecommunications projects that have proven they work. Most require preregistration and a call for participation. Included are

Newsday, a project from the Global SchoolNet Foundation; a newspaper project from NewsOntario; ThinkQuest, "helping to develop skills for the 21st century"; and others. Chapter 5, "Searching and Finding Information for the Busy Educator," focuses on search engines, tools, and strategies, with links to some of the most popular search tools such as AltaVista, Yahoo, and DogPile (a meta-search engine). *Expert sites* means those that are maintained by educators who have created mega-sites for educators with a wealth of information. Kathy Schrock's educator's page, LibrarySpot, and Cyberian are featured. In case you weren't aware of it, there are also educational search engines for homework, research, and locating people.

As a teacher, Glavac understands the importance of having a good search strategy to locate appropriate and relevant information. He discusses how to formulate a search strategy, use keyword and subject searches, and understand what you get. References and links to various search tools are provided at the end of the chapter. The final chapter, "Publish or Perish . . . No One Knows What You've Done Until You've Told Them," begins with "25 Reasons Why Every School Should Have a Web Site." From a series of tips, suggestions, and reasons, teachers can learn why having a Web site is valuable and what it can offer to their school community. If you need ammunition to get a Web site started, jot down these tips and go talk to your superintendent or principal. This chapter does not make you a Web author, but it does provide links to resources such as virtual bookstores, sites on the Web, and links to software for creating Web pages to get you started. A "Web Site Directory" lists the sites mentioned in the book, with the page numbers on which they were mentioned and their URLs. Overall, this book fulfills its purpose of introducing busy teachers to the resources available on the Internet. The fact that the sites are reviewed and recommended by a fellow teacher relieves you of having to decide if they are worthwhile or safe to use in your classroom.

Dig That Site! Exploring Archaeology, History, and Civilization on the Internet

Gary M. Garfield and Suzanne McDonough

Englewood, CO: Libraries Unlimited, 1997. (http://www.lu.com/).
135p. ISBN: 1-56308-534-8. Softcover, $25.00.

Designed for history, social studies, or civilization classes, this workbook provides the student with the excitement of the Internet alongside more traditional classroom activities. It would work well with a textbook on history or social studies. The material is arranged by the seven continents and focuses on historical places such as Israel, Athens, Egypt, Easter Island, and many more. Each chapter instructs students about customs, history, art, and civilization for the visited site. The individual lessons contain objectives, time required, materials, procedures required to complete the assignment, and URLs of the appropriate Web sites.

If you've been thinking about how to start using the Internet in your social studies class, here's a tool that makes it easy to jump in and to make the study of "ancient history" fun and exciting. Appendices include a personal site journal, suggested journals, organizations and resources, and a site index with Web addresses. *(Courtesy of Multimedia Schools Magazine, Information Today, Inc., Medford, NJ).*

Educating with the Internet: Using Net Resources at School and Home

Nancy Skomars

Rockland, MA: Charles River Media, 1998. (**http://www.charlesriver.com**). 404p. ISBN: 1-886801-70-3. Softcover, $29.95. (Includes CD-ROM).

It seems almost an unwritten rule that any Internet book must include an introductory "History of the Internet/World Wide Web" section. Here's one that doesn't follow that rule, and it's a refreshing change. Beginning with 12 key terms to understanding the Internet, this guide offers more of a "gentle" Internet introduction than some others.

The book contains three parts: "Using the Internet in Your Classroom," "Sites for All You Teach," and "Living with the Net." Beginning with an introduction to hardware requirements, the author offers suggestions for minimum requirements as far as memory, speed, modems, and telephone lines—very practical information necessary to get up and running. If you are already up and running, you may want to skip the chapter on getting connected, where you will learn about Internet service providers. There's a nice set of tips on what you should expect from an ISP, such as software, browser choice, technical support, modem upgrade, e-mail address, and TCP/IP connectivity. The book follows a logical and organized approach to using the Internet. Once you choose your equipment and get connected, then it's off to the races.

The next section introduces Web browsers, with examples of Internet Explorer and Netscape Navigator. No in-depth details, just the basics about what you will encounter upon opening a browser (menus and main features). If you are truly a novice, then you may need some more detailed information. Otherwise, this will get you going.

Next up are some lessons to put to use the things you've learned. The first lesson lets you practice browsing, to get comfortable with moving around. Step-by-step directions make the lessons easy to follow as you browse through various subjects. Once you get browsing down, then it's time to move on to a more organized means of locating information: searching the Internet.

Four search tools are briefly examined, including AltaVista, Lycos, Yahoo, and search.com. Strictly speaking, Yahoo is not technically a "search engine," but rather a subject directory with a search engine feature. Yahoo's main strength is its organized subject categories, not necessarily its search features. But this is a minor point, as the goal here is just to get started using a search tool to locate information.

Once you have the basics down, you can get started integrating online sources into the curriculum. Some good tips suggest thinking about what your next lesson is and how it might allow use of online resources; also, students can think about how an Internet site might aid them in a paper or project.

One thing that helps set this book apart is the very personal approach the author takes. She often offers tips from her classroom, such as how to evaluate the information by cross-referencing sites you find, how to avoid inappropriate sites, and how to think about the information you find. Her lesson plans come from successful classroom implementation. Instead of detailed descriptions of Internet tools, the author spends her time discussing how she uses these tools.

The heart of the book is the lesson plan chapters with many sites listed. They are well organized around specific subjects found in the classroom. Grade levels indicate the appropriateness for various age levels. There are many great ideas for lesson plans, a valuable time saver for busy teachers and a starting point for teachers new to the Internet. Skomars illustrates how she used the Internet as a source for new information for lessons, as well as a parallel resource for studying works like *Great Expectations* and *Romeo and Juliet*. Along with lesson plans comes a chapter with sites for parents and teachers who wish to expand their education in professional development areas, as well as adult education resources.

Besides lesson plans and activities, more than 1,300 sites in many different subject areas offer a wide selection to teachers and students, from educational subject-oriented ones (such as social sciences and literature) to sports, health, recreation, and many more.

The CD that accompanies the book contains an HTML TemplateMASTER CD, making it easy for teachers to prepare their own Web pages. Internet Watchdog software is also available on the CD. A folder with material on sites, lesson plans, safety software sites, teacher resources, browser information, and best-of-best sites provides teachers with hands-on resources.

With so many Internet guides available, a new one needs to offer something different to be successful. Skomars's personal approach to presenting the material makes this directory and guide a useful tool not only for locating appropriate sites, but also for providing ideas to teachers for integrating the Internet into a classroom setting with well-detailed and organized lesson plans.

Educator's Internet Companion: Classroom Connect's Complete Guide to Educational Resources on the Internet

The Staff of Classroom Connect

Lancaster, PA: Wentworth Worldwide Media, 1995.
(http://www.classroom.net). 271p. ISBN 0-932577-10-5.
Softcover, $39.99.

Educators familiar with the Classroom Connect newsletter will find similar concise and easy-to-read information about Internet sites in this publication. The *Educator's Internet Companion* was designed to present the "very best education-related resources." The authors, who know they are writing for busy educators, describe what to expect from each chapter. Accompanying the book are a diskette (MAC or Windows) and a video.

Chapter 1 contains more than two dozen lesson plans, which incorporate Internet resources into the teaching of subjects from chemistry to the United States government. Chapter 2 provides "virtual guided tours" of excellent Internet sites, with a brief site description; the navigation tool needed (WWW, Gopher, Telnet); type of account or connection (SLIP/PPP, for example); and the navigation software used. Captured screens illustrate how to navigate the site. An extensive list of Internet addresses, mailing lists, and newsgroups constitutes Chapter 3. Chapter 4 concentrates on World Wide Web sites, giving site address, a brief description, and a screen capture. Chapter 5 lists organizations, corporations, and government agencies that provide telecommunications grants.

The appendices offer a brief introduction to Internet search and navigation tools. Appendix C discusses the importance of developing acceptable use policies (AUPs) for those schools with Internet access. Two Internet sites with AUP information are listed.

Designed as a handy reference for educators who are beginning to search for useful sites for classroom teaching, this book provides excellent introductory material for teachers incorporating Internet resources into the curriculum. Keep a copy on the shelf of your school library or on your desk. However, individuals not already familiar with the basics of Internet connections and commands should not rely on this publication for an expansive introduction to the Internet. *(Courtesy of Multimedia Schools Magazine, Information Today, Inc., Medford, NJ).*

Educator's Internet Yellow Pages

Ron Place, Klaus Kimmler, Thomas Powell, and Ron Chapman

Upper Saddle River, NJ: Prentice-Hall, 1996.
(http://www.prenhall.com). 304p. ISBN: 0-13-232356-7.
Softcover, $26.95.

As more and more teachers recognize the value of the Internet in the classroom, finding appropriate resources becomes a very important factor in the process. Busy teachers do not always have time to surf the 'Net, hoping to find just that right lesson or project. What's the alternative? Search engines? Yes, they can tame some of the vast wasteland of information out there, but it still takes time. If you are too busy right now to spend the time to become an expert in searching the Web, try one of the "yellow page" books out there. In fact, try this one. It's directed to the education community and, though a bit dated (1996), still focuses on education topics where other directories may not.

Part One, "Internet Basics," provides an introductory section with a bit about connecting, a brief history of the Internet, and some facts about Internet tools. Part Two, "General Education Resources on the Internet," lists sites by type (Gopher, Telnet, Web). Part Three contains the heart of the book, with more than 260 pages of resources listed alphabetically by subject area beginning with art and ending with social studies. Sandwiched in between are the other typical school curriculum areas, such as languages, sciences, music, math, etc. All of the entries are listed by subject and then subdivided by type of site. Each entry lists the name, URL, and a brief description.

If this book were updated today, there would be less emphasis on the Gopher, Telnet, and FTP sites and more on the World Wide Web. The Web has grown tremendously in the past three years. Nevertheless, *Internet Yellow Pages* is written in an easy-to-read style and will certainly save busy teachers time in locating resources that can be used in combination with their regular lesson plans. Appendices include Appendix A, with "Educational Resource Materials" such as books, guides, government documents, and more. Appendix B, "Subscriptions," contains addresses and descriptions of resources you can subscribe to in the form of mailing lists, newsletters, and electronic journals. Appendix C, "Resources for Elementary School Communities," provides links to important resources that can help elementary teachers in their quest to become proficient using the Internet in their schools. Appendix D, "More Projects," annotates even more project possibilities; and Appendix E, "Educational Conference E-mail Contact List," provides information on technology conferences around the country.

E-mail: Electronic Mail Using Netscape Navigator

Philip R. Reinhardt

St. Paul, MN: Technology 4U, 1996. (http://www.technology4u.com). 38p. Spiral notebook, $15.00.

This tutorial is exactly what the name implies: a guide to learning Netscape's Mail component. The basics of electronic mail addresses, covered in the first chapter, can be applied to any mail system. After that, the rest of the book is a step-by-step look at Netscape's mail features. Screen shots illustrate the menus, buttons, and messages. An extensive bibliography of books, a glossary, and online resource guide complete this notebook. Not many hands-on activities are included except for one or two in Chapter 4. There's not much here that you couldn't learn by simply using Netscape. But if you're busy and just want everything in one place, or don't have time to prepare your own lesson plans for teaching Netscape mail, you might want to check it out.

44 Internet Activity Pages for French Class

Thomas W. Alsop

Auburn Hills, MI: Teacher's Discovery, 1998. (http://www.teachersdiscovery.com). 47p. Spiral notebook, $19.95.

44 Internet Activity Pages for Spanish Class

Thomas W. Alsop

Auburn Hills, MI: Teacher's Discovery, 1998. (http://www.teachersdiscovery.com). 47p. Spiral notebook, $19.95.

The Internet has opened up a whole new world for students to practice their foreign language skills. Writing to key-pals via e-mail; visiting foreign Web sites and reading in the language about the people and their culture; and even hearing the language spoken are all possible on the Internet.

These workbooks, for both Spanish and French, take advantage of the Internet's resources. Each lesson plan consists of activities on reproducible pages. The 44 worksheets are divided into three parts. Part One presents activity pages with ideas for learning about the country's culture. Students study the country's history, arts, sports, cities, museums, food, writers, artists, and festivals. Each activity begins by asking students to narrow down a topic within the broad subject under study. Students select a search engine and then, using that search engine, locate a Web site that offers the information they need. Next, they are requested to summarize and present the material to class members in the form of a radio or television broadcast. Part Two contains lessons 38 to 42 and focuses on electronic mail. Students locate key-pals in countries and write to them in French or Spanish, telling them about hobbies, family, and favorite activities. Part Three, which includes lessons 43 to 47, has students create a newspaper in Spanish or French and then create brochures to publicize it. An additional activity involves students in the creation of Web pages to promote the study of foreign languages. Other activities feature creating Web pages to tutor other students in Spanish or French; to display postcards from various foreign countries; and a weather Web page. Internet permission forms for teachers, parents, and students are part of the workbook as well. They spell out responsibilities each student has while using the Internet at school and/or home.

In this same series from Teacher's Discovery, there are also activity books for English, social studies, and science classes. They follow the same pattern of lessons except for the topics studied. For example, the unit for English class studies fiction, nonfiction, poetry, and drama.

As a supplementary workbook for homework or used in the classroom, these workbooks also promote group collaboration among students. This compilation of lessons plans makes it easy for busy teachers to integrate the Internet into their curriculum without having to create all their own activities.

Gopher It! An Internet Resource Guide for K-12 Educators

Gail Cooper and Garry Cooper

Englewood, CO: Libraries Unlimited, 1996. (**http://www.lu.com/**).
122p. ISBN 1-56308-486-4. Softcover, $20.00.

Gopher It! is a helpful tool for busy educators who are primarily accessing Gopher sites rather than the World Wide Web. It's unusual to find a book devoted only to Gopher, but the authors chose this tool for its ease in learning, speed in accessing, and the serious nature of many of the resources. Government agencies, educational institutions, and foundations are the main sponsors of sites listed in the book.

Organized alphabetically within more than 250 subject categories, topics range from African and American Studies to Youth at Risk, and cover a broad range in between. There are a ton of cross-references that seem a bit tedious at times, but on the other hand, you can hardly miss finding your favorite topic, no matter what you call it.

Each entry begins with the Gopher address, followed by the path you take to access the source. Descriptive summaries of each place are particularly helpful in learning about the site's resources.

Gopher sites tend to be overlooked today in favor of the glitzy World Wide Web. This handy guide shows that there are still valuable resources to be found at Gopher sites on the Internet. *(Courtesy of Multimedia Schools Magazine, Information Today, Inc., Medford, NJ).*

How to Create Successful Internet Projects

Timothy McLain

Lancaster, PA: Classroom Connect, 1997. (**http://www.classroom.net**). ISBN: 932577-73-3. 101p. Softcover, $29.95.

More and more teachers are incorporating the Internet into their classrooms. If you are contemplating such a move, as well as applying project-based learning, Classroom Connect's book helps explain what's involved and how to relate it to your customary classroom activities.

A special section, "Beginner's Tales" from various teachers who have successfully implemented the concept of project learning, illustrates the power of the Internet in classrooms. Successful projects from kindergarten through high school are included.

Chapter 2 contains five different models for Internet projects, ranging from correspondence and information gathering to problem solving, Web quests, and online conferencing. Project tips and tricks for each type of activity, along with URLs for examples, illustrate each model.

Chapter 3, "Internet Project Examples by Curriculum," provides more than 50 examples broken down by subject content.

The final section gets you started creating your very own project with an idea sheet that can jump-start the process. Finally, success stories provide important feedback to teachers who are just beginning.

The combination of case studies, valuable information, and further resources makes this a practical resource for teachers. For busy educators who don't know how they can begin the process, this guide shows how to get started and even come out a winner in the end. *(Courtesy of Multimedia Schools Magazine, Information Today, Inc., Medford, NJ).*

ICONnect: Curriculum Connection on the 'Net

Chicago, IL: American Library Association, 1996. (http://www.ala.org/).
16p. ISBN: 0-8389-3462-5. Spiral-bound, no price given.

This little booklet offers library media specialists a tool to locate relevant Web resources in a quick and easy fashion, as well as providing guidance in setting up, evaluating, or designing a Web page. Web sites, listed by curriculum area, include art and music, foreign languages, language arts, math, science, and social studies sites. The "WWW Tools & Resources" section contains sites for librarians to visit for practical ideas in developing their school library media pages. The Web evaluation form in Section One is a very handy tool to help make informed decisions about the worth of Web sites. If you are a real novice to the Web's resources and some of the fatter volumes of Internet education books seem a bit daunting, this little spiral notebook may help you break the ice. Otherwise, you'll probably outgrow this source quickly and need something more substantial. *(Courtesy of Multimedia Schools Magazine, Information Today, Inc., Medford, NJ).*

Integrating the Internet into the Science Classroom (Grades 7–12)

Sarah A. DiRuscio

Auburn, CA: Forefront Curriculum, 1997. (http://www.4front.com).
113p. No ISBN listed. Spiral notebook, $14.95.

Forefront Curriculum has published several workbooks to introduce the Internet into the classroom. This volume targets grades 7 to 12 for use with a science curriculum. The language is nontechnical and topics include student safety, acceptable use policies, Internet rating systems, filtering software, and the National Science Education Content standards. Much of the introductory material could be applied to any subject. The author follows the concept that students need to integrate certain skills into their knowledge base before being let loose on the Internet. The N.E.T. Integration Tools are guided navigation, content evaluation and testing, and applying knowledge. Each has a required checklist of skills to be mastered by following the step-by-step lessons and guided activities throughout the book. A "Guided Navigation Worksheet" provides teachers with a way to customize activities and select their own Web sites to incorporate into the lessons. There are also prepared activities, such as "Funny Frog Facts" and "The Extinct Gastric Brooding Frog," which combine a science lesson with practice in navigating the Web. Other science topics include the ocean, Leonardo da Vinci, space exploration, and the environment. The evaluation tool component uses a guide to evaluating Web sites along with a Web evaluation worksheet prepared by Dr. Nancy Everhart.

Besides evaluating sites, students also learn about search engines and subject directories. The top search engines are listed with their Web addresses, along with an activity to compare them. Boolean operator basics are taught in a keyword searching activity. The final component, "Testing/Application," explores electronic mail, including e-mail addresses, sending mail via Netscape or Internet Explorer, sending a file, and collaborative project ideas. Again, interactive lessons provide the practice to master these concepts. Section Four, "Curriculum Online," is the place to find Web sites for science lessons. The author has divided the material by subject and included several Web sites for each division, along with a mini-review for many. Besides Internet resources, books and other materials to aid teachers are listed.

For busy science teachers, this workbook is a helpful tool to get started learning how to incorporate the Internet into the classroom with interesting activities and well-constructed lesson plans.

Integrating the Internet into Your Classroom: Teaching with the CCCNet Curriculum

M. D. Roblyer

Upper Saddle River, NJ: Prentice-Hall, 1997. (http://www.cccnet.com). 78p. ISBN: 0-13-700253-X. Softcover, $12.00.

The Computer Curriculum Corporation (CCC) has a Web site that can be used as a resource by instructors, their students, in-service trainers, and trainees for integrating the Internet into a curriculum using Prentice-Hall/Merrill College textbooks in teacher education programs. This booklet puts together suggestions, step-by-step lesson plans, and illustrations to help educators get started.

The book is divided into three parts. Part One, "Introducing the Internet!," consists of an overview of the Internet, how to use the CCCNet Web site, and two sample lesson plans in science and math. Part Two, "Linking CCCNet with Classroom Activities," helps teachers see how to integrate online resources with textbook resources. Part Three, "Insights on Implementing Integration Strategies," focuses on getting started with technical requirements for connecting to the Internet, procedures on CCCNet's Web site, and how to prepare the classroom for online resources. Also included are several integration templates for courses to get you started. Appendices include troubleshooting and a handout for students. A glossary of Internet terms and an index of lesson strategies complete this guide.

One note: The sign-on procedures seem to be out of date. Following the steps on the first page did not get the same screen as indicated in the directions.

If you use Prentice-Hall/Merrill college textbooks, this may be worth the $12.00 to get started integrating the Internet into an already existing curriculum.

Internet ABC's for Elementary Students

Sarah A. DiRuscio

Auburn, CA: Forefront Curriculum, 1997. (http://www.4front.com).
72p. Workbook (softcover), $11.95.

Forefront Curriculum's series of workbooks for integrating the Internet into the classroom includes this title for elementary students. With more than 30 Internet activity worksheets, elementary school students can master the basics and have fun at the same time. An introductory chapter found in all the workbooks covers Internet basics. Internet skills such as navigating, using Netscape and Internet Explorer, and managing bookmarks are learned by making virtual trips to the White House as well as the popular Exploratorium Museum. A cute exercise using Mr. Potato Head (actually, he appears to have become Mr. Apple Head) encourages children to practice with the mouse and double-clicking. The Web site called "Blue Dog Can Count" teaches addition and subtraction skills. Some of the same science activities found in the two other workbooks are included here, along with others geared to younger children. For example, a tour of the White House with Socks the cat helps teach about the president; a visit to Sea World provides a resource for learning about animals. Colonial Williamsburg is featured in a history activity.

To teach electronic mail, students send a message to the president. They choose their best work and send it as a file to the teacher for practice in sending attachments. Sections also include many online curriculum resources, as well as information about copyright and multimedia.

For elementary school teachers who want to get started incorporating the Internet into their classes, this little workbook has learning materials and activities that should delight young students.

Internet Activities for Language Arts (Intermediate)

Shirley A. Gartmann

Westminster, CA: Teacher Created Materials, 1999.
(http://www.teachercreated.com). 144p. ISBN: 1-57690-407-5.
Softcover, $12.95.

Today the Internet is being used more and more by classroom teachers. It's recognized as a tool that can break down walls and expand opportunities for creative learning. It allows students to make use of current information often not available in textbooks.

Written for busy teachers, this workbook presents activities that can help supplement already existing language arts lessons. It allows teachers to make use of the Internet in their classrooms without having to prepare original plans them-selves or having to locate the Web sites. Written for intermediate students, it can be adapted for students above or below that level. The material is appropriate for individuals or as part of a collaborative project for small groups.

Before beginning with the activities, a short introduction presents the basic equipment requirements necessary to use the book. There is also an explanation of some of the benefits to be derived from incorporating Internet activities into a learning environment. The author points out how using the Internet can help foster problem-solving skills as well as allow students to become part of "real-world" situations.

The Internet can provide a way to present material not found in texts; help locate experts in a particular field; bring government information into the class-room; help locate up-to-date, newly published reports in a timely manner; and much more. Because safety issues are a big concern to parents and educators, acceptable use and policy considerations are presented so that teachers may decide these issues before going ahead with the Internet as a teaching tool. There are safety rules for students to accept as part of being able to access the Internet at school. The author also offers some very helpful ideas for maximizing the use of the Internet as well as planning for instruction. It's very important to make goals and decide some things ahead of time so that your experiences with the 'Net will be successful. In a practical vein, there are a few pages devoted to Web browsers and troubleshooting Web addresses. These are very good tips for teachers who may need to spend a little bit of time getting more comfortable with the Internet.

A helpful section covers search engines and how to define a search strategy. These will be important factors in a student's success in finding resources throughout the workbook activities. Knowing how search engines rank their results will also help students understand why they received certain responses and how to refine their searches. With all this in mind, the first activity is a search engine and directory exercise that lets students set up a search, define keywords to enter, and choose a search tool for their work. Another lesson asks students to decide between using a subject directory, such as Yahoo, or a search engine, like AltaVista. Such exercises will help sharpen a student's awareness of the differ-ences between the tools.

All the activities focus on various language-arts-related topics, including genealogy, Egyptian hieroglyphics, folk tales, fables, myths, Native American leg-ends, and more. There are also activities such as writing good descriptions, writ-ing a first-person account, thinking in sequence, and newspaper and word activi-ties. Each topic contains several lessons, which allows the teacher to select those most appropriate. Examples include making a family tree and writing about how you are related to your various family members, and locating sites that teach about storytelling and then evaluating what you find. Some lessons require essays or fill-in-the-blank answers. Charts are used to help students report their information in a logical and organized manner. In a more creative vein, students are asked to write a limerick or create a newspaper story (or even write a feature for a newspaper). The wide variety of exercises should suit most classrooms. This workbook will help students learn and, at the same time, have some fun. They will also see how important the Internet has become and why it's necessary for any person who plans to work in the next century to be information-literate.

Internet Activities for Math (Intermediate)

Walter Sherwood

Westminster, CA: Teacher Created Materials, 1998.
(http://www.teachercreated.com). 144p. ISBN: 1-57690-192-0.
Softcover, $12.95.

Math can be a tough subject for some children. Getting them motivated to learn when it's not their favorite subject is often challenging. How can the Internet help teachers teach math? Here's a workbook that can show you how. Imagine being able to teach math topics where you can go and find the most current and relevant information, or use an Internet site to make learning math a game. The 22 lessons are ready to go for the classroom. The workbook assumes several things, such as that both teacher and students have a working knowledge of how to navigate the World Wide Web and locate sites. There's no basic introduction as part of the workbook. You will need to spend some time with your class getting them ready if they are not full-fledged "internauts." One other point the author makes is to take a run through the lessons to make sure Web sites are current. They can change rapidly, so spending some time beforehand can assure you a successful lesson. This set of activities is labeled intermediate, but there is no designation about grade levels on the workbook or the lessons themselves.

Depending on the number of computers available, the material could be used by individuals or as a group activity. Each activity has a list of objectives to be met by students, along with necessary materials, Web sites, the approximate time it will take, and some tips on "Teaching the Lesson" that will help with ideas for guiding students through the material. There are "Selected Answers" to assist you as well.

Activities include a vocabulary-building game in which students locate mathematical terms and then scramble them for their classmates to unscramble. They also use the Internet to find out what the terms mean. "Baseball Math" uses the sport to figure out distances, and "Dicey Numbers" helps students practice skills such as adding, subtracting, etc., by using a "dice roll server" on the Internet.

"Math Around the World" uses the Internet to teach about math history by having students construct a timeline of important events in mathematics. "Size Is Relative" helps students understand how to compare sizes of objects. "Prime Time" uses a Web site to explain prime numbers and even search for the largest prime number.

A workbook like this helps teachers present rather ordinary material in a very special way, making learning more relevant and even more fun. The activity sheets may be reproduced for a single class to use. What a great way to help busy teachers get started using the resources of the Internet for teaching math!

Internet Activities for Social Studies (Challenging)

Shirley A. Gartmann

Westminster, CA: Teacher Created Materials, 1998.
(http://teachercreated.com). 144p. ISBN: 1-57690-405-9.
Softcover, $12.95.

This is another in the series of TechKNOWLEDGE workbooks by Teacher Created Materials, written by the same author of *Internet Activities for Language Arts*. It follows a similar pattern, but this one is for intermediate elementary or middle-school students. It offers a range of lesson activities, but also has an introductory session that offers some information to get teachers ready to use the lesson plans.

The goal of this workbook is to present teachers with "effective instruction regarding the Internet and World Wide Web" for social studies classes. As the Internet evolves into an important teaching tool, it's necessary for classroom teachers to learn how to integrate it effectively into a curriculum. To aid in the understanding of why the Internet is so important, the first part of the book looks at why teachers should use the Internet and what the Internet can do for them.

There is a list of 16 benefits to using the Internet, including exchanging information around the world, locating very current information, providing a variety of instructional options, being able to contact experts in a field, and helping students prepare for the changes coming in the workplace. Besides these benefits, the Internet is also contributing to changes in how teachers teach in the classroom. The old lecturer who seemed to pour information into students' heads is stepping back and becoming a guide while students assume an active learning role. Problem-solving skills and collaborative learning are two outgrowths of use of the Internet as a teaching tool.

The issue of unacceptable material on the Internet cannot be ignored. Parents and educators must be aware of the pitfalls of having a basically unregulated resource like the Internet at students' fingertips. Developing an acceptable use policy will go a long way in providing direction for a project using the Internet. Who will create the policy, who will be able to use the network, and how to create a succinct yet focused policy are all real issues to be dealt with. Parents as well as educators must assume a role. A list of safety rules for students to follow can also help spell out what is expected while online at school.

Before using the activities in this workbook, teachers should set aside some time to make sure they are ready to go; that is, check out their Internet skills and make sure they are confident about using it themselves before attempting to teach others.

The 30 lesson plans in this workbook offer students a new way to learn through collaborative efforts and to increase their project-based learning. Careful consideration should be given by anyone who plans project-based learning with the Internet.

There is a very nice "Technology Lesson Plan" that provides a way to organize the activity. The first few lessons show teachers how to practice some of the ways to use the Internet, such as electronic mail for key-pals and how to write e-mail (a section that offers suggestions for a good e-mail writing style). Lots of e-mail sources and mailing lists provide good resources. Getting comfortable with Web browsers is a must, so there is a lesson that helps teach about Web addresses and how to evaluate a Web site. Web search tools are covered, as is a lesson on devising a good search. These are all important to successful integration of Internet activities. Many of these same lessons can be found in other workbooks in this series. In this "challenging" level, more material is covered than in the "primary" or "intermediate" levels.

The social studies lesson activities begin with one on using a map and compass and finding one's way around, measuring distances, and using other tools. The ancient world is the main subject covered among the 30 lessons. There are activity sheets that may be reproduced for a single classroom to use. Topics covered are the seven wonders, ancient architecture, ancient civilizations such as Egypt and Mesopotamia, river civilizations, gods, the pyramids, the Olympics, and much more. There are a wide variety of exercises that will keep students interested and excited. For teachers who want lessons with already prepared worksheets and Web sites that have already been checked, take a look at this series of workbooks.

Internet Activities for Social Studies (Intermediate)

Kathleen Kopp

Westminster, CA: Teacher Created Materials, 1998.
(http://teachercreated.com). 144p. ISBN: 1-57690-404-0.
Softcover, $12.95.

The Internet activities for this workbook are for use by teachers as a supplement or part of the curriculum in social studies. There are three levels in this series of guides: Primary, Intermediate, and Challenging. This one is labeled intermediate. There is no real grade level attached to the book, so it's difficult to say what ages would benefit most from it; perhaps early elementary.

Before the lesson activities begin, there are a few pages of introductory material, such as the basics about the Internet, with some information on exploring the World Wide Web and navigating. For anyone who is just starting out, it will be necessary to read a more thorough introduction of the Internet before adding these activities to the curriculum. A "Classroom Management Tips" section offers suggestions for using the material with an entire class or within smaller groups. Many activities do lend themselves to the small group work that can foster collaborative learning. The workbook might also be used as a center lesson that would allow all students to have time on the Internet. The way it's used will probably depend on the type of Internet connection and number of computers available. Another helpful suggestion is to use WebWhacker, a software program that permits downloading of Web sites for later use offline.

The lesson plans begin with a search engine activity to locate children's social studies links. Here several of the more popular search tools are listed, along with some social studies sites to help students get started. Each activity contains an objective, materials needed, focus Web sites and destination URLs, and alternative Web sites, followed by a pre-Internet activity, suggestions for teaching the lesson, and a post-Internet activity if needed. A fun unit on pirates lets children explore the Internet and learn something about the topic as well. Other subjects include "Inventors," featuring such notables as Alexander Graham Bell, Thomas Edison, Samuel Morse, and others. Then "People in U.S. History" introduces various presidents, Susan B. Anthony, Martin Luther King, Jr., Rosa Parks, and others. "Geography and Landmarks" opens the door to some famous locations in the United States, whereas "My World" expands to other countries (including Canada, Greece, and Russia, among others). There is also a "Thematic Topics" section that presents interesting subjects such as aviation, baseball, the Vikings, current events, etc.

Individual activity worksheets are varied in scope, from objective, fill-in-the-blank questions, to essay questions asking students to write about a topic under investigation, to charts that require students to locate facts and fill in the chart, to oral presentations for classmates about a researched topic, etc. The activities appeal to elementary-age students and are obviously lower in level than the "Challenging" workbook, which requires a different and higher skill level.

For social studies teachers, this workbook offers a very good example of just how great the Internet can be as a learning tool. Because of all the work done in creating the activities, teachers will be able to get started much sooner. Using the worksheets effectively will require some time to make sure that everything works smoothly and that all Web sites work, but after that, seeing the fun students will have while logged on to the 'Net will go a long way toward making the effort worthwhile.

The Internet and Instruction: Activities and Ideas, 2d Edition

Ann E. Barron and Karen S. Ivers

Englewood, CO: Libraries Unlimited, 1998. (**http://www.lu.com/**). 244p. ISBN: 1-56308-613-1. Softcover, $28.50.

This second edition of the author's popular work updates the first with additional Web resources and a more detailed look at searching the Web. The purpose of the book, as stated by the authors in the preface, is to help teachers expand and improve their teaching by incorporating the Internet into their curriculum. Its target audience is K-12 educators, librarians, media specialists, or administrators who want to make use of the vast resources of the Internet. Another goal is to help simplify and demystify the terms and concepts associated with the 'Net and provide practical activities and lessons that can be used in the curriculum. Designed to be used as a guide or resource tool, or even textbook, the book offers a broad array of information. Throughout are detailed graphics, illustrations of hardware, and reproducible black-line masters for the lessons and exercises.

The authors also state that the chapters were written independent of one another, so the material is also a practical choice for in-service workshops. As a text, it's appropriate for either an undergraduate or graduate technology curriculum. The book fulfills its goals very well.

Among the early chapters is an excellent one that chronicles the benefits of the Internet through examples of school projects in use. There is a lot of technical information about the Internet that isn't always easy to understand. But the authors have done a good job of presenting information about how to get connected and all about bandwidths in an easy-to-understand manner. The chapter on getting around on the Internet explains the main Internet tools, such as electronic mail, LISTSERVs, newsgroups, Gopher, FTP, Telnet, and the World Wide Web. The chapter on searching the Web has new material on search tools and includes masters for analyzing Web resources with a neat checklist, a Web planning worksheet, and a search practice that helps you practice your searching skills and compares results with various search engines.

The meat of the book presents learning activities that can be used for classes from elementary up through high school. Lessons are arranged by subject and cover a very broad scope. In this second edition, science and mathematics activities are given their own chapters. Other broad subject categories are language arts, social studies, geography, art, music, and theater. Each activity offers a Web site from which to work, along with a description of it, and then presents a subtopic that students can work on. For example, in "environmental science," a subtopic is recycling or global warming. Suggestions are given for a project that students can work on. The information skills required are also listed. Often, additional Web sites are also included at the end of a topic. Sprinkled throughout are worksheets in the form of charts, fill-in-the-blanks, or just more detailed lesson suggestions.

For busy teachers, this book is a gold mine. The time required to prepare such detailed lessons and activities would be prohibitive for many educators. With this book in hand, you can get started not only understanding more about the benefits of the Internet and how it works, but also integrating it into a curriculum right away. The lessons are written in a very practical style, with clear and easy-to-follow instructions. The authors are obviously very aware of what educators need and want in an Internet book. They have put together one of the best in this second edition.

Internet Directory for Teachers

Grace Jasmine and Julia Jasmine

Indianapolis, IN: IDG Books Worldwide, 1997.
(**http://www.idgbooks.com**). 404p. ISBN: 0-7645-0219-0.
Softcover, $24.99. (Includes CD-ROM).

Written for teachers who want to get started using the Internet in their classrooms, this book serves as a "tour guide." The authors' intention is to provide a resource for teachers who want to use lesson plans to make it easy to incorporate the Internet into a class curriculum. The book is divided into four parts. Part One, "Students," divides up the resources into several subject areas, including "Famous Authors" ranging from Maya Angelou to Laura Ingalls Wilder. "Biographies" highlight historical notables, including John Kennedy, Harriet Tubman, Anne Frank, and many more. Other subject areas covered are "Extra Curricular, After-School Fun," language, math, science, social studies, and sports. The entries include a main site representative of the person or topic as well as the Web address, and "Other Stuff to Check Out," which includes newsgroups or mailing lists of interest. Each entry contains icons to indicate an age level and other information about the site. Part Two, "Teachers," focuses on general topics, such as holidays, home-school connection (families, homework, Internet safety, etc.), and methods (discipline, classroom management, etc.). "Modern Miscellany/Celebrities" highlights some famous people in the fields of sports, movies, music, and television, including Princess Diana, Madonna, Michael Jordan, and John Travolta. "Teacher Resources" will help with classroom lesson plans for science, languages, newspapers, math, and other areas, plus some professional development sites that include associations and organizations. "Theories and Trends" covers some of the major movements and ideas circulating in education, such as charter schools, alternative assessment, new math, and more. "Treasures for Teachers" help teachers locate sources for learning more about the Internet: search engines, online projects, directories, finding software, creating Web pages, etc. Finally, if you're ready to take a vacation, the section on "Vacations" highlights different countries ranging from Alaska to the Caribbean to Vietnam. Part Three, "The Part of Tens," includes the "ten best" sites for activities in K-2, grades three to six, junior high school, high school, and Internet safety for teachers. Part Four, "Appendices," offers information about hardware issues, Internet tools such as e-mail, and help with browsers and search engines, plus sites that provide even more information online. The accompanying CD is explained in Appendix B.

Each of the entries in the various chapters contains a title with the site's URL in bold, and icons that tell you much about the site, such as age group recommended, whether it's heavy with graphics and/or sound, or if you need plugins. You may have to whip out your glasses to figure out what the icon is. Their name of "micons" is very descriptive. Most entries have a very nice descriptive summary of the site, sometimes with URLs of links the authors find particularly interesting. It's obvious the authors have spent quality time examining each site. For busy teachers who want a ready source of curriculum possibilities, this is another worthy effort by the folks at IDG Books. Sure, sites change and go away, but if you want a jump-start to locating exciting and relevant resources on the Internet, this directory fits the bill.

Internet.edu: A Sourcebook for Educators

Robert H. Raese

Arlington Heights, IL: Skylight Training and Publishing, 1997.
(http://www.iriskylight.com). 220p. ISBN: 1-57517-072-8.
Softcover, $26.95.

The Internet with its vast resources is often an intimidating place to the educator who is just beginning to step out onto the Information Superhighway. *Internet.edu* is a book created by a teacher with more than 30 years' experience to help educators realize the potential of the Internet as a curriculum resource. Any teacher from elementary school through middle school and high school can use the information in this book. The author demonstrates all that the Internet can offer to teachers by presenting his selection of Web sites that exemplify excellent resources for the classroom.

The book is organized into two main parts called "The Basics" and "The Details." Part One offers three chapters, beginning with a look at the "glut of information" out there as Chapter 1 asks "Can the Internet Be Tamed?" To help visualize the Internet's resources, Raese uses a library as a model, with a floor plan of Internet tools. Another model, the Tree Model, uses its branches as the Internet tools; a final view is the now-familiar highway model. The World Wide Web is the preferred method of access in this book, but the author recognizes that not all schools have the latest technology available. Chapter 2, "The Virtual Library Card Catalogue," focuses on the best search tools for locating information, and Chapter 3, "Educational Resources," zeroes in on the best educational resources with lesson plans and projects for teachers.

Part Two, "The Details," takes the explorations further using e-mail, the World Wide Web, Gopher, FTP, IRC (Internet Relay Chat), and Telnet as tools. Each has its own chapter. The author realizes that some of the tools are not used as heavily since the Web has come along. There are also chapters dealing with acceptable use policies and a discussion of safety issues when bringing the Internet into the classroom. Teachers can learn more by following some of the exercises prepared for these topics.

Appendices include Appendix A, "Using the Internet.edu Link at IRI/Skylight," with directions on how to link to the site for this book. Appendix B details "The Structure of an Internet E-mail Address," with examples and explanations of URLs. Appendix C gives "Directions for Downloading a Graphic File." The step-by-step directions seem to be missing a step: the one where you point your mouse on the graphic, hold down the button, and then choose "File" and "Save as...." Appendix D briefly explores "CU-SeeMe—An Emerging Internet Technology," giving links to locate more about it as well as obtain the software. Appendix E, "An Archie Search," explains how to use this Internet tool. Appendix F, "Subject Area, Grade Level Ratings, and For Teacher Explorations by Chapter," gives the grade levels and subject areas for the various activities by chapter. Includes a glossary and bibliography, too.

The Internet Guide for English Language Teachers

Dave Sperling

Upper Saddle River, NJ: Prentice-Hall, 1997. (http://phregents.com). 176p. ISBN: 0-13-841073-9. Softcover, $19.95.

This is not strictly a curriculum guide, because it does contain information about the Internet and intends to help English teachers get started using the Internet's resources. The heart of this book, though, is a terrific collection of hundreds of sites related to teaching English and English as a second language.

Written by the creator of Dave's ESL Cafe, a popular Web site, this guide for English language teachers manages to cover a lot in a relatively few pages. Chapter 1, "Welcome to the Internet," covers a brief Internet history, getting connected, Web browsers, Web addresses, a list of terms such as *Java*, and helper applications. For further information, you can check out the Web sites listed. The writing style is very friendly, rather as if the author were talking to you. The topic of search engines is covered in Chapter 2. Much of the material consists of Web sites to various search engines and directories. It's a valuable tool for anyone seeking English-related resources on the Web.

Internet in the Classroom: A Practical Guide for Teachers

Philip R. Reinhardt

St. Paul, MN: Technology 4U, 1997. (http://technology4u.com). 148p. No ISBN listed. Spiral notebook, $25.00.

Five building blocks—Internet Knowledge, Teacher Resources, Students Online!, Curriculum Integration, and Additional Resources—are the main focus of this workbook for successfully integrating the Internet into a classroom. The book presents lesson plans, activities, hands-on practice, fact files, and fun quotes to master the skills.

The workbook is simply designed with fun graphics that will appeal to kids. "A Knowledge Rubric for Educators" covers the specific goals within the building blocks for beginners, intermediates, or experts. After taking the "What's Your IQ? Quiz," students will learn where they stand on background information. The next step is to move on to the activities, which cover subjects such as

Internet addresses and Internet tools (such as RealAudio and CU-SeeMe). Lesson plans accompany the various components to get students actively involved in learning. Section Two tells teachers about timesaving resources on the Internet, including LISTSERVs, the World Wide Web, search engines, bookmarks, downloading files, software, and more. A final activity allows teachers to think about planning a unit with a worksheet provided in the book. Section Three, "Students Online," discusses acceptable use and provides a form that students sign before beginning to surf the Internet. Suggestions for working with parents, plus online safety resources, offer additional information. HTML and Web design are briefly covered as well. The book includes some technology management tips that take into account the varying levels of access to computers. Lesson plans, along with a research planner and scavenger hunt, allow students to apply the information learned. Section Five puts all of the previous sections together with "Curriculum Integration," offering 50 project ideas, noting common pitfalls, and giving guidelines for integrating the Internet into a classroom. The final section of "Additional Resources" highlights glossary terms, and includes an extensive bibliography that should be helpful to teachers who wish to explore the topics in more depth.

For a teacher, planning lessons and activities is probably second nature. But most teachers are also very busy. A workbook like this can save valuable time and make it easier to get started sooner. The ideas, tips, and activities are a great way to take advantage of someone else's expertise. A Web site with additions and updates goes along with the book.

Internet Lesson Links

Austin, TX: Teaching Technology, 1996. 63p. No ISBN listed.
Spiral-bound, $12.00. (Includes floppy disks).

Teachers who want to get a jump-start on locating lesson plans can use this little reference guide for more than 900 lessons, projects, and activities found on the Internet. Macintosh or Windows disks accompany the book and supply bookmarks for these sites.

A brief history of the Internet, along with some glossary terms and a bit about connecting, provides novices with a little background before beginning the subject content of the lesson plans. Entries are for broad curriculum areas, such as math, health and physical education, social studies, science, art and music; each includes the categories, title of lesson plan, grade level, summary of the lesson, and an Internet address. Remember, sites are constantly becoming out dated, so don't be surprised to run into some dead ends. *(Courtesy of Multimedia Schools Magazine, Information Today, Inc., Medford, NJ).*

The Internet Resource Directory for
K-12 Teachers and Librarians, 98/99 Edition

Elizabeth B. Miller

Englewood, CO: Libraries Unlimited, 1998. (http://www.lu.com/).
403p. ISBN: 1-56308-718-9. Softcover, $25.00.

This annual directory of Internet resources is geared to teachers, librarians, students, and even parents who want to find quality Internet resources. It's not intended to be a comprehensive compilation of sites, but rather a selective and evaluative one. Its purpose is to help teachers provide up-to-date information in their lesson plans. With 400 new entries, most of them Web sites, the guide has enlarged its scope as well. Multicultural, gender equity, applied sciences, and school-to-work sections have been expanded. It's now possible to locate resources through cross-references as well, and with the larger subject index and a new site index, finding exactly what you need is even easier.

Organized into ten chapters, with two on professional resources ("Resources for Educators" and "The School Library"), the material covers just about any subject area found in schools.

Each entry lists the name, access information, the URL and path, login (when applicable), and other instructions. A contact name is given when available. The annotations are descriptive. There is a nice mix of Web sites, discussion lists, and Usenet groups. Because Gopher sites are becoming fewer and fewer, there are not many new ones, and many of the older sites are warning that they do not update their sites.

For busy teachers and librarians who want to use high-quality, informative, and current Internet resources, all the work is done for you in this guide. It's a valuable tool to have when you are making your lesson plans for the school year.

Internet Resources for Educators

Timothy Hopkins

Westminster, CA: Teacher Created Materials, 1999.
(http://www.teachercreated.com). 279p. ISBN: 1-57690-458-X.
Softcover, $24.95. (Includes CD-ROM).

Many teachers want to use the resources of the Internet in their classroom lessons, but don't have time to find just the right sites to use. This resource guide is a collection of hundreds of Web addresses of recommended education Web sites—just what busy teachers need. The subject areas include art, classroom management, diversity, education laws, funding, general education, language arts, geography, lesson plans, magazines, mathematics, organizations, social studies, research and reference, and special education. Each site has a short description along with space for recording notes as you use the sites. Because Web sites change so often, there is a Web site that accompanies this book, with monthly updates for addresses. There is also an accompanying CD-ROM that has links to all the Web lessons in the book.

There's no history of the Internet or introduction to using the Web in this book. If you are completely new to using the Internet, you'll need to start with another of the many Internet books for educators that are available. The book also assumes basic navigation skills with a Web browser, and it's probably a good idea to get the latest browser software to make the most of some of the sites. This is a great resource for anyone who wants to get started incorporating the Internet into lesson plans or for parents who want to know about educational sites for their children.

Internet Skills for School Success

Sarah A. DiRuscio

Auburn, CA: Forefront Curriculum, 1997. (**http://www.4forefront.com**). 72p. No ISBN listed. Softcover, $11.95.

This workbook is intended for use by students in middle and high school to develop Internet skills. The seven skills taught include "Navigating the Internet," "World Wide Web," "Electronic Mail," "Gopher," "Newsgroups," "Mailing Lists," and "File Transfer Protocol (FTP)." Further chapters cover "Multimedia Resources on the Internet," a "Teacher's Guide to the Internet," a "Student's Guide to the Internet," an "Internet Glossary," and "Student Certificate." A brief introduction to the Internet and a bit about safety on the 'Net precede the first activity. The author uses certain icons throughout to indicate whether an activity has step-by-step directions, is a hands-on activity, is a challenge to students, is a technical term, is a student learning objective, or is a cool Web site.

Each skill begins with background information to introduce the lesson. For example, skill one—"Navigating the Internet"—first briefly explains about a browser, the Web, and a URL before presenting exercises to practice the new skill. The exercises are hands-on, covering basic elements such as Netscape buttons, hyperlinks, bookmarks, and printing. Both Netscape and Internet Explorer are used. There are many screen prints, illustrations, and graphics along the way. Identifying the skills necessary to successful Internet use is important for students. This workbook sets it all out and makes learning them "cool."

The Kid-Friendly Web Guide

Laura Leininger and Chris Rowan

Palo Alto, CA: Monday Morning Books, 1997.
(http://www.mondaymorningbooks.com). 96p.
ISBN: 1-57612-023-6. Softcover, $11.95.

Geared for grades three through eight, this guide is divided into two main parts called "Search Techniques" and "Projects." There is also a "Resources" section that is similar to appendices.

By far, the "Projects" section is the heart of the book. "Search Techniques" covers some very basic material such as addresses, searching using keywords, browser tips, and tips for successful searching. But the section only takes 10 of the 96 pages. Children (and their parents) who are completely new to the Internet and surfing the Web will need another resource to build up their store of information.

Each project begins with a brief description of the topic followed by directions for completing the assignment. The projects contain several components that add to the child's learning experience, including "Researching," which begins the project by giving directions on what to look up. One or two suggested keywords help students get going. "Starting Points" supplies Web addresses for suggested sites. "Collaborating" offers tips to expand the project and link students to experts in the field. "Publishing" presents ideas for students to create more projects using computers or more traditional tools. "Extension" extends the lesson to more possibilities for research, and "Literature Links" offers print resources to follow up on the unit.

The final section, "Resources," provides several "appendices," including safety issues, putting together a Web site, netiquette information, key-pals, search tools, teacher links, and Web journals. A glossary is also included.

For a busy teacher, this book may offer valuable assistance for getting started using the Internet in the classroom. The assignments are creative and detailed in such a way as to be ready to use. The book is lacking in one area: the physical arrangement of the material. There are no divisions between the three sections of the book. When the "Search Techniques" portion ends, the "Projects" section starts right away with the first project. There is no indication of the subject area or anything. There are no divisions to separate the various subject categories, either. You'll need to look in the table of contents to see where one subject ends and the next one begins. To be fair, it's not like you can't figure out that when "Origami: A Window on Japan" ends and the next project is titled "Web

Authors," you have probably moved from art to language arts. But it would make it easier to browse with at least a heading to indicate the topic. Including such divisions would make this "Kid-Friendly" book even friendlier.

Kids.exploring.on.the.net: Super Sites to Visit and Fun Things to Do

Diane Sylvester

Santa Barbara, CA: Learning Works, 1998.
(**http://www.thelearningworks.com**). 128p.
ISBN: 0-88160-305-8. Softcover, $14.95.

Busy teachers who want to get started using the Internet will like this little book. It's full of ideas and Web sites that can be incorporated into regular lesson plans, and is organized into three broad subject categories titled "Family Fun," "Homework Helpers," and "The Amazing and Unusual." Each section has carefully selected Web sites as well as suggestions for more project ideas. This is not an Internet book in the sense that it teaches you how to use the Internet. But it does have a brief introductory chapter, "All About the Internet," with basic topics such as e-mail, smileys and emoticons, abbreviations and acronyms, plus a bit about being a good "Netter" and a glossary of terms and phrases that introduces you to some of the jargon. Because the World Wide Web is the major tool for locating curriculum sources, there's a bit about it as well. The main focus is on Web addresses and what to do if one doesn't work. Finding sites is one thing, but knowing if they are reliable or even credible is another. Realizing this, the author has included a form students can use to evaluate sites found.

Let's take a look at the heart of the book: the Web sites and suggestions for curriculum projects. "Family Fun" subjects include celebrations, nutrition and diet, sports, national parks, pets, zoos, and gardens. Each subject area lists appropriate sites with short descriptions, a title, and an address. There are about 7 to 10 sites for each subject (sometimes more). The choice of sites is really very kid-friendly. For example, in the nutrition section, besides a site on diet, nutrition, and recipes, you'll find Ben & Jerry's, Jolly Time Popcorn, and one on french fries. Besides the Web sites that go with each topic, there is a section of "Fun and Creative Things to Do On and Off the Internet" with more suggestions for research projects. These include ideas such as identifying a famous person whose birthday is that day and researching more about the day. In connection with celebrations, there's an idea for thinking of a theme for a party, creating invitations, and deciding whom to invite. "Homework Helpers" suggests activities and projects related to science, reading, writing, current events, history, and government.

Because science fair projects are increasing in popularity, there are a number of suggested sites that offer a look at what makes a good project. Looking for facts about the states or cities? There are some excellent and well-known sites here; the same goes for "Reading and Writing," where The Children's Literature Web Guide and The Internet Public Library are highlighted. The final section is "The Amazing and Unusual," with lots of fun and educational choices. Mummies, volcanoes, pirates, bats (the animal), and more make up this list of curriculum sites.

Getting started with younger kids on the Internet is a goal many teachers have. Here's a handy little guide to get going. With projects and plans already spelled out, any teacher ready to incorporate the Internet into lessons can relax a bit and use the ideas in this book for starters.

Kids on the Internet: A Beginner's Guide

Kim Mitchell

Grand Rapids, MI: Instructional Fair/TS Denison, 1998. (www.instructionalfair.com). 124p. ISBN: 1-568-22626-8. Softcover, $10.95.

The Internet provides a way for teachers to open their classrooms to the world. But this can also seem rather overwhelming to educators. The goal of this book is to teach students how to make use of the Internet in a friendly, non-threatening way. Beginning with a brief introduction to the Internet and the World Wide Web in simple terms, the author breaks down what they are and how they are used.

The book is divided into several parts that can be presented in order or based on students' skills. The exercises do not necessarily build on each other, so it's possible to choose which is most suitable for a student's skill level. It's not necessary to follow the exercises in order unless a class consists of all beginners, in which case it makes sense to move through them in sequence. The exercises are generic, in that they do not have to be used with a particular online service provider; this is good because schools may have a variety of types of connections to the Internet. The purpose of the exercises is to help teachers and students find out how the Internet can enhance their learning.

The exercises consist of a wide range of activities that help introduce students to the Internet. A great variety of exercises include topics having to do with acceptable use policies, logging on, equipment needed, how to navigate the World Wide Web using hypertext, learning to use search engines to locate information, URLs and how they work, home pages, bookmarks, electronic mail, and even what to do when the system is down.

The exercises have several parts to them. First, a section of teacher information gives some tips to teachers about the lesson. Next, an activities section provides a list of words students need to know to understand the topic they are studying. After the vocabulary list is an exercise that allows students to practice the new terms by filling in the blanks in a story. Sometimes there may be a continuing exercise that lets students locate a real-life example on the Web; for example, while studying acceptable use policies, they may look at an acceptable use policy on the Web. A brainstorming sheet provides students a way to create their own work (when applicable). Again, the acceptable use policy is an example. In a brainstorming activity for this topic, students would create their own policy. The exercises are step-by-step and allow students to work at their own pace. Others permit students to work together in a group.

One exercise called "Ready, Set, Go" lets the students fill out a checklist to take with them when they are going to be online in the lab. It records how they spent their time. Also, an interesting concept is to have students work out an activity to use when the Internet is extremely slow or even down. In the search engine section, there are activities that let students get their feet wet searching on the Web, with their teacher's help. "Journey of Discovery" leads students through a practice using search engines with self-directed questions, then continues with Part Two that enlarges upon their skills. Students can practice their skills through an exercise in which they search for an author of their own choosing. Learning how to use Web addresses lets students choose sites from Yahoo and then enter the URL on an exercise sheet. They visit government sites, entertainment sites, and some sports sites. Then they practice understanding URLs by trying to figure out some for major companies such as Pepsi, Nike, Coca-Cola, etc.

Teaching Internet skills is an important part of many classrooms today. This guide is a great resource for teachers who want some ready-made activities to teach the Internet. It offers hands-on activities for students to practice their Internet skills. Busy teachers don't have to prepare the activities, but can concentrate on goals and how they want to incorporate the activities into the curriculum. An answer key is provided at the end of the book.

Kids@school.on.the.net

Karen Krupnick

Santa Barbara, CA: Learning Works, 1997.
(http://www.thelearningworks.com). 128p.
ISBN: 0-88160-303-1. Softcover, $14.95.

Because the Internet is such a vast and constantly changing place, it's often difficult for teachers to keep up with sites that might enhance their regular curriculum. Here's a little guide that makes it easy to accomplish. With lots of Internet-based activities for elementary school students, the time required to get ready to use the Internet in the class is much shorter. The activities are fun and will keep kids interested in learning. Best of all, the work is already done. You don't have to find the best sites yourself; just look through and choose those worksheets that complement your lesson activities. A Web site has been set up to accompany the book. You can use it to go to any of the sites listed in the activities.

A nice little introductory chapter, called "You're on the Superhighway," contains teacher resources as well as some basic information about the Internet and its tools. Netiquette, e-mail, mailing lists, Telnet, IRC, Gopher, FTP, and, of course, the World Wide Web are all covered. Brief descriptions are just enough to get you started. "Where do you go first?" provides sample sites to begin exploring. These will be helpful to the Internet "newbie" because they are some of the best-known Web sites containing a vast array of education-related material. EdWeb, Classroom Connect, ERIC, and Web66 are some of the sites listed. A special section, "Sites for Students," presents several of the best "for kids" sites out there. Both of these sections will enhance your knowledge of what's out on the Web and provide you with some good examples of collections of education materials on the 'Net. If you still have some questions, then check out "Frequently Asked Questions about the Internet." Here you'll find some common situations encountered by educators, with helpful answers. Topics range from "where do I start?" to safety concerns to basic error messages.

"You're on the Superhighway: Internet Activities" begins the Internet activities and lesson plans. Content is arranged by subject area and includes math, social sciences, language arts, science, art and music, special days, cross-curricular units, and some fun Internet treasure hunts. One note: the topics run together with a small header at the top listing the subject. There are no introductory pages or dividers between subjects. One page is an exercise in "Moebius Magic" for math and the next page is "How many miles?," which begins the social studies activities. This is not a big deal, just inconvenient. You're moving along and all of a sudden you've switched topics. The table of contents lists the lesson titles and page numbers, so just take a look there to see where one subject begins and another ends. "Internet Treasure Hunts" contains clues for kids to follow along with various links to end up at a point where they have completed the hunt.

Whether beginners or experienced, kids will find that using this book makes learning fun as they move to a Web site to locate answers, read the material, or continue a project. The book is liberally dotted with cartoons and illustrations that will appeal to kids.

NetAmerica: Travel the 50 States on the Information Highway

Gary M. Garfield and Suzanne McDonough

Torrance, CA: Good Apple, 1996. (http://www.frankschaffer.com/).
112p. ISBN: 1-56417-852-8. Softcover, $13.99.

Written by teachers for teachers, this tour of the United States presents teachers with projects they can use in their classes to study the 50 states. Written for grades four through eight, the authors first introduce the Internet and how it can be used in the classroom. Tips on how to get telecommunication access for your class include suggestions for sharing plans with your PTA group, contacting corporations for support, and talking with your superintendent about your project ideas. Before beginning the road trip, there is a checklist of what the student will be seeing on the computer screen that is a basic guide to Netscape's browsing features. Search engines are explained very briefly and perhaps are somewhat oversimplified.

The bulk of this guide is sharing lesson ideas for teaching the 50 states. The chapters are in alphabetical order beginning with Alabama. Each lesson contains a main home page for the state where students can begin to gather information. Subsequent links help students learn more about people, places, and things.

In general, the book will supply busy teachers with key Web sites for each of the 50 states. It's not meant to teach Internet skills, so if students are not comfortable with Internet basics like navigating the Web, teachers will need to spend time on these skills first.

Net Lessons: Web-Based Projects for Your Classroom

Laura Parker Roerden

Sebastopol, CA: O'Reilly Publishing, 1996. (http://www.ora.com).
306p. ISBN 1-56592-291-3. Softcover, $24.95.

A follow-up to the book *Net Learning*, this volume continues with a "roadmap" to success in using Web-based projects. The target audience is classroom teachers, both novice and experienced. After an introductory chapter that sets "The Lay of the Land," the author describes ways in which teachers can create curricula that make the most of the Web's potential as a learning tool.

Chapters are filled with practical information, including tips and specific lesson plans to get started. "The Big Twelve" offers activity types to try in the classroom. Examples include key-pals, Web mentors, Web collaboration, and more. There are plans and worksheets to show teachers how to actually begin to implement ideas. The worksheets seem especially helpful in getting started.

In Part Two, "From Theory to Practice," actual lesson plans are presented. The plans are arranged by subject and include objectives, prerequisites, and procedures. More than 100 are described. Subject categories include art, music, language arts, math, science, and social studies. The book's very practical approach makes it a great starting point for teachers who wish to incorporate Internet resources into the curriculum. The book contains appendices with worksheets and lists of Web sites by topic area. An accompanying CD provides access through America Online. *(Courtesy of Multimedia Schools Magazine, Information Today, Inc., Medford, NJ).*

NetStudy: Your Complete Guide to Academic Success Using the Internet and Online Service

Michael Wolff

New York: Dell, 1997. (http://www.bdd.com). 342p.
ISBN: 0-440-22429-2. Paperback, $6.99.

This *NetStudy* book was one of several published by Michael Wolff's New Media, which is no longer in business. Touted as the "most complete guide to educational sites on the Web," the more than 300 pages of sites seem to indicate that this is not just a marketing ploy. This is not a guide on how to use the Web. Except for a few pages of frequently asked questions that address some basic topics (such as what the 'Net is, and how to get connected, choose equipment, use e-mail, and read newsgroups), the rest of the book lists and reviews education-related sites. Although the book is somewhat out-of-date, the comprehensive coverage of education sites still makes it a useful tool today.

For anyone already familiar with the Web who wants to locate a specific site, use the index, where every site in the book is included. For those less familiar with the Web's resources in education, it's possible to browse the 11 parts of the book. These include the following subject areas: "Back to School," "English," "Mathematics," "Science," "Social Science," "History," "Foreign Languages," "The Arts," "Electives," "Physical Education," and "School Library."

"Back to School" features the more general education sites of interest to educators, students, and parents, featuring virtual classrooms, home schooling, starting points, homework help, etc. "Teacher's Lounge" features resources for teachers, such as ERIC, education projects, educational links, publishers, and lesson plans. A special section for parents highlights resources of interest to families. Besides Web sites, discussion lists are featured in the "Teacher's Discussion Groups" section which completes the "Back to School" chapter. "The School

Library" chapter presents reference sources such as dictionaries, conversion charts, Zip Codes, encyclopedias, library catalogs, and more. Obviously, some of the library catalog addresses are out of date at this point, so these may not be as useful today.

Within each of the subject-specific chapters are subtopics. For example, if you are interested in social studies sites, there are Web pages under geography, federal government, civics and current affairs, economics, "ologies" and "osophies," ethnic studies, women's studies, and comparative religion. Just a note: "Ologies and Osophies" are the anthropologies, philosophies, etc. There is a "Starting Points" and a "Teacher's Lounge" section in each chapter, which focus on subject-specific sites and specific resources for teachers. Each chapter begins with a brief, lighthearted introduction. Sites feature reviews with good solid information as well as a touch of humor that creates a nice balance.

With the publisher out of business, it may be difficult to find this title. However, if you can, it's worth the $6.99 just to see all the educational possibilities contained in the book, even though they are somewhat dated by now. The collection is vast and will certainly help teachers and students locate subject-specific sites.

The School Administrator's Handbook of Internet Sites

Leslie A. Ramsey, ed.

Alexandria, VA: Capitol Publications, 1996.
(http://www.cappubs.com/). 174p.
ISBN: 1-56925-045-6. Softcover, $54.00.

This guide is a directory of 270 sites on the Internet of interest to school administrators. The book is organized by subject area and includes topics such as curriculum, government, grants, professional development, etc. Some of these sites would be of interest to educators in general. Each entry lists the name of the site, its Internet address, and a paragraph or so describing the content. It's easy to tell if the site is a Web site, Gopher, mailing list, or other type by the large capital letter (W for Web, M for mailing list, etc.) underneath the title. The entries are easy to read and locate with an index in the back. At a rather hefty $54, this book is a bit pricey, considering how rapidly things go out of date on the Internet. If you are a busy administrator who just doesn't have time to surf the Internet and compile your own list of sites, then you might find this handy to have at your computer. Otherwise, there are a lot of other education-related Internet resource books that have more sites and cost a lot less money. *(Courtesy of*

*Multimedia Schools Magazine, Information Today, Inc., Medford, NJ). **Note:** A sec-*
ond edition was due out in 1998.

Simple Internet Activities (Intermediate)

Alain Chirnian

Westminster, CA: Teacher Created Materials, 1999.
(**http://www.teachercreated.com**). 96p. ISBN: 1-57690-460-1.
Softcover, $11.95.

Geared to the teacher who wants to be able to incorporate the Internet into
the curriculum, this collection of activities offers a variety of exciting lessons that
can be completed by students on their own or as part of a group. There are a variety of subject areas that include art, language arts, science, math, and social studies. There is no introduction to the Internet; it is assumed that you have a basic
knowledge of the Internet and navigation skills using a Web browser.
Furthermore, the author recommends having the latest browser version, to take
advantage of the latest technologies such as Java. It is also recommended that
you install helpers and plug-ins, such as Shockwave and RealAudio, to get the
most out of some of the Web sites.

Each activity is prepared so that it can be completed in a standard class period, and the lessons are self-contained. The lessons include "Teacher Notes,"
"Objectives," "Materials Required," and "Web Sites." The time required and
notes on teaching the lesson are part of each activity. A nice feature is the inclusion of a Web site for updates to the Web addresses in the lessons. This will be a
handy resource and make the book more valuable as a curriculum tool.

Surf's Up! Spanish Website Workbook

Linda Moehle-Vieregge, Rodney A. James, and Eliud Chuffe

Guilford, CT: Audio-Forum, 1997.
(**http://www.agoralang.com/audioforum.html**). 235p.
ISBN: 0-88432-953-4. Spiral notebook, $14.95.

Written by experienced educators, this interactive workbook uses the Web
in a structured environment as a supplementary tool for learning beginning
Spanish. The great thing about this book is that it can be used as a teaching tool
for students or by an individual with access to the Internet who is learning
Spanish independently.

Teachers have recognized the value of the Internet as a teaching tool and
this is certainly true for language acquisition. The World Wide Web's ability to

provide a graphical interface, as well as access to sound and multimedia, makes it the perfect tool for language teachers with Internet access. Web sites can be kept current by adding new material and revising information—things that make the Web more useful than many textbooks.

The authors have included activities that are "universal" in appeal and work with most basic foreign language programs or textbooks. This makes the workbook an ideal supplementary activity book. The sheets can be torn out and handed in by students as homework assignments. Answers can be found at the workbook's Web site.

There are 50 activity sheets. The authors have been careful to make it possible to finish each activity within a normal class period. Each activity is preceded by a cover page that introduces the topic's theme, gives a Web address, and states the goals of the exercise. As well, the level of proficiency in Spanish is indicated by a symbol. In general, exercises can be used by anyone with little or no proficiency, up through those with a more advanced knowledge of Spanish. Most sites present the material in Spanish. To help with some of the technical aspects, a "Techno-Tips" section presents such information as the importance of typing the URL exactly, what to do if you have a problem accessing a site, and suggestions about plug-ins that may have to be downloaded. The "Comments" section provides the authors' ideas about the site and the activities or experiences with the site. There is also a "Related Websites" section when applicable, and a blank page where students can make notes as necessary.

Lessons cover a wide variety of topics, such as geography, science, culture, the arts, literature, language, music, politics, sports, religion, and more. The exercises include puzzles, objective questions that require reading of the material on the screen, and fill-in-the-blank sections, as well as more open-ended types of questions that may require writing more in Spanish. Aside from improving their language skills, students will surely also be able to improve computer skills, including navigating the World Wide Web. Best of all, the sites are preselected by qualified experts, saving busy teachers time. At the end of the workbook are more than 400 Web sites with links to more sites of interest to the Spanish student. This is an excellent resource for busy Spanish teachers. Or, if you just want to take advantage of the Internet to improve your Spanish, pick up a copy and have some fun while you do so. There are additional workbooks for French and German that follow the same organization: *Surf's Up! French Website Workbook* and *Surf's Up! German Website Workbook*.

Surf's Up! Website Workbook for Basic French

Linda Moehle-Vieregge, Mary Ann Lyman-Hager, Stacy DuBravac, and Travis Bradley

Guilford, CT: Audio-Forum, 1997.
(http://www.agoralang.com/audioforum.html).
256p. ISBN: 0-88432-934-8. Spiral notebook, $14.95.

The concept of this workbook is wonderful. It's a really handy tool for those who want to learn or refresh their French. The Web is a great resource for language learning. *Surf's Up* allows students to broaden their learning environment by accessing information on the Internet. Its emphasis on reading comprehension, critical knowledge, and the ability to experience authentic French materials are invaluable. The exercises could be adapted for an individual learner or for a curriculum in a classroom setting. After some basic Web information, the authors jump right into the lessons.

Each lesson has an introduction with goals, level, technical tips, and general comments. The activities chosen are fun as well as educational: from reading about scientists to learning about cities and regions of France to Celine Dion, the French-Canadian pop superstar. You may need to keep a French dictionary handy for the exercises I tried, but they were fun. Although there are no answers in the book, you get a Web address where you can find them.

The usual caveat about changing Web addresses applies here too. Teachers might want to double-check the exercises for accuracy. Still, a workbook that lets you make use of the incredible interactive capabilities of the Internet makes learning more fun and interesting. *(Courtesy of Multimedia Schools Magazine, Information Today, Inc., Medford, NJ).*

Teaching the Internet: A Guide for Teachers and Parents

Christine Pace

Stevens Point, WI: Xanadu Press, 1996.
(http://coredcs.com/~cpace/xanadupress.html).
47p. No ISBN listed. Spiral notebook, $12.95.

This little spiral notebook offers a collection of lesson plans, projects, and activities for parents as well as teachers who want to incorporate the Internet into either the classroom or work with kids at home.

Each lesson plan contains objectives, materials needed, and an explanation of the procedure to teach the lesson. Some lessons also include crossword puzzles or activity pages. Answers can be found at the end of the unit. The last two sections provide a list of popular Web sites and a journal to jot down favorite places of your own. The lessons are creative and the activities are fun. Of course, once the Internet hooks you, you'll want to find a more detailed source of curriculum ideas.

If you are a harried teacher or parent or an Internet "newbie" who is a bit overwhelmed by all the Internet material, and perhaps still a bit daunted about exploring on your own, this little book will get you started with some fun ideas for using the Internet. A bit pricey at 47 pages and $12.95, however. *(Courtesy of Multimedia Schools Magazine, Information Today, Inc., Medford, NJ).*

Teaching with the Internet: Lessons from the Classroom
Donald J. Leu, Jr., and Deborah Diadiun Leu

Norwood, MA: Christopher Gordon Publishers, 1997.
(http://web.syr.edu/~djleu/teaching.html). 227p.
ISBN: 0-9-26842-59-5. Softcover, $25.95.

The intent of this book is to give teachers ideas about integrating the Internet into their curriculum using real-life examples from the classroom. The book's three main parts are: "Welcome to the Internet: Getting Acquainted," "Teaching in Content Areas with Internet Resources," and "The Internet Classroom: Putting It All Together."

Each chapter begins with an "e-mail" message outlining the chapter. Following this is "Lessons from the Classroom," a unit offering classroom experiences related to the particular chapter under discussion. Various sources provide these experiences, including LISTSERV discussions, personal experiences, and even the authors themselves. These first-hand lessons provide a nice look at real-life Internet use and offer teachers an opportunity to learn from them.

Section Two focuses on specific subject areas such as science, social studies, and mathematics; it contains worksheets as well as activity assignments and projects, along with central Web sites. Each part presents "Lessons from the Classroom," "Central Sites," "Activity Assignments," "Projects, Internet Inquiry," and "Instructional Resources on the Internet." One chapter in Section Three presents material on how to make sure to include all students, with emphasis on access to sites for visually impaired students. In another chapter, basic HTML is discussed.

All in all, this book covers much of the same territory as many other "teaching and the Internet" books, but it packages the material in a very "real-life" and practical way with classroom examples. The material comes alive for prospective teachers who want to take the leap to using the Internet in their classrooms. *(Courtesy of Multimedia Schools Magazine, Information Today, Inc., Medford, NJ).*

Using the Internet and the World Wide Web in Your Job Search

Fred E. Jandt and Mary B. Nemnich

Indianapolis, IN: JIST Works, 1997. (http://www.jist.com/jist).
308p. ISBN: 1-56370-294-4. Softcover, $16.95. (Includes floppy disk).

Though it is not really geared just to the education community, students who want to learn how to find a job using the Internet and World Wide Web will find this a very useful and informative guide.

The authors' goals are to help prospective job seekers, not only to locate jobs but also to learn how to get connected and become proficient Internet surfers in the process. The 14 chapters cover material about why the Internet is an important tool for locating jobs, how to get connected, how to use the World Wide Web for classifieds, and how to use commercial services, as well as how to create an electronic résumé and what an Internet interview is. There is a specific chapter for college students plus some advice for employers. Besides Web sites, some Gopher sites and newsgroup resources are also included.

The chapter on college students covers places to look for a variety of jobs, ranging from entry level to others in education or a specific discipline such as mathematics. Appropriate Web sites are described and URLs given. Online placement offices are highlighted as good sources, including the University of California at Irvine and Ball State University. Using the correct netiquette is important, and a chapter with general guidelines helps prospective job hunters learn the rules of the road.

Lots of resources plus practical advice make this guide a unique tool for anyone who wants to take the job search to the Internet and World Wide Web.

Using the Internet to Research . . . Ancient Egypt

Jane Bourke

Greenwood, WA: Ready-Ed Publications, 1997.
(http://www.iinet.net.au/~edubooks). 28p.
(Internet Cyber School series). ISBN: 1-86397-146-7.
Softcover, no price given.

Part of the Cyber School series published by an Australian publishing company, this workbook contains reproducible activities and exercises for students aged 10 and older. There are a number of different titles in the series having to do with various subject areas, mostly in the sciences. Each book follows a similar structure, so children will feel comfortable moving from one subject to another in the series. The author's goal is to help children successfully learn to use the Internet.

Several learning outcomes are part of the book's activities. Students should know how to use research skills to respond to questions, extrapolate information from Internet references, and use Web sites to increase their knowledge of the topic under investigation. Finally, it's important to become familiar with several search engines for locating information, as well as using links to broaden the scope of research.

The book is Australian in origin, but except for some links to Australian and New Zealand Internet sites, the activities can be applied anywhere. The workbook is meant to be used cover-to-cover. Teachers can decide at what point of entry to begin. After completing the research skills activities in the first workbook, teachers may elect to begin with the first subject-oriented exercise and skip the research lessons. The point is that teachers should guide students in their use of the exercises. Each workbook has the following activity sequence: materials/practice in research skills; information and practice in using the Web; an address book where students can record the latest and best sites to visit; focusing activities; and expanding activities.

The three "Net Research" lessons cover using a search engine, using Internet addresses, and finding fast facts online. The directions for these lessons aren't exactly step-by-step. Sometimes they are a bit vague and don't work as smoothly as they should. For example, there is no indication of which browser to use, but the directions state to use "Net Search," a Netscape Navigator button. The exercise has you go to Yahoo; specifically, Media, then "Current Headlines." But the problem is there is no "Media" by itself, though there is a "News/Media" on Yahoo's menu. But then there are no "Current Headlines" to find as indicated in the next step. Luckily, there is a Web site that accompanies the series. There are updates and changes to the exercises in the book, so check it out for the most current steps to follow.

The activities explore the Pyramids, the Great Sphinx, Egyptian religion, mummification, art and artifacts, and famous people such as Cleopatra, Khufu, and Tutankhamen. Exercises might revolve around answering questions by filling in the blank or writing a narrative. Others are more creative and involve drawing, creative writing, and more. Answers are included in the back of the workbook.

Using this workbook as a supplementary resource for the study of ancient Egypt shows exactly why the Internet is such a powerful tool in the classroom.

The sites explored during the activities illustrate the interactive and powerful potential of the Internet to bring a new dimension to learning in the classroom. Students can see the power of the Internet with these well-developed and interesting sites. Getting the most from the workbook does require a certain level of navigation skill by students. There is no tutorial or explanation of the Internet or World Wide Web except for some preliminary comments about safety issues. If students are not ready to surf the 'Net, it will be necessary to provide instruction in this area before undertaking the activities.

Using the Internet to Research...Our Amazing Planet

Jane Bourke

Greenwood, WA: Ready-Ed Publications, 1998.
(**http://www.readyed.com.au**). 28p. (Internet Cyber
School series). ISBN: 1-86397-149-1. Softcover, no price given.

The Cyber School series of workbooks, from the Australian publishing company Ready-Ed, contains a variety of topics, mostly in the area of science. This one, on "Our Amazing Planet," consists of activities centering around the Earth, such as the ozone layer, Antarctica, endangered species, volcanoes, rain forests, and more. It has been revised and updated.

Each title in the series has a similar structure, so that students will become comfortable with the format as they move through the various books. Generally, there are three introductory lessons on research skills: using a search engine, Web addresses, and locating some basic facts. After students work through them in one workbook, they can skip those sections in subsequent books. To make the most of the workbook, activities should be followed in sequence throughout.

The activities teach students certain skills that include information and practice in research skills, using Web pages for maximum benefit, using an address book to record new and interesting sites, and using Internet sites to gather information that is represented on the screen. On the first level, lessons may include fill-in-the-blank or objective questions that require specific answers. A higher level of using information is also part of the activities and includes exploring the sites in more depth by using links. Tasks in these sections are more open-ended.

The activities are structured around the use of a Web page created for the book. At this site you can use the links mentioned in the exercises rather than having to type in the URLs directly. Some of the exercises will require direction from teachers; if students are not skillful Web navigators, it will be necessary for them to learn those skills before beginning the exercises. The Web site also updates material in the workbook. It's a good idea to check it out to see what has been changed.

The lessons provide students with a real means to understand how to obtain information from the Internet. They are fun and interesting. The information is very current, which is important for topics covered in this workbook. If you are a teacher or parent who wants to be able to provide some educational uses of the Internet to your children, these ready-made activities will offer a fun way to learn more about the Internet as well as interesting subjects.

Using the Internet to Research . . . The Kids Internet Explorer

Jane Bourke

Greenwood, WA: Ready-Ed Publications, 1998.
(http://www.readyed.com). 28p. (Internet Cyber School series).
ISBN: 1-86397-164-5. Softcover, no price given.

The Cyber School series is a set of workbooks that allow students to learn more about using the Internet for research. This book, "The Kids Internet Explorer," targets children aged seven to nine who are just beginning to use the Internet. The activities are created in a way that helps students stay on track as they move around the World Wide Web. It is assumed that students can navigate the World Wide Web and have a basic understanding of what it is. No background or introductory material is offered. The lessons cover a variety of topics, mostly in the science area. "The On Line Sites for Kids" page presents a good starting point for collections of kids' activities and places of interest.

Activities are very directed and focused. For example, in learning about worms, children are supposed to click on the various "worm cousins" on a Web page and then write two amazing facts about each type of worm. In the lesson on cockroaches, kids draw their interpretation of the bugs they see on the site and then draw and label a "Madagascar Hissing Cockroach." A couple of the sites are commercial, including one for Pocahontas and Toy Story, both from Disney's site.

If you want a fun book to help kids explore and learn to use the Internet to gather information, this series is a good one to have on hand.

Using the Net to Enhance Your Classroom Instruction (Grades 6–12)

Sarah A. DiRuscio

Auburn, CA: Forefront Curriculum, 1997.
(http://www.4front.com). 119p. No ISBN listed.
Spiral notebook, $14.95.

Another of the Forefront Curriculum workbooks by Sarah DiRuscio, this one takes a more general approach to using the Internet for grades 6 through 12. It does not focus on one subject area but can be applied to most classroom settings. The same principles found in *Integrating the Internet into the Science Classroom (Grades 7 through 12)* can be found in this workbook as well.

An introductory chapter explains what the Internet is, how information is sent, how to connect, hardware requirements, safety issues, acceptable use policies, and filtering/access software. Applying a concept of N.E.T. Integration tools, the author discusses the six levels of mastery: "Master the Navigational Skills," "Conduct Effective Research Using the 'Net," "Develop Internet Based Lesson Plans," "Electronic Mail & Activities," "Host a Collaborative Project," and "Publish Student Work & Classroom Web Site." A checklist of skills necessary for each level, along with a guide containing activities, helps students complete the six levels. The activities and lessons are a fun way to work through the skills. Section Three is a treasure trove of online curriculum resources for teachers and students. Several of the same lessons found in *Integrating the Internet into the Science Classroom* are also used in this workbook. Guided worksheets allow teachers to create individual lesson plans, and the Web activities incorporate interesting and fun sites while maintaining a specific curriculum objective for each one.

If you've been reluctant to get started using the Internet because of the amount of work needed to plan and make up lessons, check out this little workbook for a wealth of ideas and activities and take the plunge into the world of the Internet.

Virtual Field Trips

Gail Cooper and Garry Cooper

Englewood, CO: Libraries Unlimited, 1997. (**http://www.lu.com/**). 168p. ISBN: 1-56308-557-7. Softcover, $24.00.

Remember when the only kind of field trip you knew about meant getting permission slips signed, asking parents to chaperone, and getting everyone ready to board those buses for an all-day drive? *Virtual Field Trips* intends to provide the same field trip experiences but without the hassles and without leaving your classroom.

This collection of Internet sites has something for everyone, no matter what your subject area may be. The 13 chapters are organized into rather broad categories, including "Historic Time Travel," "Worldwide Travel," "The Natural World," "Outer Space," "Culture and Sports," "Art Museums and Galleries," "Mathematics and Logic," "On-line Classes and Schools," "Meet Famous

People," and "Field Trips for Primary Grades." Within a chapter, sites are arranged alphabetically and are briefly annotated. The entries are simple, with titles in bold followed by the Web address, and then the annotation. "See" references plus an index will help you zero in on the exact site you want.

Needless to say, having a copy of this book could be a real time-saver for busy educators who want to take advantage of the Internet's interactive adventures, but just don't have the time to explore and select their own virtual field trips.

Wading the World Wide Web: Internet Activities for Beginners

Keith Kyker

Englewood, CO: Libraries Unlimited, 1998. (**http://www.lu.com/**). 170p. ISBN: 1-56308-605-0. Softcover, $18.00.

Wading the World Wide Web is written by a middle school teacher. The term *wading* is meant to imply that you won't get in over your head in this book. This guide is for educators and students who wish to learn how to successfully incorporate the World Wide Web into the classroom and enjoy using the resources that allow them to expand the classroom's walls.

The two-part book consists of a couple of basic chapters that highlight information about the Web and how to implement it into a school setting. The second part consists of 41 exercises that use the Web as a resource for lesson plans.

Chapter 1, "Welcome to the World Wide Web!," contains a history of the Web, its main characteristics, hardware issues, and browser features. There are also details about URLs (those funny-looking Web addresses) and service providers, plus more. The bibliography at the end of the chapter contains some nice resources for further information. Chapter 2, "The World Wide Web in School," targets the school and its use of the Web. Teachers will find this a valuable source of information if they are still at the point of getting started. The author, as a library media specialist himself, understands the process and issues that must be dealt with. The material is very practical, dealing with hardware issues and various models for enabling Web use in the classroom. Some illustrations accompany the text as well. Each model has a section of advantages and disadvantages. Finally, there is a nicely organized chart that puts all the main features together to give an overview of each one. The remainder of the chapter touches on issues of supervision, acceptable use policies, computer stations, and how to block unacceptable Web sites. "Myths About Students and the World Wide Web" explores various questions that might arise, such as "All kids will be excited by the Internet" and "Everything on the World Wide Web is fun," among others.

Part Two, "Teacher Plans and Activity Sheets," organizes a variety of lessons into a teacher plan plus the exercise. The plan sets up what to do before beginning the exercise and what to do after completing it. The exercises consist of the site name, Web address, and directions for the lesson activity. There are also two more advanced activities, called "Super Surfer" and "Kowabunga Dude!," for students who are ready to move on to other activities. These can be done outside the classroom.

Subjects include language, literature, the sciences, arts, health, fitness and nutrition, sports and the outdoors, cultures, government, biography, and some general-interest topics. Each activity is one page and can be reproduced for classroom use. An "Answer Key" provides teachers with an easy way to check answers, except when the question is open-ended and cannot have one specific answer. The author maintains a Web site to update the activities and Web addresses.

A number of activity books for teachers are now available. This one has a very clean presentation, is well written, and is easy to use. The one-page format makes the activities easy to reproduce and the accompanying Web site assures a means to easily update your favorite lesson plan. For any educators who are still somewhat reluctant to jump in, perhaps "wading" is just what they need to get started.

A Year of the Internet Thematic Units

Austin, TX: Teaching Technologies, 1996.
(**http://www.teachtech.com/k-12**). 106p.
Softcover, $27.99. (Includes floppy disks).

Another title from Teaching Technologies, this title also provides the teacher with a handy reference tool for using the Internet in the classroom. Units are supplied for the months September through May and match the holidays or special occasions of the particular month when possible. Themes are on apples, pumpkins, turkeys, polar bears, presidents, weather, chocolate, and sports. Each one offers multiple activities for the seven intelligences (according to Dr. Howard Gardner), so that subjects can be taught for various learning styles in the classroom. With the sites bookmarked, this tool makes it easier for teachers to incorporate the Internet into their daily lesson plans. My only complaint is that the directions for using the Mac disk must have been written by a Windows user—and at $27.99 and about 100 pages, it's a bit pricey. *(Courtesy of Multimedia Schools Magazine, Information Today, Inc., Medford, NJ).*

Chapter 5://The Internet in Juvenile Fiction

Introduction

Everyone had a favorite book or series of books they read as a child. Whether it was way-back-when with Nancy Drew and the Hardy Boys, or more current series such as Jonny Quest and Goosebumps, mysteries and adventures appeal to children. Today, the mystery being solved has a new component—technology and especially the Internet. Teenagers are often avid game players and Internet surfers. It was only a matter of time before someone realized this and came up with series that use the Internet as a theme or backdrop. There are a variety of Internet fiction books out there for children. In some cases the story has an international flavor with groups of friends who met over the Internet. Others revolve around one or two friends who have a shared interest in computers and the Internet. Mysteries are a popular genre to showcase the Internet's exciting tools. There are even a few romance novels that now incorporate the Internet into the story.

The Internet can almost be a main character in some titles. In others, it's a supporting player, and in some its role is small. However, each title at least mentions some aspect of the 'Net or uses it as a plot device.

The books reviewed are all works of fiction. Most characters in them use the Internet alone, unsupervised, and almost any time they want. This type of unsupervised access may not set well with some parents and teachers.

Attack of the Evil Cyber-God

Brad Quentin

New York: HarperCollins, 1997. (**http://www.harpercollins.com**).
103p. (The Real Adventures of Jonny Quest #8). ISBN: 0-06-105722-3.
Ages 9–12. Softcover, $3.99.

Jonny Quest is a popular adventure television show. And now there is a series of novels surrounding the science fiction hero as well. In *Attack of the Evil Cyber-God*, Jonny and his father, Dr. Benton Quest, must bring down an evil monster who is stalking the Internet before he destroys civilization. Written for the preadolescent group of nine- to twelve-year-olds, this science fiction book with a touch of the Internet provides some twists and turns and lots of adventures.

Jonny is playing an online game called "Castle of Dread" with his father one day, when he notices something funny. Parts of the game are missing. Hadji, Jonny's adopted brother and best friend, is a whiz at computers and programming. He takes a look at the source code and discovers that code is indeed missing. Because this is science fiction, there are lots of possibilities to get to the bottom of the mystery. In this case, Jonny and his father decide to "jack in" to QuestWorld and then to the Castle of the Dread, so they can see what is going on. Soon they are sitting in the computer room in the AD (Alternative Dimension) recliners that will take them into cyberspace. Once they enter the Castle of Dread, Jonny is even more convinced that something or someone has been trashing parts of the game's software. As they look around, suddenly a loud BOOM echoes around them, followed by even louder footsteps. It sounds almost as if the giant in "Jack and the Beanstalk" were coming. Unfortunately, it's worse than that. A huge monster is coming their way. Before he can get to them, they are transported back to the real world. When they study the downloaded image of the monster, Dr. Quest realizes that they have encountered a Cyber-God. And you'll never guess how he grows: he has created himself and stays alive by eating binary code taken from computer games. To continue to live, he will eventually destroy the whole Internet and subsequently the world, once he begins attacking databases, government sites, hospitals, and everything else. Jonny and his father set about making a plan to "kill" the Cyber-God. This will involve returning to cyberspace and trying to get any leftover parts of the computer programs to help them fight the monster. Can you imagine such "superheroes" as Pegasus, the winged horse; Samuel Clemens and his riverboat; Fred Friendly; the Help module from a financial planning software package; and Thelma the Typist, from a typewriting tutorial? As Jonny and his father gather leftover ships, planes, and bombers to attack the Cyber-God, nothing seems to be slowing him down. They've got to come up with an answer before the Cyber-God breaks through the wall and comes into the real world.

Younger kids will enjoy the vivid descriptions of the Cyber-God. If you can imagine a huge monster made up of all the parts of the programs he's eaten, you'll get the idea. There are also vivid descriptions of what it's like to be in cyberspace, as Jonny and his family move around trying to combat the evil monster. And of course the suspense: what will work to end this monster's reign? What will happen if he manages to break down the wall and get into the password-protected parts of cyberspace?

The Internet is a main theme as the means for accessing the game "Castle of Dread." The Quest family has its own network, QuestWorld, at the compound overlooking the Atlantic Ocean. For any Jonny Quest fans, this will be a must read. If you haven't read any others, try this one if you like the 'Net and cyberspace.

Bad Intent

Jordan Cray

New York: Aladdin Paperbacks, 1998.
(http://www.SimonSaysKids.com). 225p. (danger.com@6).
ISBN: 0-689-81477-1. Ages 9–12. Paperback, $3.99.

Number six in the danger.com series, this one explores the goings-on at Bloomfield High School, which is known for its successful sports teams. But the school is in the spotlight now for another reason: four of its star football players are on trial for murdering their coach. A secret gang called the "24 Point Club" followed a pattern of stealing an object from their intended victim, painting it black, and then sending it back with the message, "SOMEDAY YOU WILL DIE." They tormented or terrorized at least three girls. No one was seriously hurt until Coach Cappiatrano, the football coach, found an e-mail message in the locker room about an upcoming meeting of the club. Evidently he went and confronted them, and was later found shot in the head at his house.

The story is told through the first-person narrative of Brian Rittenhouse, the school's student body president. Even though Brian is president, he's not one of the in crowd. He was elected president as a junior because his best friend, Mal Bouchard, delivered a great campaign. He and Brian have been best friends since elementary school.

Another plot component involves the "Water Fountain," an in-school electronic bulletin board that has become very popular because of some anonymous postings by "LoneLobo." LoneLobo is someone who doesn't hesitate to express his feelings, good or bad. He has become almost a cult figure among students. Lobo is funny, sarcastic, and angry, and sends out random messages about the doings at school. Brian greatly admires him because Lobo doesn't hesitate to speak out. Brian is one who always says the right things at the right times. Sometimes he wishes he were more like Lobo.

Without giving too much away, the plot revolves around several issues. First are the football players under arrest for the coach's murder. A former alumna, Detective Hanigan, is investigating because rumor has it that the leader of the 24 Point Club was not arrested and is still out there. Next, Brian has a major crush on Dawn Sedaris, a cheerleader who doesn't see him as anyone more than a pal. She wants to find out who Lobo is and enlists Brian's help to do so. There's a subplot with Brian and Dawn as he tries to figure out a way to get her to see him as more than a buddy. Brian's campaign to be reelected class president is also a part of the story, along with his relationship with Mal.

The plot moves along in one direction and then bang, something totally unexpected happens. The first couple of chapters are rather slow-moving, but as the plot develops, and certain things are revealed, the pace picks up.

The Internet is not very important to the plot here. E-mail or bulletin boards are used for communication among LoneLobo and the students, but that's about it. Anyone looking for a lot of technology will be disappointed. But if you want a suspenseful read with unexpected goings-on, then give it a try.

In this title of the danger.com series there aren't really any characters that are very likeable. There's very little humor and most of the story is considerably more serious and a bit darker. And don't count on a nice neat ending, either.

Blackout in the Amazon

Bruce Balan

New York: Avon Books, 1997. (**http://www.AvonBooks.com**). 152p. (Cyber.kdz #4). ISBN. 0-380-78517-X. Ages 9–12. Paperback, $3.99.

The Cyber.kdz are together again for another mystery. This time the story revolves around Tereza, who is from Brazil, and Josh, who lives in Seattle. Tereza is planning a vacation in the Amazon with her mother and invites Josh along. Josh has found out that a solar eclipse will take place at the same time as Tereza's trip. Soon Tereza, Tereza's mother, and Josh have made their way down the Amazon and arrived at the camp where they are to spend their vacation. Along the way, they have met a reporter named Marisa.

One night Josh discovers that smugglers are transporting trees illegally cut in the Amazon forests. He and Tereza decide to find out who they are. In their attempt, they put themselves in serious danger and must rely on their cyber-friends, Deeder and Sanjeev, and the Internet to get them back safely.

This book is written for children ages nine to twelve. Kids can learn bits and pieces about Brazil and the Amazon as they read. Of course, there are also references to the Internet and especially e-mail. All of the Cyber.kdz are experts at using the Internet and its tools. Because of the references to the Internet and the use of e-mail, this book may not appeal to children who have little or no interest in technology. However, it's a fun way to introduce children to some of the special things about the Internet, such as being able to correspond around the world. It also introduces children to multicultural ideas and languages.

For teachers and parents, this series is a great opportunity to get kids off the computer for a while to read a book that uses the Internet to solve mysteries and adventures.

Cyber Feud

Michael Coleman

New York: Bantam Skylark Books, 1996. (**http://www.bbd.com/id**). 124p. (Internet Detectives #4). ISBN: 0-553-48643-8. Ages 9–12. Paperback, $3.99.

Cyber Feud is the fourth title in the Internet Detectives series, which uses Abbey School in Portsmouth, England, as its setting. The series revolves around a group of friends connected by the Internet.

Twenty-five years ago, Josh Allan's father was wrongly accused of setting a fire at Abbey School and was forced to leave. Josh had no idea about this until circumstances brought these facts to his attention. Josh, along with his friends, begins a quest to prove his father innocent. The Internet becomes a powerful ally in his pursuit of the truth, as the trail leads to various locations around the globe. But as they seek to find information, someone seems to be one step ahead of them. How can that be? And then Josh is accused of a crime. Can it be that the same thing is happening again, this time to Josh?

As the three friends use their electronic tools to try and prove Josh's father's innocence and learn what really happened, it's possible to see how effective the

'Net is in finding information, sharing it instantaneously, and communicating around the world. Each time an e-mail message is read by one of the students, a screen shot is used in the book. This helps to visualize when something is happening through the Internet. Other Internet-related facts and tools are also involved. The importance of changing passwords, so that hackers cannot figure them out; mailing lists as a source for locating particular groups of people with a similar interest; the ability to attach files and send them in an eyeblink across the world; and how to use a scanner for making digital images are a few in the story.

The series combines a fun-to-read mystery along with a useful information source about what the Internet can do. If you have a child or student who likes mysteries, why not show him or her these books? At $3.99, it's a pretty good deal.

Cyber Scare

A. G. Cascone

Mahwah, NJ: Troll Communications, 1997. (**http://www.troll.com**). 138p. (Deadtime Stories). ISBN: 0-8167-4396-7. Ages 9–12. Paperback, $3.50.

Deadtime Stories is a series of humorous thrillers for children aged nine to twelve. *Cyber Scare* combines mystery, thrills, and cyberspace in a terrifying online computer game called "Monster Mash." Roy and his cousin, Danny, are really into computer games. One night they are saddled with Ernest, another cousin, whom they would rather just avoid. In Roy's room is his pride and joy, a computer with all the latest software and hardware. This night the monitor is already flashing with an e-mail message from someone named Vlad, someone Roy encountered in a chat room for horror fans. Roy doesn't want anything to do with him, but Danny is intrigued and types in the password to visit Vlad's castle. But just at that moment Ernest comes into the room and Danny runs to claim the lower bunk bed for himself. The computer catches Ernest's eye and he goes over to it. Not knowing anything about computers, he reads the message "Type Enter to Continue" and begins hitting keys. Suddenly, a huge wind tears through the room, followed by a creepy green mist. The mist is coming from Roy's computer. The next thing they know, Ernest is blown into the maelstrom and sucked into the computer.

How are Danny and Roy going to get Ernest back before his parents come the next morning? It looks like the only way is to play the terrifying game of "Monster Mash." As they look at the monitor, Ernest appears on the screen, standing on a drawbridge. To get him out of the computer, they must meet and defeat the vampire, Vlad.

The rest of the story follows Danny and Roy as they play the game to rescue Ernest. Along the way they encounter trolls, skeletons, rats, bats, mummies, and blood-sucking creatures. Ernest is everyone's geeky cousin. He's overweight, a pain in the neck, and cries all the time. As he has to make his way through the various chambers, rooms, and moats, he finds himself losing many levels of his life force. In other words, he's dying. When he gets down to one life force, that's it. He's really dead. Besides Ernest's problems inside the computer, some of the scary things seem to be coming out through the hard drive into Roy's room. But this is just a virtual reality game, isn't it? Read the story and see.

Cascone injects humor alongside the often scary and violent tricks played on Ernest. But it's a computer game, so when Ernest loses his head or falls in a moat or gets his blood sucked out, it just takes the right move of the joystick to bring him back to life. For any kids who like online games, this will be an adventure they won't want to put down until they find out what happens to Danny, Roy, and Ernest. Deadtime Stories don't always have nice neat endings, so be prepared.

Cybercops & Flame Wars

Ted Pedersen and Mel Gilden

New York: Price Stern Sloan, 1996. (http://putnam.com).
141p. (Cybersurfers #4). ISBN: 0-8431-3979-X. Ages 9–12.
Paperback, $3.99 (out of print).

Get ready for another cyber adventure with Jason Kane and Athena Bergstrom, the two "brilliant teenage hackers" in the Cybersurfers series. Set in Ft. Benson, Washington, a rural northwestern town, Athena and Jason have forged a real friendship since their first Internet adventure. This particular book focuses on Athena as we get to know her family a bit better.

What has she done? Outraged by a flame from a cybersurfer called "Rebel," Athena has responded with her own and is now caught up in a situation she can't control. He sends hundreds of e-mail messages to her account at school and causes the system to crash. But Rebel doesn't stop there. The next thing you know, her family becomes involved. They are receiving strange, harassing phone calls. Her father's credit card and checking accounts have been tampered with. As the final straw, a policeman comes to the door to arrest Athena's brother, Ralph, for armed robbery!

As Athena tries to figure a way out of this awful situation, she learns that things are a lot worse than she thought. It's more than just her family that's at stake. And it's up to her and Jason to figure out how to stop this cybermaniac, "Rebel."

In this book, we meet a couple of new characters. Susan is a new student at Ft. Benson, a "babe" who seems to have her eye out for Jason. She manages to cause some tension between Jason and Athena, who are mostly "just friends." Bruce Archer, the nephew of Ms. O'Malley, the school principal, is a computer expert working at Lock-Me-Tight Systems, a computer security firm. He surely does know a lot about computers and seems very friendly to Athena. Jason is not very happy about that.

Once again the Internet is an integral part of the adventure. The problems and situations that can arise when someone is able to manipulate data and control computers from afar are demonstrated here. The issue of security for networks and systems is also part of the plot, and interactive Internet games receive some attention. You might want to read the Internet notes guide at the end of the book first if you are new to the Internet. The glossary is rather substantial in presenting words and phrases that need explaining. It's also a helpful part of the book. Geared to readers aged nine to twelve, this series will appeal to children with an interest in the Internet or computers. Each title presents another aspect of the Internet as part of the adventure.

Cyberspace Cowboy

Ted Pedersen and Mel Gilden

Los Angeles, CA: Price Stern Sloan, 1995. (**http://www.putnam.com**). 144p. (Cybersurfers #2). ISBN: 0-8431-3934-X. Ages 9–12. Paperback, $3.95 (out of print).

This is the second title in the Cybersurfers series featuring Athena Bergstrom and Jason Kane, students at Benton High School. Jason and Athena forged a relationship in the first book, *Pirates on the Net*, when they worked together on an Internet project. *Cyberspace Cowboy* finds them once again involved in the Internet at school. This time Jason has been asked to create a MUD (multiple user dimension) so the local kids can spend time chatting online among themselves in a safe environment. Athena is not familiar with MUDs, so Jason fills her in on what they are. He shows her one called Zenobi, and before you know it Athena is hooked on the game-playing environment of the MUD. She meets an online persona named Cowboy, and after he saves her from various harmful possibilities in the MUD, she wants to know more about him. But the Cowboy is not forthcoming with any personal information.

As Athena tries to track down more about Cowboy, readers can learn about applications like Finger (to locate people using the Internet) or how to use the Web to locate information at a local university or college. Athena describes the "live picture" of the University of Washington on their Web site as well as the fact that it has links off-campus. Athena is a good detective and figures out the real identity of Cowboy. Athena and a reluctant Jason then visit the Bellevue Community College, where "Cowboy" works as an instructor. After sitting in on one of his classes, Athena approaches him, but he leaves abruptly. His behavior seems very strange. When Jason and Athena return home, Jason helps Athena "surf" around a bit for more information. What they find creates a dangerous situation for Cowboy as well as themselves.

In this series the Internet is at the core of the plot. Each of the stories revolves around an aspect of the Internet. In this one, it's a MUD. The MUD creates the environment of the mysterious Cowboy and causes Jason and Athena to delve further and further into the Internet for their answers and their solution to the problem. Along the way we learn about MUDs, Telnet, downloading files, and a bit about security issues. If you have students interested in computers and the Internet, this book will supply them with some fun hours reading and learning about Internet tools. The "Internet.notes" section at the end of the book supplies definitions for the various Internet tools that are mentioned in the book, and a glossary will help you with any of those strange-sounding words or phrases.

Double Trouble

S. F. Black

Mahwah, NJ: Troll Communications, 1997. (http://www.troll.com).
110p. (Cyber Zone #5). ISBN: 0-8167-4427-0. Ages 9–12.
Softcover, $3.95.

Have you ever wished you had more time to do things? That you had a double to help you out? This title in the Cyber Zone series examines what happens when Chris Fenton, who is always late for everything and totally disorganized, makes such a wish...and it comes true.

Chris never seems able to keep up with everything he has to do. Whether it's basketball practice or band, remembering his best friend's birthday party or a presentation for history class, he just can't seem to get it together. After an especially trying day where nothing goes right, Chris decides he's going to change.

Chris is just entering the Internet age. His father has bought him a computer and Chris's best friend, Josh, along with Josh's sister Jenna, are coming over to help him set it up. Although Josh is a computer whiz, Chris has never even surfed the Internet. But there is one Web site Chris wants to visit: TimeSolvers. This infomercial on television features Professor Chronos, who promises to help you use your time wisely. This is just what Chris needs to get going and be more organized. But weird things happen when Chris pulls up the site. First, there's a message with his name on it. How could that be? It's his first time on the 'Net. This is pretty creepy and Jenna is ready to exit the site, but not Chris. All of a sudden, he realizes it's probably Josh who has set it up to play a trick on him. So he clicks "yes" to answer a survey about using his time. When he's done, the computer informs him that he's an ideal candidate and can receive a free double for trial use. Without thinking, Chris clicks "ok." Then noises and strange sounds explode from his computer and a bright light seems to wash over him. In a moment, the computer screen flashes the message "Successfully copied." When nothing seems to happen, Chris begins to think it was just a prank.

But the next morning, his worst nightmare comes true. He looks in the kitchen and sees himself chatting with his parents. How can Chris change things back before his double completely takes over his life?

This is a clever story that involves computers and the Internet. Any kids who enjoy computerese will get to experience what it's like to be inside a computer. Various computer terms come up, as well as references to Web sites, the Internet, and electronic mail. In this particular novel, the main character is not a computer whiz (though his best friend is). It's a nice portrayal of a fairly typical kid who likes the Internet but isn't all that crazy about computers. Surfing the 'Net can be hazardous to your health, as you'll find out when you follow the adventure of Chris and Josh, who are in "double trouble." Chris is a likeable protagonist and one that kids will be able to relate to. He's messy, unorganized, and always late. He's not a hero, but has strengths when needed. You'll want to read on to see how they resolve things. It's suspenseful and fun at the same time.

Escape Key

Michael Coleman

New York: Bantam Skylark Books, 1997. (http://www.bbd.com/id).
128p. (Internet Detectives #2). ISBN: 0553-48621-7. Ages 9–12.
Paperback, $3.99.

With the popularity of the Internet continuing to grow, the concept of a mystery series for children using the Internet is a good idea. *Escape Key* is number two in the Internet Detectives series for children aged nine to twelve. In this book, we find new friends Rob, Tamsyn, and Josh—all students at Abbey School in Portsmouth, England—entangled in another mystery, this time over a missing man wanted by the police. They think they may have spotted him at an airport. Once again, the Internet is their main tool for solving the puzzle.

Waiting at the airport for his father's flight, Rob, along with Tamsyn, plays a game of "I Spy" and in doing so happens to pick out a man who turns out to be wanted by the law. After finding out that he is probably the con man who took money from one of their Internet pals, Rob, Tamsyn, and Josh set out to find him. Through e-mail, discussion lists, and Internet Relay Chat, they are able to learn more from their pals Tom, in Australia; Lauren, in Canada; and Mitch, in New York. Each of them has a part in solving the puzzle.

There is not a lot of action or real danger in this book. But there is quite a bit of electronic communication using e-mail among the friends. There is usually a screen shot when e-mail is used so that you can see it and know it's an electronic message. Throughout the book each of the friends uses his or her own computer.

Reading this book provides a look at what you can do with an Internet connection. In this case, the "key-pals" send files and photos across the world and regularly use e-mail. Internet Relay Chat is used to carry on a live conversation between Mitch in New York and Loren in Canada. You can see how to find flight schedules and make reservations through the 'Net. There's an Internet show that takes place in England. So, if you want to provide your child or student with an opportunity to read more and to learn about some of the features of the Internet, this series would be a good place to start. Along with learning about the Internet, it's also a fun mystery to read.

Faceless

Scott Ciencin

New York: Random House, 1997. (**http://www.randomhouse.com**).
203p. (The Lurker Files #1). ISBN: 0-679-88235-9. Ages 9–12.
Softcover, $6.99.

Faceless is the first in a series of novels set at Wintervale University, a fictitious college town in North Dakota. The series revolves around a presence on campus who calls himself the Lurker. Through his selective chat room, The Ratskellar, he controls the lives of students, who do his bidding in the physical world. The print version is based on a serial from Random House's Web site.

Gia Gibson is a freshman at Wintervale with lots of hopes and dreams for her future as a journalist. But one day Gia's life takes an abrupt and dangerous turn. Her roommate, Peggy, hasn't returned. Gia is sitting at her computer one night when all of a sudden, she sees disturbing images of her friend in some kind of cyber lair. What has happened to Peggy? After this strange and rather terrifying incident, it seems that Gia's a marked woman. She is stalked and harassed by someone calling himself "Dethboy." All of a sudden Gia is an outsider. Her friends seem to have deserted her and she's not sure who she can trust. But Gia has to find out what's happening before she finds herself among the missing. Her friend Wally is one person she can go to, or so Gia thinks. But even he begins acting strangely.

The plot of this series is a bit hard to take. There are so many twists and turns that it's sometimes confusing as to who is doing what to whom. There seem to be two factions involved with Gia—the Lurker and the Fraternity. Keeping them straight is a challenge in itself. A lot of the action is online, with characters assuming user names such as "Goldeneye," "Night Beast," and "Ripley."

There doesn't seem to be anything going on except parties, rallies, and stalking incidents. No one goes to class, and the library is only used to escape from "Dethboy" or to hide kidnapped students. On the one hand, the plot is confusing and the characters' relationships even more disturbing, but somehow just when you want to put the book down for good, it kind of grabs your interest. The ending obviously leaves room for more in this series.

There is a lot of chatting online, as part of the plot; perhaps in an effort to simulate the online world, the author uses a Courier-like font that appears to be coming from a computer. The rather chopped-up format of the paragraphs, along with the typewriter-looking font, don't really contribute to the readability of the book. It's actually a bit distracting at times. A Windows disk comes with the book; Mac users will have to order one. It offers some profiles of characters and lets you read diary entries and get a bit more information about the Lurker.

If you do want to check these books out, read them in order. Don't read the last one first or you'll already know what happens to Gia and Wally—that is, if you can keep everything straight.

Firestorm

Jordan Cray

New York: Aladdin Paperbacks, 1997. (**http://www.SimonSaysKids.com**). 194p. (danger.com@2). ISBN: 0-689-81431-3. Ages 9–12. Paperback, $3.99.

Randy Kincaid is almost 16. He's a typical teenager who lives in a Florida beach town and likes to skateboard and surf but isn't that crazy about school. When it rains continuously for several days, Randy can't surf the waves, so he decides to "bond with his laptop" and surf the Web. He has recently had his computer overhauled by a classmate, Maya Bessamer, a computer whiz. The first time Randy logs on and clicks on his "favorite places" icon, he is taken to a chat room he's never been to before. Generally, Randy avoids chat rooms, because he finds them boring. But his best friend recently told him that it's a great way to meet girls. So Randy decides to hang around for a while. When he's identified and asked about his stats, he lies and says he's 19 and works as a mechanic at a raceway. As Randy listens in on the chat, he really doesn't think much about the strange topics under discussion. One of the chatters, SwampFox, posts a poem that makes no sense to Randy. He stays on a while longer and then logs off. The next morning he is reading the newspaper and sees an article about the bombing of a day care center in Knoxville. As he reads the report, something jogs his memory. He can't believe it, but is it possible that the chat group had something to do with the bombing? Something about the poem and certain sound-alike words send shivers down his spine. But Randy thinks it's just his imagination. That night he logs on again to the chat room and once again the conversation seems almost to be some kind of code. He jots down the phone number mentioned and after logging off tries it. It doesn't work. The next morning, Randy reads about another bombing. This time two people were killed in Mississippi. The targets have all been places associated with immigrants. Randy can't shake the feeling that he has found a group of terrorists who are responsible for the bombings. Somehow he's got to break the code and figure out what's going on. When he figures out what they are doing and how they are communicating the information, he tries to warn the police, but no one takes him seriously. Then he decides to talk to Maya. After she hears Randy's story, she decides they should work together. Randy and Maya set up a plan to monitor the chat room and then set a trap. Randy makes contact with one of the members who wants to meet him, but something goes terribly wrong and Randy and Maya are almost killed when a bomb planted in the diner goes off. All of a sudden, Randy is a suspect in the bombing. And the group knows who Randy is and where he lives. Now he's got to find out who's behind this or he may be the next victim.

The plot has some twists and turns and an exciting finish to it. There's a lot of adventure and mystery throughout as Randy and Maya try to find the bombers before someone else is hurt. It's a good read for kids who have an interest in the Internet and like a suspenseful plot. There's a touch of romance as well. The language is contemporary and Internet slang is thrown in every now and then, along with a good dose of humor. There's a Web site that goes along with the series danger.com. You can read about the characters and even visit a bulletin board or find out more about the author. This series is fun and leaves you wanting to turn the pages to find out what happens.

Flavor of the Day

Elizabeth Craft

New York: Archway Paperbacks, 1998. (http://www.simonsays.com).
184p. (@café #4). ISBN: 0-671-00448-4. Young Adult. Paperback, $3.99.

The fourth novel in the @café series features a continuing romantic saga of a group of teens working at an Internet café. This one takes up where *Make Mine to Go* left off. You'll probably enjoy the series more if you read them from the first one.

Sam Barton's mother has overdosed on pills and alcohol. She has been despondent over the imprisonment of her husband, which has left her to take care of Sam and his younger brother, Eddie. Sam's girlfriend, Natalie, was on her way to break up with Sam the night his mother was taken to the hospital. Now it's impossible to do, even though Natalie realizes she loves Dylan, Sam's best friend. At the hospital, Sam meets a young woman named Hallie, whose father is very sick. Hallie and Sam seem to hit it off. They have similar situations that make them almost soul mates.

Another romantic problem revolves around Blue (Sara Jane) O'Connor (Dylan's sister) and Jason Kirk, her best friend. Their relationship was complicated by a blind date in which each of them became aware of more complicated emotions. Of course, neither expressed those feelings to the other. Thus, Jason is dating Celia; Blue has met Christian and thinks she just may be ready to "date." The problem is that Blue sees Jason with Celia. Blue is jealous and when Jason sees Blue with Christian, he is also jealous. At one point, Jason decides to take a big step and tell Blue how he really feels. At the same time he decides to unburden his feelings to Blue, she has decided that maybe Christian is someone she could fall in love with. As you can tell, something will probably go wrong.

A third romantic relationship sitting precariously on the rocks is that of Tanya Childes and Major Johnson. She loves him, but he is not looking for a relationship. Tanya thinks she has accepted this, but when a female answers his phone, Tanya is stunned and hurt. To get rid of her hurt, she tries to find another guy to replace Major, to take her mind off him. But it doesn't work.

After Sam's mother is well enough to leave the hospital and go to a rehabilitation facility, Sam decides to throw a party on his houseboat one Saturday night. The party serves as the catalyst for several of the characters. First, Dylan and Natalie cannot control their desire for each other, and toward the end of the evening they share a kiss in one of the bedrooms. Just at that time, Sam walks in and is devastated to find his best friend kissing his girlfriend. But Sam has a more serious problem than his romantic woes. The police have come to arrest him for allowing minors to drink. He is placed under arrest. What will happen to Sam now? His two best friends have betrayed him. How will he survive the hurt and anger he feels? Is there someone he can count on? What will this do to Natalie and Dylan's love? Will guilt over being caught by Sam destroy it?

At the same party, Tanya sees the girl who was with Major and confronts her—turns out they are just friends. Now Tanya must figure out what to do. Is there any chance that she and Major can have a real relationship? And finally, Jason has gotten his nerve up to tell Blue how he feels. She doesn't seem to be responding to his indirect communication, so Jason just blurts out how he feels. Right at that time, Christian walks in. Blue has not said anything and now it's too late. Will Jason ever know how Blue feels?

There's not as much action at the Internet café this time, and very little use of the Internet at all in the plot. There are mentions of the Web and e-mail, but none of these characters is really an Internet junkie.

Teens following the saga of @café will probably wait breathlessly to see what happens to Natalie and Dylan, Jason and Blue, and Major and Tanya. Teenagers, especially girls, will love to follow the romantic entanglements of this hip crowd of San Francisco teenagers. They're cool and attractive and love is all around them.

Gemini7

Jordan Cray

New York: Aladdin Paperbacks, 1997. (**http://www.SimonSaysKids.com**). 196p. (danger.com@1). ISBN: 0-689-81432-1. Ages 9–12. Paperback, $3.99.

Gemini7 is the first novel in a new series of adventure stories involving the Internet, written for kids aged nine to twelve. Jonah Lanier and Jen Malone are both 16. They live and attend high school in Milleridge, Pennsylvania, where they've been dating since seventh grade. Lately Jonah has been wondering about whether he's missing something.

Taking a cruise on the Internet one day, Jonah meets and begins flirting online with several girls. Soon he has six or seven online relationships going. But one in particular stands out.

Her online name is Gemini7 and her real name is Nicole. Jonah and Nicole spend a lot of time chatting and sending e-mail. One day Jonah downloads her photo and can't believe his luck. She's a "babe": long blonde hair, blue eyes. She's into MUDs (multi-user dimensional fantasy games) on the Internet and hacking. As Jonah's relationship with Nicole heats up, he rationalizes that he's not hurting Jen. But he's spending more time online with Nicole and finding excuses not to be with Jen.

Things get more complicated when Nicole shows up one day on Jonah's doorstep. But even before she appears, there have been some strange things going on. First, Jonah's father gets a promotion, when his rival is fired because of an e-mail message sent to everyone at the company; and Jonah gets a B instead of a D on his report card. But then the bad things start happening. Jonah's father is in a mysterious car accident; Jen, who by now is not speaking to Jonah, almost gets killed on a rope swing; and a family cabin blows up. Jonah begins to think his "dreamgirl" is becoming a real-life nightmare.

The plot is pretty predictable, but still manages to keep you interested and wanting to know how it's all going to end. Along the way Jonah makes you think about what happens when you get too involved with someone online, and examines the issue of the impact the Internet can have on real lives. Through Jonah, we see the debate about whether having an online relationship is "real." Somehow he can justify his life offline as separate from his online one...until they come together with disastrous consequences. Young readers might learn a few things from this fictional experience. Jonah learns that when you have a committed relationship with someone, meeting new girls online is the same as cheating. He also learns which type of relationship is more important.

The story is part mystery, adventure, lots of action, and romance, with the Internet intertwined as part of the story. In fact, without it as the catalyst, there would be no story. Teenagers will relate to the lives of Jen and Jonah. The writing is lively, with lots of teen lingo that manages to sound pretty natural. Plus there are enough twists to keep you guessing for a good deal of the plot.

Ghost on the Net

Ted Pedersen and Mel Gilden

New York: Price Stern Sloan, 1996. (**http://putnam.com**).
141p. (Cybersurfers #3). ISBN: 0-8431-3978-1. Ages 9–12.
Paperback, $3.99.

Can you contact people who have "gone beyond" on the Internet? That's the question to be answered in this third book of the Cybersurfers series. Jason Kane and Athena Bergstrom are 14-year-old computer whizzes at Ft. Benton High in Washington state. They've worked together on a couple of projects that got rather more complicated and dangerous than they thought. This time it's Halloween, and Athena and Jason become involved in a mysterious situation that arises following a séance held at school one day. Athena is excited about the séance, but notices that Jason wants nothing to do with it or the holiday.

Halloween rolls around a few days later and instead of holding an old-fashioned séance, Madame Schiff, the medium, decides to do it the modern way—through the Internet. The next few minutes are strange and scary, with all kinds of strange, unexplainable sounds. Jason seems very upset by the session and, when questioned by Athena, finally admits that Halloween is not his favorite holiday. His mother died eight years ago in a car accident on Halloween.

Before he and Athena can leave the room, a very strange thing happens. The computer seems to come to life, and all of a sudden there is a message that leaves Jason shaken. "Jason. Stop MetaCorp. Love, Mom." Jason is confused and a little frightened. He knows there is no way his mother is communicating with him from the dead—or is she?

In their quest for information, Athena learns of the mysterious circumstances surrounding Jason's mother's death. She was killed in a traffic accident, but no driver was found in the truck that totaled her car. And Athena comes up with the name of a reporter who was also writing about MetaCorp.

Jason and Athena meet with the reporter and find that Mrs. Kane was close to exposing the company's wrongdoings and possibly causing its ruin. In light of this, was her death really an accident? How can Jason finish what his mother started? The plot is enjoyable and moves quickly, and we learn more about Jason and his family that adds to the story.

As with other titles in this series, Jason and Athena must use the Internet to help them solve a mystery. The World Wide Web is a source for locating information about MetaCorp and its founder. Gopher is a tool that helps Jason track down newspaper articles. Athena uses an Internet Relay Chat (IRC) group to find out more about paranormal activities in order to explain the mysterious messages appearing on Jason's computer. Could Jason's dead mother really be sending messages?

There's no problem reading these books out of order. Each is a complete story. For anyone new to the Internet, a handy "Internet.notes" section at the end provides a means for learning more about some of the tools discussed and, of course, a glossary helps provide definitions of words and phrases used in the book.

The Great NASA Flu

Bruce Balan

New York: Avon Books, 1997. (http://www.AvonBooks.com). 162p. (Cyber.kdz #3). ISBN: 0-380-78516-1. Ages 9–12. Paperback, $3.99.

This really should be the first title in the series because it explains how the Cyber.kdz met and formed their online club. It's not clear to me why this wasn't explained in the first book of the series. In a "Note to the Reader," the author says that "this is the story of how seven kids came together to create a great friendship...and a pretty cool club."

Deeder Van Hout lives in Holland with his family, and is a computer whiz, especially at tracking down viruses. He is the first one of the Cyber.kdz. Deeder's father is a specialist in artificial intelligence, assigned to a NASA special project. His father has developed an artificial intelligence program, called SLIDE, that helps with shuttle launch decisions. He has a contract with NASA to put the system into use at the next space launch. Because he will be in Florida for four months, Deeder is allowed to go with him after school is out. Deeder is corresponding with Tereza at this point and tells her about the trip.

In Florida, Deeder keeps busy by helping his father check file access codes, or working on his coding for breaking a nasty virus he's found, or walking around the space center.

The day of the launch arrives and as the countdown progresses, SLIDE begins to indicate various malfunctions in the stages of launch. The problem is that the center's own Launch Processing System (LPS) indicates things are normal. What could be causing the discrepancy? Mr. Van Hout tries to verify that the system is functioning correctly, but can't seem to find anything. As the liftoff gets closer, the launch director demands that control be turned back over to LPS. But things get worse. SLIDE won't relinquish control. Finally, they are able to return control to the LPS, but SLIDE has proven a failure. The launch is halted and the blame squarely put on Mr. Van Hout and his program.

Back in Holland, Deeder's father is depressed about his failure. Deeder is determined to help his father. He wants to know what happened and turns to his online friends: Tereza from Brazil and another computer whiz, Sanjeev, from India.

While trying to find out about the NASA files, they realize they don't know enough about NASA's setup and need help. Through an e-mail, they meet Josh, the next Cyber.kdz to get on board. He's the science expert. Finally, they meet Becky and Paul from New York. Paul is a computer games expert at the tender age of 10.

As they begin to penetrate NASA's computer network and discover the source of the trouble, they realize that someone has planted a virus. Finding the source involves their many computer skills and in the end reveals the truth about what happened.

There are a lot of technical concepts in the story. Chat rooms, various software for setting up a secure online chat environment, and server software may not be something all children will be familiar with. Language such as finding "the main routers" and "hackin' a filter to sort out packets..." and "we'll have to spam 'em all..." is not commonly known to most kids unless they are really into computers. The Internet is a big part of the plot because it's the main source for communications, and of course the World Wide Web is the main source to locate information.

Although this book has a certain entertainment value, the plot does revolve around a lot of technology that may not be as interesting to some children. But for children who enjoy the series, this one is a must because it introduces the group.

Hot Pursuit

Jordan Cray

New York: Aladdin Paperbacks, 1997. (**http://www.SimonSaysKids.com**). 224p. (danger.com@4). ISBN: 0-689-81434-8. Ages 9–12. Paperback, $3.99.

This volume of the danger.com series is a fast-paced one with lots of twists and turns. It keeps you guessing—for a while, anyway. The millennium and all that is threatened by the change to 2000 are part of the plot.

Randy Corrigan is in a lot of trouble. He's a "cybernerd" who has played one too many pranks with his computer. He's managed to get himself expelled from school (on purpose) by shutting down the school's electrical system. Randy is waiting to go to college and doesn't want to be in high school anymore. This was his way of ending his high school career a little early. But he didn't count on the consequences of talking to a reporter for a local newspaper. Somehow, his declarations of other hacking incidents have caused the FBI to come knocking at his door.

Randy is a typical computer geek who doesn't make friends and turns to his computer to fill the void of having no social life. His friends are his computer hardware and software. It didn't help that he and his mother moved nine times to nine different states, either. Randy's father died while his mother was carrying him. Randy has developed almost no social skills. To avoid more trouble, his mother is packing Randy off to California for the summer to stay with a friend. But before he can go, he receives a message from JereMe, a name the FBI had quizzed him about. And who is the Millennium Caravan, and how do they know so much about Randy? He's now on the FBI's Most Wanted list and running for his life. He meets up with Sabrina Sebringo, who is heading to California. They team up to try to straighten out Randy's life before it's too late.

But just as he begins to trust and perhaps even fall in love with Sabrina, his trust is shattered. Instead of rescuing him from the FBI and keeping him safe from the Caravan, she has actually brought him right to their front door. And guess who Sabrina is…JereMe. Her father is the leader of the Caravan. What can he do now? The compound is isolated and far away from possible help. There seems to be no escape. What Randy finds out about the true intentions of the Caravan makes him break out in a cold sweat. He has to do something before they carry out their deadly plans.

Randy seems rather annoying at first. It's easy to say he's just a trouble-maker, hacking into computers and causing systems to crash. But as the story unfolds, Randy reveals some strengths and learns about trust and more about himself. His life will never be the same. But then it wasn't what he thought in the first place.

Teens will enjoy the suspense and action. There's also some romance along the way and touches of humor that pop up throughout the story. This is a pretty good page-turner and reads quickly.

I'll Have What He's Having

Elizabeth Craft

New York: Archway Paperbacks, 1997. (**http://www.simonsays.com**). 196p. (@café #2). ISBN: 0-671-00446-8. Young Adult. Paperback, $3.99.

This is the second in Elizabeth Craft's @café series about a group of high school students in San Francisco. *I'll Have What He's Having* takes up right where *Love Bytes* ended. If you haven't read the first one, the author does recap events and explain who people are.

This series reads rather like a soap opera for teenagers. It's all about relationships and love. There's not much of a plot except as it pertains to each person's love life, and things tend to get a little complicated, as in most soaps. In this title, Natalie is trying to get over the crushing blow of learning that Mathew Chance, the boy she was crazy about, is interested in her sister, Mia. Dylan O'Connor, the young owner of @café, is in love with Natalie. Natalie used to love Dylan but never thought she had a chance, so she never said anything to him. Now, it turns out that Sam, Dylan's best friend, announces that he is in love with Natalie and sets out to do something about it. Dylan does not want to hurt Sam, so he remains quiet about his feelings. Meanwhile, Blue (Sara Jane O'Connor), Dylan's sister, is having problems in her friendship with Jason Kirk. Blue and Jason have both renounced dating. They were best friends until a blind date, where it seems they both discovered they had "more than friend" feelings. Of course neither will admit that, so the situation gets complicated and takes some wrong turns. Jason meets Celia, a beautiful but strange young woman, at another coffee bar. Celia is aggressive in pursuing Jason. Naturally, when Blue finds out she stops talking to Jason. Things are not looking good for these two friends. Tanya, Natalie's best friend, is in love with Major, whom she met while visiting a prison. No, he's not a prisoner, but was doing a video on prison conditions. Major is not looking for a relationship. Tanya is but knows she has to pretend not to care.

As you can see, love is in the air in various forms—mostly as unrequited or misunderstood or hopeless, but rarely working out. Issues that most young teens deal with are part of the plot. These are the kinds of relationships that teenagers, particularly young girls, will relate to: sitting by the phone, waiting for that special someone to call; trying to decide if you should call him; kissing someone you're not sure how you feel about; deciding if he's just a friend; having stronger feelings for someone, but afraid to mess up a good friendship; and trying to find that special someone who will make your life complete. All of these emotions are played out in this installment of the @café series.

How does the Internet come into play? First, @café is an Internet café with computers for people to use while they drink their coffee. All of the main characters work at @café. It has its own Web site. Each chapter begins with a Web page discussing a topic that will be followed through in the succeeding chapter. Because this is the Internet age, several characters use chat rooms to talk about their problems. Jason uses e-mail to try to communicate with Blue when she ignores him at work.

There is one plot development that has nothing to do with love. As Natalie is looking in an online chat room that has to do with vegan recipes, she sees a note posted by a Delia Broderick. That was her mother's maiden name. Natalie whips off an e-mail, excited that she might have found a relative. What Natalie learns will change her life forever.

This is a series young teenage girls will love to read. The guys and girls are all good-looking, "cool" people with typical teenage problems that anyone aged 13 to 18 will be able to relate to. Once they read the first one, they'll want to see what happens in the next and the next.

In Pursuit of Picasso

Bruce Balan

New York: Avon Books, 1998. (http://www.AvonBooks.com). 151p. (Cyber.kdz #5). ISBN: 0-380-79499-3. Ages 9–12. Paperback, $3.99.

The Cyber.kdz are a group of friends connected around the world by the Internet. They formed their group to help solve problems among themselves and to fight crime and solve "high-tech mysteries."

This story revolves around Loren, whose great-uncle was accused of stealing priceless art masterpieces during the Second World War. As the story opens, Loren learns that the Louvre has found an old letter that may prove where the artwork is hidden and give some details about the theft. But they will not publish the letter for the public to see. Loren, who has been reading his uncle's diaries, cannot believe he would have stolen the paintings. He wants to try and prove his great-uncle's innocence. But how? Getting his father to discuss it is impossible.

Loren unburdens himself to Becky in an e-mail telling her all about his great-uncle's plight. Becky thinks about it and comes up with a plan. Here's where you have to suspend belief. Her plan is for Deeder and Sanjeev to disable the Louvre elevator so that Loren and his father will have to go and repair it. Then Loren can take some time to locate the letter. Oh yes, Loren's father is an elevator repairman in Paris.

Loren is able to read only part of the letter. After going over the few sentences he can read, he realizes that his great-uncle has used a code in the letter that may tell where the paintings are. Finally, Loren thinks he's discovered the formula for the code. It seems the paintings may be in Evian somewhere near a fountain. Unfortunately, Evian is too far for Loren to travel by himself, and his father does not even want to discuss the subject of his great-uncle, so Loren is stumped.

Here's where it's necessary to interject some background. Steve Roberts, a self-professed "technomad," is taking his BEHEMOTH, a specially built 580-pound computerized recumbent bicycle, around the world. He has designed this vehicle to include a sophisticated computer system. It includes six computers and has all the necessary connections for Steve to live and work while riding his bike. He is traveling around Europe at this time. Deeder has sent an attachment of a newspaper article telling the other kids about Steve Roberts's journey. Suddenly, Deeder remembers that Steve Roberts is not going to be far from Evian on his tour. He sends Steve an e-mail with an attachment of the background information and Steve agrees to help them.

Finding the paintings in Evian is relatively easy compared to how Steve is going to keep them and get them safely back to Paris. Two men appear and Steve realizes they are after the paintings. Will Steve be able to get them safely back to Paris? How can the Cyber.kdz help him over the Internet? Will Loren be able to clear his great-uncle's reputation after 50 years?

This series always uses the Internet in imaginative ways. Sometimes they are quite technical in nature—breaking into servers and hacking into Web sites. In this book a lot of e-mail messages are sent and there is much chatting online among the kids and Steve Roberts. At one point, Tereza uses e-mail to guide

Steve to Paris on secondary roads and bike paths to avoid his pursuers. It's fascinating to read what Steve Roberts's bike is able to do. It boggles the mind to think of him riding his recumbent and sending e-mail at the same time. But then, 5 teenagers who can find 11 French masterpieces that have been missing for more than 50 years is, well, *incroyable*, as the French say. Once again the Cyber.kdz come to the rescue of one of their own and solve a seemingly impossible mystery by using the Internet and its resources.

There is enough mystery and adventure at times to hold the interest of kids who aren't especially into all the technology as well.

In Search of Scum

Bruce Balan

New York: Avon Books, 1997. (http://www.AvonBooks.com).
163p. (Cyber.kdz #1). ISBN: 0-380-78514-5. Ages 9–12.
Paperback, $3.99.

This is the first book in a series called Cyber.kdz, written for children aged 9 to 12. The main characters are an international group of 7 kids, ranging in age from 10 to 16, who met on the Internet and have formed a secret online club. The kids include Tereza (Brazil), Josh (Seattle), Sanjeev (India), Deeder (Netherlands), Becky and Paul (New York), and Loren (France). Paul is the youngest member of the group at age 10. Each has particular talent with computers that enable them to do a lot of complicated and seemingly impossible things involving the Internet to solve problems that arise.

There are basically two plots going on. One revolves around a crisis in Josh's life. He and his family recently moved to Seattle after his father left them for another woman. Josh is angry at his father, upset about leaving Los Angeles, and worried about his mother.

Luckily, he can communicate online with his friend Tereza, who offers support. But one day she doesn't hear from him and after the silence continues for several more days, she is concerned. So is Josh's mother, because one day Josh does not come home. When Josh's mother finds an e-mail to Tereza, she contacts Tereza, hoping that she has heard from Josh.

How can the Cyber.kdz help? Well, you know it has to involve computers and the Internet in some way. And it does. Using e-mail, live chat sessions, their hacking skills, and MUD playing expertise, eventually Josh is "found" by Paul, the youngest member of the group. Josh finally admits he has gone to Los Angeles to confront his father. Josh learns some things about his father that he didn't know and sees him in a different light.

The support from his Internet pals presents a very positive model of friendship and shows how relationships can form through online communication. Though living in all parts of the world, this group of friends is always there, ready to help each other when problems arise.

A second subplot revolves around another member of the group, Deeder, who found a virus sent to a mailing list. Deeder's passion is killing viruses, so he wants to make sure this one is taken care of. But Deeder gets more than he bargained for and needs the help of his online friends in New York, when he learns who the anonymous sender is. Turns out he's found an international group of terrorists that is about to bomb the United Nations. What can the kids do to stop this deadly plan?

The book uses quite a bit of technological jargon throughout with no real explanation. It's obvious that the author assumes a certain level of computer awareness by the reader. Slang computer talk is interspersed throughout the e-mail correspondence among the kids. Anyone who isn't a heavy-duty computer user—or even those who are—may find terms and phrases they don't understand. For example, "sliding the talkway," "threading the Net," "spinning the Web," and "thread sled" are all used at one time or another. Also, if you are unfamiliar with Internet tools, references to MUDs, Telnet, and FTP will not mean much.

In this adventure, the Kids use a multitude of computer skills to help solve the threat by terrorists. Hacking into the FBI's server and the New York City Fire Department computer may seem a bit "over the top," especially when you consider their ages, but (let's face it) teens are certainly some of the more active hackers in real life.

Even though this is the first book in a series, the author never explains how everyone met, and he occasionally refers to a previous incident about which we know nothing. The use of foreign phrases is interesting. Kids can learn a few salutations and phrases in Portuguese, Dutch, and French.

Young cybersurfers who are into computers will enjoy this interesting group of "cyber.kdz" and their Internet escapades. Kids will also relate to the personal issues Josh has to deal with. One tip: first read the glossary at the end so you will have a basic understanding of the terms used. And then have a good time finding out how they stop the terrorists from blowing up the UN and see how Josh resolves his own personal problems.

The Internet Escapade

Joan Lowery Nixon

New York: Disney Press, 1997.
(**http://www.disney.com/DisneyBooks/index.html**). 86p. (Casebusters #11).
ISBN: 0-7868-4088-9. Ages 9–12. Softcover, $3.95.

Casebusters is a mystery series created by Edgar Award-winning writer Joan Lowery Nixon. Written for children aged 7 to 11, the books focus on Brian and Sean Quinn, brothers who have an unusual hobby: they are the Casebusters and they solve mysteries. In *The Internet Escapade*, Sean and his friend, Matt Fisher, have pulled a couple of annoying pranks in the computer lab at their school, Redoaks Elementary School, where Sean is a fourth-grader. Both are sent to the principal's office, where Mr. Burns, the principal, tells them they will be in trouble if this happens again. When Sean gets home, he decides to play a game on his father's computer. Instead he sees a mysterious e-mail message that tells him Mr. Burns will soon have problems of his own. Sean is concerned about the creepy message and tells his older brother, Brian. Brian can find no user name or address. The next day, Mr. Burns calls Sean into his office when it is determined that someone has put a virus on the computers in the lab. Sean protests his innocence, but knows the only way anyone will believe him is to find the person responsible. When Sean continues to receive mysterious and threatening e-mail, it's time for the Casebusters to get busy and find the culprit.

Sean is a good example of how younger children can learn to use computers. His school has a computer lab and he knows how to use e-mail. His older brother is a member of a computer club that comes to the elementary school to help out with problems and projects. At one point, when Sean receives the first anonymous e-mail, Brian explains to Sean about anonymous remailers that strip off the header and address and forward the message. How can Sean redeem himself and get back into the good graces of his principal? Can the Casebusters solve the mystery?

This is a cute story with a cyber-related plot. Children who follow the series will enjoy this one, especially if they are into the Internet and computers.

Invasion of the Body Thieves

S. F. Black

Mahwah, NJ: Troll Communications, 1997. (**http://www.troll.com**). 110p. (Cyber Zone #4). ISBN: 0-8167-4344-4. Ages 9–12. Paperback, $3.95.

Ian Steiner is a sixth-grader who's a whiz with numbers. He's also interested in computers and space aliens. His substitute teacher, Mr. Carson, kind of reminds him of one, with his big ears and strange appearance. Ian has just gotten hooked up to the Internet and has a computer in his room. Ian spends his time playing games in MUDs and interacts in some chat rooms where he's met some friends.

One day after Ian logs on, a funny thing happens. His computer screen goes blank for a moment and then a series of numbers flashes across the screen. Ian thinks a hacker may have broken in, or perhaps a virus is on his computer. But as he looks at them closely, he realizes the numbers are some kind of code. When he manages to decipher the message, and types it into the computer, it says, "Greetings from outer space...." At this point Ian thinks it's a cute trick. He continues to type in numbers to represent words and soon finds he can automatically translate the numbers into their words. What is happening? Then Ian realizes this is a joke—it must be his friend Mike. When he types in a message to Mike, his computer goes crazy with humming noises that grow louder and louder. And then a face appears on the screen...a very familiar face. It's Roy Carson, his substitute teacher, with a green and scaly face peering out at him. Roy begins talking to Ian, who is dumbfounded because his computer doesn't have a sound card— it can't produce sounds. So how can he hear any sounds? Ian is torn between being really scared and thrilled that he will be the first person to have communicated with an alien from outer space. And Roy's got a good story too.

He wants Ian to help him and his country, Zaz. The Zazians have developed a game that they want to see if Earthlings will like. All Ian has to do is get his friends to play it. If Ian will agree to try the game and encourage his friends to play, this could be the beginning of a great relationship between Earth and Zaz. Ian is not sure, but when Roy promises to show him how to bridge time and space, how can Ian say no?

Ian begins playing the game, called "Bug Out," that night and before he knows it his mother is calling him. Ian is totally unaware that several hours have passed. After dinner, he can't wait to get back to the game. Ian calls his best friend, Mike, and tells him the Web page address to find "Bug Out."

The next morning Mike is as enthusiastic as Ian. They agree to meet in the computer room at lunch to play. They recruit another friend, Tanya. Something strange seems to happen to people who play the game. They become addicted to it from the start. Soon Ian has many of his friends playing the game. All Ian seems to be doing is playing "Bug Out." One day when he comes home from school, he notices that his mother is sitting in front of the television, just staring at it. Something strange is happening with his parents. They seem distracted and sit in front of the television watching game shows all the time. Ian hasn't paid particular attention because all he has been doing, basically, is playing "Bug Out," going to school, then eating junk and playing some more. One evening, after a visit from Roy, Ian doesn't feel so great, and he realizes he hasn't eaten a decent meal in days. Why haven't his parents been cooking dinner? He races downstairs'and sees them sitting on the sofa in their pajamas. The refrigerator contains spoiled food. What is happening? What has happened? Ian begins to realize that the game he's been playing is causing his friends and family to undergo drastic changes. When Mike and Tanya appear at the door one night looking very curious and somewhat green, Ian is really scared. They are turning into aliens.

Ian realizes that the combination of playing "Bug Out" and eating sweets has the power to change regular people into green aliens. When he realizes that almost the whole town is involved, he knows something has to be done. How can he stop this alien takeover? How can he bring normalcy back to his town before it's too late?

The story is full of humor. The descriptions of Mr. Carson as an alien are great, along with the idea that playing a computer game and eating sweets will make you turn into a garbage-eating alien. Poor Ian, he's the typical kid who seems always to get into trouble and who never gets noticed by his peers...until now.

Written in the first person, the plot is revealed through Ian's eyes. By the end of the story, he has learned a valuable lesson about showing off, and he also decides to limit his online time playing games.

It Had to Be You

Stephanie Doyon

New York: Bantam Books, 1996. (**http://www.bbd.com**). 181p.
(Love Stories #10). ISBN: 0-553-56669-5. Young Adult.
Paperback, $3.99.

Love stories have to keep up with the times. Teenagers are big users of the Internet. Many probably know more than their parents do about surfing the 'Net. Here's a story about some typical teens who have the usual teenage angst about dating, school, and life in general. Written in the first person, *It Had to Be You* is a romance novel written for children aged 12 and up. The setting is Westfield High School in Maine, where best friends Rebecca Lowe and Leslie Weaver are beginning their junior year. As you would expect, the topic on both their minds is boys.

This year their school is getting e-mail and will be able to post messages to a bulletin board. However, the network is only within the school, not to outside networks. Even so, Leslie is excited. She understands that e-mail can be fun and a great way to communicate. Rebecca is less enthusiastic, as she's never been that interested in technology. She wonders why anyone would want to send something electronically instead of writing or calling. This is a nice way to introduce both attitudes about electronic communication.

In their first computer class, Leslie shows Rebecca how to choose a user name and select a password for her e-mail. Leslie is all set to post a message to the bulletin board. She's decided this is the best way to meet some guys. She also sends a message for Rebecca.

Rebecca is the leader of a jazz band called Synergy. The group of students meets at a café called Java Joe's to rehearse after school. This year the band has a new sound man, Jordan West, who is replacing a member who moved away. Meeting Jordan for the first time, Rebecca is not sure about him. He's really good-looking, but he seems too smooth. And his ideas seem to be taking away from Rebecca's role as leader of the band. The band likes what Jordan has to say about things. This makes Rebecca get her defenses up and sets the tone for her relationship with Jordan. Every time she sees him, sparks fly. She seems to find something wrong in everything he does.

The second day of school, Rebecca and Leslie meet Antonio Ramirez, who is an exchange student from Spain. His dark good looks and suave manner make him an instant hit with all the girls at school. Leslie convinces Rebecca that she should ask Antonio to the homecoming dance, but Rebecca is not sure she has the nerve.

Rebecca's not having much luck with her e-mail. No responses so far. So Leslie decides to send another message and this time Rebecca's gets some answers. One e-mail from "Carlos" catches her eye and thereafter Leslie convinces her to reply. This begins an online relationship that blossoms into love for Rebecca. But how can she be in love with someone she's never met? One day, Rebecca notices that the last e-mail she received from Carlos indicates he couldn't have been far away from her. By coincidence, Antonio is in the lab. Rebecca thinks she's figured out who her online love is, Antonio. It all makes sense: the name Carlos, the fact that he's traveled. Now Rebecca pictures Antonio every time she sends or reads an e-mail.

In the meantime, Leslie has also connected to the Internet from home with her family's computer. She has met someone in Manchester, England. Once again, Rebecca is the practical one, voicing skepticism about who this person might really be. But Leslie is very excited about it and wants Rebecca to try chatting with Carlos too. As Leslie introduces Rebecca to what an online chat is like, the pros and cons of chat rooms are presented. Rebecca, as the skeptic, wonders about weirdoes and how you know whether the person is telling the truth. What about being in a private chat room with someone? She's uncomfortable with that idea. However, Leslie convinces her to come over and use her computer to chat with Carlos on a Saturday night. Rebecca is converted. She sees how easily you can slip into a pretend world, create your own reality, and use your imagination. Rebecca and Carlos chat for hours and she finally asks him to the homecoming dance. Now Rebecca can't wait for the day to come when she will be with Carlos/Antonio. But when it's time for the dance and she waits for her cyberlove, who appears? Not Antonio, but Jordan West. How can this be? Rebecca is dumbfounded. Why is he here instead of Antonio? Jordan is equally surprised, but he declares his love for her. She believes that Jordan has intentionally misled her into thinking her online companion was Antonio, just to humiliate her. Now Rebecca doesn't know what to do. Can Jordan be the one? Or is Antonio her true love? Rebecca must sort out her feelings and come to a decision.

The characters in this romantic novel seem down to earth. They share many of the real-life concerns and problems faced by many teenagers. While the Internet is a large part of the plot, there are no technological wizards here. The Internet is kept more in perspective as to how it affects them. Basically, e-mail and chat rooms are the main Internet resources in this story. It is a bit hard to swallow that a school would not get an outside connection but only have a local area network within its own building, but given the plot, having a full Internet connection wouldn't have produced the same results. Maybe it's a little poetic license. Chat rooms are part of the twists of the plot and provide a look at the pluses and minuses associated with them. A few safety tips are thrown into conversations as well. Written in the first person from Rebecca's perspective, we get to see how she feels and deals with the people around her. She's got a sense of humor that shows in various chapters. She's also capable of being embarrassed and makes mistakes that many teens will be able to identify with. Teenagers, especially girls, will enjoy this novel.

Know Fear

Scott Ciencin

New York: Random House, 1996. (http://www.randomhouse.com). 204p. (The Lurker Files #2). ISBN: 0-679-88236-7. Ages 9–12. Softcover, $6.99.

Following on the heels of *Nameless* in The Lurker Files is *Know Fear*, which continues where *Nameless* left off. This cyber serial revolves around the unknown Lurker, an online presence who controls the lives of students and faculty at Wintervale University. In *Know Fear*, the story focuses on Josh Stewart, a big basketball star in high school. He's enrolled at Wintervale and has become known as the champion of "Apocalypse Man," a game at which he is able to beat most challengers. But Josh is not winning on his own. One day Josh realizes that the Lurker is behind most of his wins. Eventually, Josh rebels against the Lurker and begins working with Calle Ann, a computer whiz who is trying to bring down the Lurker.

For most of the plot, it seems that Josh goes from one threatening situation to the next. Once again, it's confusing and very difficult to keep up with everything and everyone. There's no telling who's good and who's bad. Josh seems to be someone who wants to do what's right, but he also seems helpless to do anything that doesn't end up turning out wrong.

Much of the conversation occurs online in chat sessions between the Lurker and other characters under online names. That's a mystery in itself. Who's using what name online?

Every time it seems that Calle Ann might be getting one up on the Lurker, something happens and you realize he's still got the upper hand. For some reason, this second novel just does not hold your interest like the others. There's no real character development and the whole plot is just one incident after another, which gets quite tiresome. If there were some clues along the way that helped you try to figure out who the Lurker is, it might at least make you want to continue reading, but nothing provides any real information about who he might be.

This series began as an online Web site that was very popular. The novels are a print version of the online serial. The large type and attempt at making it look like it's coming from a computer may help some people read the print more easily, but in some ways it's just distracting. If you like convoluted mysteries with an Internet background and can get through the stilted, conversational style of writing, maybe you will be able to finish all three novels.

Lost in Dino World

S. F. Black

Mahwah, NJ: Troll Communications, 1997. (**http://www.troll.com**). 125p. (Cyber Zone #2). ISBN: 0-8167-4280-4. Ages 9–12. Paperback, $3.95.

Here's a fun story with some special characters and a lot about dinosaurs. Brooke is a sixth-grader with long brown hair and ordinary looks, but with a photographic memory and an "A" record in school. Faith is a pretty sixth-grader with long red hair, freckles, and nothing but boys on her mind. Faith and Brooke are best friends. Brooke's father is a paleontologist at the local college. Her mother is also a paleontologist. Guess what Brooke wants to be when she grows up? As the story opens, Faith and Brooke are looking in "Fossils," a "weird secondhand store" in town. Faith wants to find a dress for the Halloween dance. Brooke wants to find the perfect present for her father. While trying on dresses, they accidentally knock something down. It's large and has claws and at first Brooke thinks it's alive. Of course dinosaurs can't be alive and that's what has fallen down—a dinosaur model as lifelike as Brooke has ever seen. And it has feathers on it, of all things. Mrs. Trowdon, the storeowner, does not want to discuss the model. In fact, she and her strange son act downright suspicious, according to Faith. What do they have to hide about the model? When Brooke offers to buy it, she can't get them even to discuss a price with her.

Faith is convinced there is something going on and decides that she will stay over at Brooke's and they can find out what it is. That evening, Brooke logs on to the Internet into her favorite chat room, Dino World, where she and Faith ask questions about the Coelophysis, a dinosaur that lived in the late Triassic period. Lizard Boy is one of the chat room members whom Brooke likes. He knows a lot about dinosaurs and she's hoping he can tell her something about the feathered model they saw. Faith can't keep her hands off the keyboard, so she joins in too. She blurts out their trip to the store and describes the model they saw. Everyone is incredulous. Lizard Boy asks where they saw it and what the name of the store is. As Faith begins to write "The name of the store is . . . ," something impossible happens. Brooke's computer suddenly lets out a screeching noise, then a blinding light comes gushing out of the computer, and before Brooke and Faith know what's happening they are moving faster and faster through the light into the computer. When they land all of a sudden with a thud, a bright light, and a buzzing noise, an incredibly blue sky is above them. Where are they? Funny trees and noises are all around. All at once Brooke sees something large heading directly for them—a dinosaur is heading their way, fast. Brooke recognizes the dinosaur as a plant-eating variety, not meat-eating. They're safe for now. All at once, a voice sounds and Rachel, a friend from the Dino World chat room, is there. They meet Billy Zipkin, a classmate of Brooke's and Faith's, as well. What is everyone doing there? Somehow they have been transported back to the prehistoric age. How are they going to get back? Billy managed to bring a laptop along and this may be their only means of help. It's never explained how it can have a network connection, but they are able to log onto the Dino World Web page at one point.

As Brooke leads her friends through the adventures of being lost in prehistoric times, she learns something about her own family and must make a decision that will affect her friends' safe return as well as her future.

This science fiction novel has a lot of adventures with some interesting science facts thrown in. It has taken a science adventure and added a modern component, the Internet, as a vehicle. There are numerous references to various dinosaur species and descriptions of the land that provide some educational information as well as fun reading for kids.

Love Bytes

Elizabeth Craft

New York: Archway Paperbacks, 1997. (**http://www.simonsays.com**). 211p. (@café #1). ISBN: 0-671-00445-X. Young Adult. Paperback, $3.99.

Love Bytes, the first in a series of romantic novels with an Internet touch to them, focuses on a group of teenage friends who work together at an Internet café called @café in San Francisco. Dylan, Natalie, Sara Jane (known as Blue), Jason, Sam, and Tanya work together, sharing friendships, romances, and life. Except for Dylan, who has graduated, the others still attend high school.

Dylan O'Connor is only 18 but has recently bought the @café. He's banking on it making money so that he can go to a really good college in a couple of years.

Love Bytes introduces and spends a little time on each member of the group so that you can get to know who they are and who they date or want to date or used to date. Natalie and Tanya are best friends, but sometimes boys can come between a friendship. Natalie used to have a huge crush on Dylan, but, realizing it would never happen, she has now transferred her "love" to Matthew Chance, a "hunk" whom she is determined to get to notice her. Unfortunately, Matthew has a rather checkered past and Tanya knows that better than anyone. Will he come between best friends Tanya and Natalie?

In another twist, Dylan is shocked to realize he is falling in love with Natalie, his good friend and worker. The problem is that there's an unwritten rule that you don't mix romance and work at the @café. Jason and Blue (Dylan's sister) are pals who hang out together and seem to be on the same wavelength. None of that romance stuff for them—but when Natalie wants to put an ad on the Internet to find a boyfriend for Blue, Jason's not so sure he likes the idea. Then the tables are turned and Sam decides that Jason needs to date, too. How does Blue feel now? Sam (Dylan's best friend) is in the midst of a crisis within his family. His father was convicted of insider trading violations and is now in a minimum-security prison. This has had a great impact on Sam, who must now assume the role of parent to his younger brother. He must also watch out for his mother. She is not handling the crisis very well and refuses to face the reality of their situation.

As you can see, there are quite a few subplots running through the book. The main one is supposed to be Dylan's sudden realization of his feelings toward Natalie, but to be honest, this does not seem to be the main story line. A lot more attention is paid to Natalie's interest in Matthew and the triangle with her friend Tanya. The café is the main setting for much of the action because all of the friends work there.

There are various references to the Internet throughout the book. The @café has its own Web site called "Spill the Beans." Tanya often writes a horoscope column for it. Natalie puts her favorite recipes online. Jason writes about whatever he likes. The @café has computers available for customers to send e-mail or surf the Web. When Natalie and Tanya want to find a boyfriend for Blue, they use the Internet to post a personal ad, and Blue and Jason use e-mail to get in touch.

This novel will appeal to teenagers, especially girls. It's a fun read about typical teenage romantic problems experienced by 17-year-olds. The book even includes photos of the main characters with a little blurb about each. This is a nice touch that allows you to visualize the characters as you read. This is a series, so if you want to find out what happens you'll have to continue to read the rest of the books; nothing is resolved at the end of this book. For maximum effect, it's best to read them in order.

Make Mine to Go

Elizabeth Craft

New York: Archway Paperbacks, 1998. (**http://www.simonsays.com**). 186p. (@café #3). ISBN: 0-671-00447-6. Young Adult. Paperback, $3.99.

The third novel in the @café series continues the romantic lives of a group of teenagers who work at a coffee café in San Francisco. The café is owned by Dylan O'Connor, an 18-year-old recent high school graduate who is saving money earned from the business to go to college someday. This story continues where *I'll Have What He's Having* ends.

Natalie Van Lenton has recently discovered that her mother is alive. After almost 15 years believing she was dead, Natalie is faced with the startling fact that her father has lied to her all of these years. Recently Natalie began seeing Sam Barton, Dylan's best friend. Obviously, this complicates things for Dylan, who loves Natalie, but does not want to jeopardize his friendship with Sam. When

Natalie decides she must drive to Portland to see her mother, Dylan coincidentally has to make a business trip there. The meeting is emotional and on the drive back, Dylan is a patient listener. When their car has a flat tire and they stop to fix it, the situation is tense and leads to a romantic kiss between the two. Now what? Both decide they must forget it.

There are further complications with Blue, Dylan's sister, and her longtime friend, Jason. They've both recently discovered "romantic" feelings for each other but don't want to admit it. So, Jason is dating Celia and Blue meets Christian, a folk singer. Now, Jason is seeing Celia and Blue is seeing Christian. So why isn't either one happy?

Tanya is still crazy in love with Major, a guy she met recently. He's a college student and not interested in a relationship. Things get complicated when Tanya sees him with a girl and assumes it's his girlfriend. This leads to misunderstandings and more complications.

Meanwhile, Natalie has been thinking about the kiss with Dylan. Finally, she writes Dylan a letter admitting that she feels something. Dylan can't believe his luck. She wants to talk to him about it and is going to break up with Sam. Of course, since nothing is ever simple and this is a series, things don't work out quite the way they should. Natalie learns that Sam's mother has overdosed, so there's no way she can end their relationship now.

This is a continuing saga of the love problems of six people. There are love triangles and unrequited love everywhere you turn. No one seems able to admit their real feelings or to be happy in a relationship. Many of these problems are ones that teenagers will relate to. It's easy to identify with waiting by the phone or loving someone who doesn't love you. Every relationship is "love." After two days, someone is your boyfriend and you are in love. Every emotion is intense and every moment is packed with feeling. The only plot aside from everyone's love life is Natalie's revelation that her mother is alive. How will that affect her family life with her sister and father? Will her mother become part of her life?

Throughout this series, references are made to the Internet in various ways. The setting for the novels is an Internet coffee café where people can surf the 'Net while sipping their espressos and cappuccinos. @café has a Web site to which each of the friends contributes pages, such as recipes or articles about love, relationships, and even addiction to computer games. E-mail is a tool used by them to correspond. In fact, that's how Natalie found out her mother was alive.

The books are meant to be read in order, but if you don't the author is good about recapping who everyone is and what has happened. If you read one in the middle of the series, you won't be lost, but you may learn some things that will give away what happened in earlier books. If you're into teenage romance novels, start at number one in this series.

Meltdown Man

S. F. Black

Mahwah, NJ: Troll Communications, 1997. (http://www.troll.com).
125p. (Cyber Zone #1). ISBN: 0-8167-4279-0. Ages 9–12.
Paperback, $3.95.

Matt Harper is in the sixth grade. He's one of those kids who isn't good at sports; rather, he's a klutz who gets made fun of by the jocks. Life's not much fun at school. But one place Matt feels great is online. He's into computers and games. His best friend Kevin and he spend time logged on to the Internet playing MUD (multiple user dimension) games that let you assume the role of someone else and usually involve some kind of fight against an evil character. One day Kevin and Matt log on in their school computer lab at lunch and find a new game called "Meltdown Man." And of all things, the creators live in Greenvale, New York, Matt's hometown. As they begin the game, another student, Chris, wants to join them. He's played the game before and is kind of a know-it-all.

The goal of the game is to get into Dirk Zorsan's lab to steal his secret formula. But he has an army of henchmen and soldiers plus a moat that make it almost impossible. Meltdown Man hates Dirk the most because he was responsible for disfiguring Meltdown Man. Matt's first experience playing gets him hooked. Somehow Matt seems to have all the codes down pat and wins the game the next day. No one can understand how he did it.

One day something strange happens in school. Matt is accosted by a rather frail-looking student with dark glasses who tells him to "Stop while there's still time." Matt dismisses the warning. One night he feels compelled to play even after he's supposed to be in bed. It's almost as though it's beyond his control. The next morning Matt awakens and feels awful. He notices that his eyes seem very sensitive to light and when he looks in the mirror, his eyes look like Meltdown Man's. What has happened to him? He suddenly realizes what it means when he gets mad at his younger sister and "melts" her doll. A similar incident at school with Mr. Allen, his gym teacher, has Matt panicked. Is he turning into Meltdown Man? Maybe that strange boy who stopped him in the hall can help. Wasn't he wearing sunglasses too? But when Matt learns who the boy is, he realizes he may be in a dangerous situation. Or is he going crazy?

Matt has to find out what's going on before it's too late. How can he stop this transformation into Meltdown Man? He may have to play the game one more time, only this time it's for a lot bigger stakes—his life.

Meltdown Man is an adventure that uses online games as its context, especially MUDs. The story has a theme many kids will relate to: bullies versus the computer nerds at school. What happens when you get so angry that you want revenge on the people who have mistreated you at school? The "Meltdown Man" game will also appeal to kids who like online adventure games or who have ever started playing and had a hard time quitting. Besides the humor alongside the adventure, there's also a moral to this story. Matt learns something very important that will change his life.

Monsters in Cyberspace

Dian Curtis Regan

New York: Henry Holt, 1997. (**http://www.hholt.com**). 178p.
ISBN: 0-8050-4677-1. Ages 9–12. Hardcover, $14.95.

Written for grades five through eight, this is the third installment of the Monster of the Month Club series, centering on 13-year-old Rilla Harmony Earth and her family. Rilla is home-schooled and lives in a bed-and-breakfast run by her mother and aunt. She also lives with her collection of stuffed monsters. Rilla receives a new monster each month, usually stuffed. However, when the stars line up just right, some of them come to life. Keeping these active monsters hidden in her attic bedroom is a constant challenge. The only other person who knows about the live monsters is Joshua (her one true love).

For her September selection, Rilla receives "Owl," wearing thick glasses and dressed in a cap and gown. He sure looks smart and guess what? He's alive and laughing. Rilla's life is further complicated by having the July and August monsters come to life as well. Now she's got three to keep fed, under control, and hidden.

Besides receiving her new monster for September, Rilla also has a brand new computer, compliments of her friend, Mr. Tamerow. He's set it up and given her some lessons in how to connect to the Internet. Now Rilla can send e-mail to Mr. Tamerow and meet some new friends online. There's something else Rilla wants to do, too. She promised herself a long time ago she'd try to find her father. Now with a connection to the Internet, maybe she can.

There's one small problem. Owl has taken a fancy to Rilla's computer. It seems that his diet consists of written material and he can learn anything he eats. You see, he likes to eat poetry, literature . . . anything with print on it. So, after eating a few pages of Rilla's online manual, he knows how to log on to cyberspace.

The story combines Rilla's new monsters with the online adventure of finding her long-lost father. In this installment, Rilla goes out on her first date and her Aunt Poppy gets engaged. The characters are sweet and the monsters add a humorous and touching aspect to the story. The writing has wonderful descriptions of the monsters, and Rilla's conversations to herself and her monster friends are full of laughs. Kids will also appreciate Rilla's very real teen angst about her first date with Andrew and her feelings about Joshua. The black-and-white illustrations at the beginning of each chapter add to the overall feel of this very sweet, somewhat poignant, yet funny story.

Most Wanted

Jordan Cray

New York: Aladdin Paperbacks, 1998. (**http://www.SimonSaysKids.com**). 232p. (danger.com@6). ISBN: 0-689-82040-2. Ages 9–12. Paperback, $3.99.

This is the last (at this writing) in the danger.com series and features a story that revolves around lies and murder. Andy MacFarland thought his life was pretty much set. He and his mother live in California, where Andy's a junior in high school. His best friend is Syd Gross, the daughter of his mother's best friend and business partner. One day, as he is looking at a picture of himself when he was five, he realizes he's never seen a picture of himself when he was a baby. When he asks his mother, he learns a secret she's kept from him for many years, something that will change his life forever: he is adopted. But that's not the worst part. His father, Silas Murdoch, is a convicted murderer. He killed Andy's birth mother. This news drives a wedge between Andy and his adoptive mother. He feels betrayed. His mother, who has taught him to be honest since the day he can remember, has lied to him for 16 years. How can he trust her again?

As Andy thinks about the whole situation, he knows one thing. He has to find out about his "real" father—and he does. Using the World Wide Web, he locates articles about his father and learns that he has been paroled. His father is out there somewhere. With Syd's help, he learns where his father is. Using his mother's company's e-mail address, he sends a note to the restaurant where his father works, trying to find out more about his father. After a couple of correspondences, the manager of the restaurant gets a little testy and tells Andy he should talk to Silas himself. But Andy isn't ready for this, or is he? The next night an e-mail appears—from his father. Andy replies, pretending to be one of his own friends. He gives Silas information about himself and soon finds he is drawn to this man he has never met. Maybe he's not guilty. Maybe he didn't kill Andy's mother. His mother has no idea what's happening until one day she finds e-mail messages printed out. This just pushes the wedge between him and his mother even further.

One day, as Andy is working outside, he notices a man in blue jeans walk by and then pause. Andy looks up and knows that standing right there in his front yard is Silas Murdoch, his father.

How will this affect Andy's life and relationship with his mother? The rest of the book follows what happens as Silas begins to become part of Andy and his mother's lives.

This book draws upon the Internet as the main source for finding information about Andy's father. Andy uses the World Wide Web to locate newspaper stories. He also searches for information about his father's trial, and instead of calling, he uses electronic mail to get in touch with his father's boss. His mother is the owner of a software company that makes games on CD-ROMs for girls. They have a Web site and an e-mail address.

At one point, it's stretching the imagination to picture an ex-con who has been in prison for 15 years knowing how to use e-mail and chat rooms. The characters are basically likeable, but occasionally you may find yourself shaking your head at Andy's impulsiveness and stubbornness as things get more complicated and even dangerous.

Mystery Date

Kate Williams

New York: Bantam Books, 1998. (**http://www.sweetvalley.com**). 231p. (Sweet Valley High series). ISBN: 0-553-57073-0. Young Adult. Paperback, $4.50.

Sweet Valley High is a romance series created by Francine Pascal, featuring a group of Southern California teenagers who attend high school. (There's even a television series based on this series.) There's also a Web site. *Mystery Date* centers on two Sweet Valley teens who come from different school cliques. Olivia Davidson is a poet. She loves to write and draw and couldn't care less about sports or the football types that make up the other clique—the jocks. Ken Mathews is the quarterback on the football team and sports are his life. Could two people be more opposite? At a school dance one night, Olivia realizes she is lonely. Her boyfriend and she have recently broken up and now she's ready to date again. But do you think even one guy has asked her to dance? Olivia is a free spirit. But she doesn't fit the mold of the popular kids at school, the cheerleaders like Jessica Wakefield or her twin Elizabeth. Though Jessica and Elizabeth are very different, they are both members of the elite at Sweet Valley. Ken Mathews is also at the dance solo. He was recently dumped by Jessica Wakefield and is nursing his hurt feelings. In fact, Ken wonders if he ought to spread out and date different girls who are not part of his circle of friends. As he looks around the crowd at the dance, he realizes that everyone he's dated has been from the same group of people.

That night after the dance, Olivia logs on to the Internet and visits the Virtual Hangout, a special online service for teenagers. There she goes to the Southern California chat room. This is where Olivia feels more comfortable and free to be herself. She can be one of the gang here and it doesn't matter what clique you are in. Olivia enters a favorite chat room as "Freeverse," her online name. Here she can talk with her online pals on any topic.

Ken Mathews uses the Internet to check sports scores. The next morning after the dance, he needs to find out the score for Sweet Valley's main rival, El Carro. He finds the score but wants more details, so he goes to the Virtual Hangout to see if any El Carro students have more information on the game. Ken logs on with his online name, "Quarter" for quarterback.

When he asks if any El Carro students are online, he gets a question, "A quarter of what?," which comes from Freeverse (Olivia). As they converse, Ken finds he likes Freeverse's artistic bent. She's easy to talk to. When Ken is asked what else he likes, he begins to type in "football, basketball," but then thinks better of it. He doesn't want to appear the typical jock football player, so he decides to keep silent about his position on the football team. Ken and Olivia hit it off, but Ken thinks that Olivia is an El Carro student. He has no idea that he's talking to a person he's known since kindergarten. The story explores their online friendship and is a good illustration of the importance of what a person is on the inside rather than on the outside. Every time they chat online, Olivia finds more that she likes about Ken. After communicating and visiting in cyberspace for a while, they decide to meet. What will happen when Ken finds out that "Freeverse" is Olivia Davidson and she learns that her cyberlove is a jock football player? Will they still share those special feelings of love in the real world?

Along with the online romance between Olivia and Ken, another subplot centers on the unrest and discord among several cliques at school. The jocks hate the hippies and visa versa. Things get out of hand when a football player is charged with assault. This divides the school even further. Each takes sides based on their special group. The issue of diversity and tolerance for differences is almost beaten to the ground in this "love story." It seems to go on and on. Much of the plot seems to be conversation among Sweet Valley students about who's a geek, who's a jock. The question of using physical violence when attacked verbally is tossed around among various characters.

The social dynamics of a large high school are explored here through a variety of teen types who experience the special crises that only adolescents can. The main plot incorporates the Internet as a tool for romance. Safety concerns are expressed at one point when the two online loves want to get together. The question of whether persons online are who they say they are can be a real concern. Written for ages 12 and up, there's a lot that will probably appeal to teens. Teens will want to read to find out what happens with Olivia and Ken's cyber romance, but the trials and tribulations among all the various groups seem a bit overdone in some of the scenes and drag on too much at times.

Nemesis

Scott Ciencin

New York: Random House, 1997. (http://www.randomhouse.com). 203p. (The Lurker Files #3). ISBN: 0-679-88506-4. Ages 9–12. Softcover, $6.99.

Nemesis is the third book of the Lurker series. Kyle Simmons is a freshman saddled with a roommate he can't stand, Zack Alexander. To get away from Zack and to have some time to himself, Kyle volunteers for the graveyard shift on a campus security patrol called Nemesis. There have been some serious pranks on campus and someone could get hurt. Peter Nakamura, a student, created Nemesis to protect students at night, walk them places when necessary, and keep an eye out for any possible pranks. But when Kyle attends his first meeting of Nemesis, guess who else has signed up? Zack. Looks like Kyle is stuck with his roomie forever. Two other Nemesis members are also present: Janine Wolf and Courtney Wade.

The first night out, Courtney and Kyle run into a group of vandals. Three of them are wearing ski masks and have voice-altering devices attached to their necks. Kyle manages to get close enough to yank one of the masks off, but the vandals run off through the woods. Courtney has observed it all and immediately follows the vandals through the woods. Soon she sees them stop near an old well and place something inside it. When they leave, Courtney steps up and retrieves a locked black box with an LCD light and keypad on it. She picks it up and takes it with her.

That same night, rookie Zack and Janine are paired for patrol duty. They also run into some vandals who have set a trap at the Hope Galleries. Janine unwittingly sets it off, causing debris to rain down onto Zack. The campus security officer wants Janine and Zack to go to the hospital to get checked out. Later, as Kyle relates his story to Peter, Courtney rushes in and tells them she has pictures and that she followed the two vandals who accosted Kyle. She mentions the names "Coyote" and "Ozymandias," which cause Peter to register alarm.

He explains about the Lurker, Wintervale's online menace, who seems to have an army of operators called "dethboys" to do his bidding in the physical world. No one knows if the Lurker is male or female, but they do know he rules cyberspace. His power lies in being able to do anything that someone wants—but then, like Faust, you are in with the devil. Once he grants you your wish, he's got you where he wants you.

After hearing this, Courtney does not mention the black box. Later that evening, when the Lurker communicates with his dethboys, he wants to know why the black box wasn't at the usual dropoff spot. Suddenly, he realizes that someone has stolen it. Later that evening, he finds out who has it. Courtney contacts the Lurker in a chat room under the persona "ghost," where she makes demands of the Lurker before she will return the box. This sets the stage for a series of adventures that surround the black box and involve the other members of Nemesis. When Courtney goes to get her carefully hidden box, Zack follows and knocks her out and takes the box. He's the next one to deal with the Lurker. Zack wants lots of money. He discusses his demands online as "Adonis" in a chat room. Meanwhile, after Courtney awakens, she tells Kyle everything and they decide to go to Peter.

The story seems to be one close call after another. People are drugged with dart guns, stunned with taser guns, and almost killed by falling gargoyles. The plot takes lots of twists and turns. Pranksters versus the Lurker...who is whom? Sometimes it's difficult to keep up with everyone in the plot. Who are the pranksters and what is their relationship to the Lurker, if any? What is in the black box? Why is it so important?

This series is a bit different from others that have an Internet focus. The characters here are college students and not necessarily the technology geniuses we see in the other series, such as Internet Detectives or Cyber.kdz. This series is also a bit more sophisticated in its plot than others like the Internet Detectives or Cyber.kdz. The action is a bit more violent and there are lots of fights, cars being run off the road, druggings, etc. It's all done in a pretty clean way, however.

In the Lurker Files, the characters use the Internet for communication, and chat rooms are major vehicles for the main character, the Lurker. The Internet is a focal point in this book as the main source for the Lurker's presence. He is master of the Ratskellar, a campus online chat room. There are references to chat rooms, the World Wide Web, and of course e-mail throughout. The plot keeps you wondering yet gives you no real clues. As an action novel with a little bit of college romance thrown in, kids may like this series, but may have to reread a few of the chapters to make sure they understand what exactly is happening and to whom. Perhaps the characters themselves are a bit confused too; a couple of times in conversations, they try to figure out what is happening. These are very helpful to the befuddled reader who is trying to grasp what is going on.

You may want to read this series in order. There are a number of references to past titles that may give away some things if you read this one first. It may also be helpful to read them in sequence to get a better understanding of the Lurker's power and control over Wintervale's online world. The Web site will give you more information about the characters and the Lurker.

Net Bandits

Michael Coleman

New York: Bantam Skylark Books, 1997. (**http://www.bbd.com/id**). 128p. (Internet Detectives #1). ISBN: 0-553-48620-9. Ages 9–12. Paperback, $3.99.

The first in a series of Internet Detectives mysteries written for children aged 9 to 12, this premier title introduces a group of friends who have developed a relationship through the Internet. The idea is that they help each other when problems arise, and this doesn't mean answers to homework questions. Someone is always getting into a jam or finding themselves involved in a situation that requires help from one of their Internet friends. In this first book, we meet Rob Zanelli, a young boy who is being home-schooled. His parents are very protective of him after an accident left him paralyzed. He is an Internet junkie whose parents own a software company.

The story takes place primarily in Portsmouth, England, where Rob lives. He regularly checks the Internet and reads his e-mail from pals across the world in Canada, New York, and Australia. Soon after the book begins, using his log-in name, "Zmaster," Rob meets a new Internet friend, Tamsyn, a student at a local school, Abbey School. She's new to the Internet and would really rather read a good book. Her friend, Josh, is a computer expert. Both attend the same school, where they often make use of the computer lab.

Soon after Rob and Tamsyn exchange a couple of e-mails, Rob finds himself in a dangerous situation at home. His tutor is working with a fired employee from Rob's family's software company, who wants revenge. Rob is held against his will while they try to find a new software disk ready to be marketed by Rob's family's company. Somehow Rob manages to send an e-mail message to Tamsyn that says "Get Help." But they don't know Zmaster's real name. Will Tamsyn and Josh be able to get help in time?

What makes this an Internet Detectives book is that help comes through the use of a computer, modem, and friends who are connected to the 'Net. Kids who are into the Internet will relate to all the Internet language and talk such as downloading files, surfing the 'Net, and logging on. Whenever there is e-mail, a screen shot in the book shows what it looks like. When someone logs on to the Internet, you see an illustration of it. This is a nice way to show newcomers to the Internet exactly what goes on. The book is fun to read and kids who are into the Internet will find it enjoyable. The language is kid-friendly and the characters are "cool."

A Picture's Worth

Bruce Balan

New York: Avon Books, 1997. (**http://www.AvonBooks.com**).
164p. (Cyber.kdz #2). ISBN: 0-380-79515-3. Ages 9–12.
Paperback, $3.99.

This is the second title in the Cyber.kdz series of stories about a group of cyber whiz kids who have banded together online as friends and use their computer skills to solve mysteries and help out when they learn about a problem on the 'Net. *A Picture's Worth* focuses on Becky and her brother Paul, who live in New York. Becky is not very happy at her new private school, where she's just started high school. Having to leave her best friend, Kim, who is attending public school, was hard. It's a difficult time for Becky, who is overweight and often the target of name-calling and harassment by her fellow students. Becky's favorite subject is history. In a recent oral presentation in class, she was able to use material found on the Internet to impress her teacher and win his praise. So it's a shock when report cards come out and she receives an F. It just doesn't seem possible.

One day when she's communicating with the Cyber.kdz, she tells Loren about her grade problems. He cannot believe it either and thinks something must be wrong. Could it be that someone tampered with the database and changed her grade? To find out, Becky has to get into the school and download the database files. After she does, Deeder, the virus whiz kid, figures out that someone has been into the database and made changes. But there is no evidence that can pinpoint who did it. Becky has another problem. She sent a picture of her best friend, Kim, instead of her own photo for an online album and now feels guilty about it.

How can Becky prove that someone changed her grade? How will the kids react when they find out she has sent in her best friend's photo instead of her own?

Again, this series has managed to combine an appealing mystery and a look at a typical teenager's problems and crises. Becky's weight problem and resulting lack of self-esteem in a new school are something that many kids have to face. The situation is handled with insight, showing that you don't have to be a perfect teenager to have friends and to be successful in school.

Once again the Cyber.kdz team up to help out one of their members, using their special Internet and technology skills.

Pirates on the Net

Ted Pedersen and Mel Gilden

Los Angeles, CA: Price Stern Sloan, 1995. (http://www.putnam.com). 144p. (Cybersurfers #1). ISBN: 0-8431-3933-1. Ages 9–12. Paperback, $3.95.

Jason Kane and Athena Bergstrom are high school students at Ft. Benton High, in the Pacific Northwest. Both are heavy into computers, but in different ways. Athena is a computer artist who loves to spend time creating art using her computer. Jason is a "hacker" and programmer who knows all about how to use computers to get into other systems. Jason and Athena are chosen by their teacher, Mr. Madison, to test a new gateway software to connect to the Internet at school. The principal, Ms. O'Malley, is skeptical about technology and spending money to upgrade the lab, so Athena explains the benefits of an Internet connection to her. This is a handy way to get the same information across to kids who might not know as much about the Internet as some books assume. This also serves to explain to the reader what the Internet is.

After the project is approved, Athena and Jason can't wait to get home to start "surfing" the 'Net. Unfortunately, Jason ends up getting involved in a dangerous plot to steal a secret game engine from a leading game manufacturer. How can he prove he didn't steal it without his computer? How can Athena help him prove his innocence?

The story involves a plot that will appeal to teens. There's the relationship between Jason, who is a loner, and Athena, the only girl at school who knows anything about computers, with a hint of a possible romance suggested. There's also some mystery and a little adventure. And the Internet plays a main plot in the story, too. The appealing thing is that the authors don't assume that someone reading this book will necessarily know much about it. They don't just throw in technology without explaining it. So, the characters always work explanations of Internet-related terms into their conversation. There is a nice combination of storyline between two typical teens along with the Internet that should appeal to kids today. This series would be a nice way to introduce a child to some of the possibilities of the Internet.

Shadow Man

Jordan Cray

New York: Aladdin Paperbacks, 1997. (http://www.SimonSaysKids.com).
195p. (danger.com@3). ISBN: 0-689-81433-X. Ages 9–12.
Paperback, $3.99.

Annie Hanley is 16 and recently dumped by her boyfriend, Josh, after going steady with him over the spring and summer. Pepper Oneida, all of five foot two with blonde hair and blue eyes, set her sights on Josh and managed to steal him from Annie. Now Annie's in the midst of dealing with a broken heart. It's Christmas and there's no way to avoid running into her ex and his girlfriend when you live in a small town like Scull Island off of the Connecticut coast. In the summer, it's alive with tourists, but come Labor Day, the crowds pack up and the businesses close for the winter. So, anywhere Annie wants to go for fun is the same place Pepper and Josh will be.

But when Nick, Annie's new stepbrother, arrives to spend the Christmas holidays with his father and her mother, she may get her chance for revenge on Pepper. Nick has an idea of how they can go about getting back at her. First, they manage to find Pepper's credit card number and cancel a big party Pepper's having to celebrate Josh's birthday. Nick has another idea in mind as well. He borrows Annie's PC and, after he thinks he's found Pepper's e-mail address (pepr.oni), they "spam" her by sending an e-mail message hundreds of times to her account.

But something's not right. Pepper doesn't seem in the least distracted by the many electronic mail messages. Is it possible they got the wrong e-mail address? When Annie determines they have not been sending the mail to Pepper, she wants to turn off the computer and forget the whole thing. But Nick realizes that the person to whom they've sent the mail has something mysterious he's hiding, so he decides to play along for a while. If he's up to something bad, maybe they can stop him.

Little do Annie and Nick know that by continuing this game, they are letting themselves in for a dangerous encounter, one that may put their lives in danger.

The danger.com series focuses on teens who somehow get involved in adventures that begin by using the Internet in some way. In this case, a wrong e-mail address sets up the plot that forces Annie and Nick to continue their dangerous involvement with a man who has something deadly to hide and will stop at nothing to keep them from finding out. Other than that, there's very little cyber stuff in the story. It's mostly an adventure story, with Nick and Annie trying to stay one step ahead of "pepr.oni."

Written in the first person, Annie's narration of the story and her sense of humor add a light touch to even the more serious moments. Besides the mystery, teens will relate to Annie's broken heart and her feelings toward "the other woman" who stole her boyfriend. There are some funny scenes, such as the one in which a dog named "Cannibal" chases the two into a freezer where there's more than frozen meat inside. This is a fun story to read, with two likeable teens as the main characters. The small island off of Long Island Sound makes a nice setting at Christmas time. You can almost imagine the brightly colored lights and holiday decorations. If you are into the technical world of cyberspace, this one won't fill your needs. But if you're a fan of the series and read it for more than just the techie stuff, you won't be disappointed in this one.

Speed Surf

Michael Coleman

New York: Bantam Skylark Books, 1997. (http://www.bbd.com/id).
112p. (Internet Detectives #3). ISBN: 0-553-48622-5. Ages 9–12.
Softcover, $3.99.

This is the third book in the Internet Detectives series, which features several friends who use the Internet to solve mysteries and problems that arise. Rob Zanelli, Tamsyn Smith, and Josh Allan all attend Abbey School in Portsmouth, England. Three more Internet friends include Lauren, from Canada; Mitch, from New York; and Tom, from Australia.

Rob Zanelli's parents own a software company called Gamezone, which makes computer games. They are sponsoring a yacht in a single-man race from New York to Portsmouth and Rob's buddies, Josh and Tamsyn, are excited about it. Rob shows them a Web page with all the information about the race. Brad Stewart is manning the yacht for the Zanellis and Rob has an e-mail message from him on his computer. As it turns out, all the yachts are equipped with sophisticated technology that includes an Internet connection for monitoring the weather.

Mitch, one of Rob's best friends from cyberspace, works at Cyber-Snax, a café in New York. The café has computers available for its customers to use the Internet to send e-mail or surf the Web. Rob has arranged for Mitch, an avid sailor, to meet Brad Stewart and tour the yacht while it's in New York. On the day that Mitch is to visit the yacht, he helps a customer send an e-mail message to a Web site. Mitch doesn't think too much of it except that the man doesn't have a clue about how to use the Internet. At the dock, Brad shows Mitch over the entire place while Mitch takes photos. As he's leaving he spots a painting wrapped in a newspaper. Later, after e-mailing his friends about the yacht and the painting, he learns it may be a stolen masterpiece worth $5 million. As it turns out, the painting is a copy of the original. As he stands in the museum director's office, he sees a police detective take out a mug shot and show it to the museum director. Mitch recognizes the face. It's the man who came into Cyber-Snax and sent the e-mail message. Mitch remembers the message and as Tamsyn and Josh finally figure out what it says, they realize that the stolen painting is on board the Zanellis' yacht. Is Rob's father involved? How did it get on board? And how can they prove who is behind the theft? Using their contacts on the Internet and e-mail, they set out to solve the mystery.

Each title in the series spotlights one of the "Internet Detectives," so readers can learn a little more about them. Mitch is featured in this episode. Besides the main plot of the stolen painting, there is a minor subplot with Tom, who has had his bike stolen in Australia. And Lauren and her grandmother in Toronto help break the code of the e-mail sent at the Cyber-Snax Café.

The books in this series offer a nice combination of interesting mysteries that show the Internet and its tools used in a more practical way than other "cyberspace" mysteries. You don't have to be a geek or computer nerd to enjoy the story. Surfing the 'Net, posting e-mail, and sending digitized photos are some of the ways the Internet is used. Also, when discussing ASCII text and how it works, the author manages to work in a brief sentence or two about ASCII for those scratching their heads. This makes the book appealing to anyone who would like to read about three friends in England and their cyberspace pals around the world. This series can be read in any order unless you absolutely don't want to have any information about a former episode. There are references to past activities that could give away some of the plot.

Stalker

Jordan Cray

New York: Aladdin Paperbacks, 1998. (http://www.SimonSaysKids.com). 213p. (danger.com@5). ISBN: 0-689-81476-3. Ages 9–12. Paperback, $3.99.

Mina and Camille (Camy) have been best friends since grade school. They shared everything. That is, they did until the summer before their senior year, when Camille went away. When she returned, her transformation included losing weight and realizing she was "cool." Accepted by the in-crowd at school, she cuts Mina out of her life. Mina is not "Miss Popularity" at school. Her rather caustic sense of humor and ironic comments don't go over well with some people. Camy finds a new boyfriend, Mick, one of the best-looking guys at school.

Mina and Camille have not spent time together in a long while. But one day Mina gets a call from her ex-friend asking if she'd like to go to the mall. They go in Mina's car. Mina cannot keep her barbed comments and sarcastic attitude from leaping to the forefront. Eventually, she and Camy argue and Camy leaves. Mina tries not to feel badly about how things went, but when Camy's mother calls late that night and announces that her daughter has not returned, Mina is worried and feels very guilty.

The next morning her friend has still not come home. Now it's serious. The police are called in, but as the days pass Mina fears the worst and decides to try to find some clues by checking her friend's locker. As she is sitting on the floor going through Camy's things for clues, Mick walks up. He has had the same idea. Mina's natural skepticism of him (because he is good-looking and dating Camy) doesn't get in the way of agreeing to work together to find Camille.

The story revolves around their growing friendship as they try to locate their missing friend. The clues they pick up don't look good for Camy, who may have gotten involved with an obsessive, unbalanced person she met online. It turns out that she has been corresponding via e-mail with someone called Andrew. They had decided to meet. Could this person be responsible for Camy's disappearance? It's beginning to look that way. Putting the pieces together takes them to a conclusion they can't believe. But is it too late? Can they save their friend?

Stalker is one of the best of this collection of Internet mysteries in the danger.com series. It's also somewhat more unsettling. Kidnapping and murder, especially as they relate to the Internet, are scary ideas. The issue of safety on the Internet is a real concern to parents. It is dealt with in this book and should certainly make children think about the possible dangers of meeting someone online.

The author provides us with a look into the mind of the obsessed stalker by inserting excerpts from an electronic diary throughout the book. In this manner we see what the killer is doing and thinking as well as what happens to Camy. These chapters really help intensify the emotion and heighten the suspense. We know who the killer is, but will Mina and Mick figure it out?

Mick and Mina's relationship has its moments of humor along the way. They make a good pair, with her sarcastic comments and his calm and unruffled manner. It's also possible to see Mina's potential and strength. *Stalker* is a fast-paced adventure that combines suspense and mystery along with humor and an examination of feelings and relationships. The plot keeps you guessing and then kind of takes your breath away when you learn Camy's fate. It moves quickly and kids will want to read to find out what happens.

System Crash

Michael Coleman and Jason Levy

New York: Bantam Skylark Books, 1998. (http://www.bbd.com/id).
123p. (Internet Detectives #5). ISBN: 0-553-48654-3. Ages 9–12.
Paperback, $3.99.

A blackmail threat has been posted on the Internet by someone calling himself Icarus. Rob Zanelli, Tamsyn Smith, and Josh Allen are in their school's computer lab when they run across a message from Interpol asking for help. The blackmailer has threatened dire consequences for Planet Entertainment theme parks unless his demands are met. Icarus is a 'Net-savvy individual. He's managed to hide his e-mail address and there's no way to trace him. Rob, Josh, and Tamsyn and their three cyber pals—Mitch Zanelli (no relation to Rob) in New York, Lauren King in Toronto, and Tom Peterson from Perth—are trying to find out how to stop this madman.

Rob and his family are just about to leave for vacation in Florida. Tamsyn is going along to help Rob, who is confined to a wheelchair. Josh is staying but will be housesitting for the Zanellis, which gives him access to Rob's computer.

Icarus posts another threat and then strikes at Planet Entertainment in Toronto, where Lauren and her grandmother are spending the day. No one is hurt, but it's obvious the blackmailer means business. Through other coincidences and happenings, plus some good use of the Internet, the friends figure out who Icarus is. They set up a plan to catch him, but something happens and he gets away. Now where is he heading? Which park is the target of his blackmail threat? Can anyone stop him before innocent people are hurt?

System Crash brings the Internet Detectives together again for a mystery that could be a dangerous situation. The Web is a tool to solve their mysteries that allows them to search and locate information about the terrorist. E-mail is used as an important communication tool that keeps everyone involved. By sending a photo of the possible suspect, Tamsyn and Rob can see what he looks like. To discuss what's going on, they use Internet Relay Chat to get interactive communication set up. Even on vacation, Rob and Tamsyn manage to use the computer in the business office of their hotel in Florida.

The main goal of each title in the Internet Detectives series is to solve a problem or mystery. The stories do not involve romance or relationships except among the five friends as they work toward solving the problem that has come up. They do not use sophisticated servers or hacking to solve the mystery, just their knowledge of the Web and other Internet tools that offer a means of communication and a resource for locating information quickly. The books are a light read and will appeal to kids who like the idea of using the Internet to solve mysteries. The main characters are not really very deeply defined, and some of the dialog is a bit stilted, but it's fun to see what happens and how they get there and figure things out before any of the adults do. At this writing, no other title was mentioned in the series.

Virtual Nightmare

S. F. Black

Mahwah, NJ: Troll Communications, 1997. (**http://www.troll.com**). 123p. (Cyber Zone #3). ISBN: 0-8167-4343-6. Ages 9–12. Paperback, $3.95.

It's Halloween and the setting is Sleepy Hollow, the town of the legendary Headless Horseman and Rip Van Winkle. Andy Winkler and his twin sister, Amy, recently moved here with their family when their father took a new job. Andy has made a few friends, three of whom are Mark Harrison, Ray Vandeveer, and Steve Tolbert. There's something strange about these three, Andy thinks. But he's not sure what it is.

Halloween night turns out to be a disaster for Andy when he shows up at the dance dressed up as Rip Van Winkle—along with almost every other gullible student who listened to Mark, Steve, and Ray. Somehow they convinced each of the other students to dress up in the same Rip Van Winkle costume. Andy is furious and storms out of the gym to go home. When he arrives at his house, he realizes his parents are gone for the evening and his sister Amy is still at the dance. Suddenly Andy notices a strange light coming from his room. It's his computer, but Andy knows he shut it off before leaving. He sees the Holloween Home Page displaying with a message snaking across the screen. It's from Steve. As he reads the message, all at once Andy begins to feel sleepy. His eyelids get droopy. It's almost as if he's being hypnotized. Then the Holloween Home Page comes back and the next thing he knows, his room is spinning and he feels he's being sucked into the vortex of a tornado. Suddenly he's in this black tunnel hurtling toward who-knows-where. The spinning stops abruptly and he's deposited onto hard ground. Andy looks up to see his three friends also on the ground. What are they doing here?

This is where the science fiction action begins. Andy has been transported through cyberspace back to Sleepy Hollow during the time of the Headless Horseman. His three friends turn out to be entirely different people than he thought, and Andy must play a dangerous game—and win it—to get back to the present. But the worst is that he has turned into an old man. When he reaches

100, he'll never be able to return. That doesn't leave much time, as Andy seems to grow older much more quickly in this cyberworld. He has only a short time left to solve the riddle and figure out how to return to his former life.

In this plot, the Internet is used as a tool to transport Andy back in time. He literally is sucked into his computer, much like Brooke in *Lost in Dino World*, the second in this series of adventure stories. The World Wide Web is a platform used to allow Andy to communicate with his friends through a chat room. It's also the site of the "Holloween" Home Page, Sleepy Hollow's version of a Halloween Web site where Andy's scary adventure begins. There are twists and turns throughout the story. How will Andy solve the riddles? His memory is not as good since he's aged to almost 85. What if he can't remember people?

The special bond he has with Amy is an important part of the plot. Andy uses a laptop he stole from his three "friends" to communicate with his sister during his journey to solve the puzzle and return home. It's a rather interesting concept to think of being able to use a computer in Sleepy Hollow around the late 1700s, don't you think? But this is science fiction, and kids will enjoy the adventure and root for Andy to solve the riddle so that he can go back to being a 12-year-old.

Unlike other series, this one does not carry over from one book to the next. You don't have to read them in any particular order to understand anything. Each has different characters. They all have one thing in common, however. They use a lot of science fiction and computers and the Internet play a part in the action.

Visitor from the Beyond

S. F. Black

Mahwah, NJ: Troll Communications, 1997. (http://www.troll.com). 126p. (Cyber Zone #6). ISBN: 0-8167-4428-9. Ages 9–12. Softcover, $3.95.

Here's a modern-day ghost story with the Internet as a vehicle for communication. Amanda and Jeff have just moved from New York City to a small town in New Hampshire with their mother and father. Amanda is experiencing culture shock. As a 12-year-old, she loved the city life with its many things to do. They've moved to an old farmhouse left to their father by his great-aunt, Libby. Amanda isn't happy. She liked their cozy New York apartment and this old house is creepy. The house has a history to it. A long time ago, three people died in a fire started in the attic. Rumor has it the house is haunted.

She also misses her best friends, Marriane and Tara. The good news is that Amanda can keep in touch online. Her father has set up her computer so that

Amanda can chat with her friends. The bad news is that she's receiving strange messages that aren't from her friends, and strange sounds and lights are emanating from her computer. Her brother, Jeff, is also getting strange messages, such as "Came to warn you." When Amanda types back, "Who are you?," she sees the word *Ghostweb* dancing on her computer screen.

This is the start of an adventure that has Jeff and Amanda examining their beliefs about ghosts and learning that some things happen that you just can't explain. There is a lot of suspense as Jeff becomes a pawn in the hands of one of the ghosts. Jeff is not in control of his actions at times. Once he sets fire to the grass outside his school. Amanda is deeply worried about her little brother. When Amanda also begins seeing ghostly visions and hearing voices from her computer, she knows she must do something to save her brother and herself.

Cyber Zone books nearly always highlight a relationship between two people, and in this case it's a brother-sister relationship that works very well. You have to care about the people and in this story kids will pull for Jeff and Amanda as they fight the evil "visitor from the beyond."

The Internet aspect of this book is interesting given that the main characters are 12 and 9. Each has a computer in his or her room, and there must be two phone lines, as at one point Amanda gets a phone call while she is online. Chat rooms are part of how she keeps in touch with her New York pals, and it's also how the ghosts communicate with Jeff and Amanda and how she is able to get support at a crucial time in the story. Also, this is a rural area, but Amanda makes friends with a girl at her school who is also on the Internet. Good, fast-moving story that kids will like.

Web Willy in Cyberspace: A Virtual 3-D Adventure

Keith Faulkner; images by Piers Baker

New York: Dial Books for Young Readers, 1998.
(http://www.penguinputnam.com). 20p. ISBN: 0-8037-2285-0.
Ages 9–12. Hardcover, $15.99. (Includes mask for viewing book).

Web Willy is a computer "geek" who loves lime Jell-O, surfing the 'Net, and chatting on the World Wide Web. Willie is chatting one day with his cyber-friend, Jeanette, when he finds a strange message on his computer screen. As he reads it, a strange light appears and Willy is sucked right into his computer. Once inside, he meets Mouse, his guide in cyberspace. Mouse takes him to the Webmaster, who tells Willy that a nasty virus threatens the entire Internet. Willy's programming skills are needed to save cyberspace. Willy realizes that he and Mouse must get to the CPU (central processing unit) where the fiendish virus is most likely heading. Along the way, Willy does battle with some renegade Gigabytes that try to stop him. Willy is helped by some Pixels that form a wall and let Willy "escape" into the CPU. Willy saves the day by throwing his bowl of lime Jell-O on the virus.

Web Willy is lavishly illustrated with bright, fantastic colors. The text is equally colorful and kids will love looking at the bright colors and finding out what happens to Web Willy. To make the adventure even more exciting, there is a mask that can be assembled to provide a 3-D experience. Besides the fun of the adventure, kids can learn something about computers and the Internet as well. There's a lot of Internet jargon along the way, including chatting, e-mail, pixels, mouse, bytes, and CPUs. This book reflects the new world of cyberspace today, as the Internet assumes a prominent role in our lives. A glossary of Internet terms is included.

When the Chips Are Down

Bruce Balan

New York: Avon Books, 1998. (http://www.AvonBooks.com). 168p. (Cyber.kdz #6). ISBN: 0-380-79500-0. Ages 9–12. Paperback, $3.99.

Cyber.kdz mysteries take you to exotic places. *When the Chips Are Down* takes place in India, where we get to know another member of the group, Sanjeev.

Sanjeev's sister, Sarita, argues with her parents over her boyfriend Raj, a crewman on a ship, and runs away to find him. Later that night, the family receives the terrible news that Sarita's bookbag was found on a train that has crashed. No body is found. Sanjeev feels he must find Raj and tell him the awful news.

In his quest to find Raj, Sanjeev stumbles on a very dangerous plot aboard the ship *Star of Asia*. He also finds his supposedly dead sister, alive and tied up in the cargo hold.

Sanjeev is able to hack into the ship's reservation system and books them into a cabin under a false name. He learns that there are indeed boxes of stolen computer chips on the ship. The Cyber.kdz do some research and manage to find out that several companies have reported chips stolen and the likely head of the ring. In a twist of fate, Sanjeev and Sarita find themselves seated at the captain's table, directly across from their prime suspect, Alejandri. Now Sanjeev must figure out a plan to prove that Alejandri is responsible. Sarita and Sanjeev pretend to be in the computer business together, to impress Alejandri. In their quest to bring Alejandri to justice, Sanjeev and Sarita will need to keep their wits about them and the Cyber.kdz will have to lend a hand via the Internet if their friends are to get off the ship alive.

As the plot thickens, the Internet plays a crucial role in the action. E-mail is the main communication tool among the Cyber.kdz. They also use chat rooms to communicate in real time. To help Sanjeev and Sarita, it's necessary for the Cyber.kdz to break into far-away servers. One e-mail message uses the terms *ISP* (Internet service provider) and *overground T3's*. You may feel like you have to whip out your computer dictionary at times. There is no real explanation in plain English about what they're doing, and at the end of the book not all the technical terms are explained. The kids use a lot of slang when communicating: terms like *comm, commbot, flu, GMT, scrunch*, etc. You may want to read the glossary first before reading the story.

The writing has a certain non–United States flavor that gives more character to the kids, who come from several different continents and speak different languages. But sometimes the language seems a bit stilted and the conversation a bit mechanical. Aimed at kids aged 9 to 12 who are interested in the Internet and computers, and who also like a mystery, this book gives an opportunity to combine both interests at one time. It's probably going to be a better read for someone who has a little bit of Internet knowledge and can appreciate all the technology used throughout the book.

Series Included in This Chapter (titles in alphabetical order)

@café

Flavor of the Day
I'll Have What He's Having
Love Bytes
Make Mine to Go

Casebusters

The Internet Escapade

Cyber.kdz

Blackout in the Amazon
The Great NASA Flu
In Pursuit of Picasso
In Search of Scum
A Picture's Worth
When the Chips Are Down

Cybersurfers

Cybercops & Flame Wars
Cyberspace Cowboy
Ghost on the Net
Pirates on the Net

Cyber Zone

Double Trouble
Invasion of the Body Thieves
Lost in Dino World
Meltdown Man
Virtual Nightmare
Visitor from the Beyond

danger.com
Bad Intent
Firestorm
Gemini7
Hot Pursuit
Most Wanted
Shadow Man
Stalker

Deadtime Stories
Cyber Scare

Internet Detectives
Cyber Feud
Escape Key
Net Bandits
Speed Surf
System Crash

Love Stories
It Had to Be You

The Lurker Files
Faceless
Know Fear
Nemesis

The Real Adventures of Jonny Quest
Attack of the Evil Cyber-God

Sweet Valley High
Mystery Date

Chapter 6://Internet Books for Web Page Design and Creation

Introduction

There are many books out today on Web design, Hypertext Markup Language (HTML) authoring, and creating Web pages. In this chapter I have included books that can be used by anyone who wants to learn how to create Web pages. Not many books are available strictly for educators, but whenever possible I have tried to track these down and include them. My choices include practical, hands-on kinds of books. A few go beyond the beginner's stage with Java or JavaScript. Because HTML standards seem to change every so often, the version taught in some titles may have changed. In many cases the titles included are in their second, third, or even fourth edition, so be aware that a newer one may be out. The writing and style should remain the same, with added material and new standards.

Books chosen for this section may be written for various audiences, including the general public, children, librarians, or educators. Any book covering the topic of Web design or HTML is included in this chapter regardless of the targeted audience—educators, parents, and children.

There are a variety of approaches to teaching HTML and these are reflected in the variety of formats found in this chapter. Some books are reference sources listing the tags and examples. Others are broader in scope and cover other issues related to creating a Web page or site. Others are step-by-step tutorials to teach topics in HTML. Others combine HTML tag information with material on creating pages using HTML editors.

Because much Web page creation is now done with software products that handle most of the markup for you, I have included titles for several of the more popular software products, such as PageMill, FrontPage, and Dreamweaver. I have tried to include a mix of platforms as well. Web design is also a large part of successful Web authoring. I have included a couple of titles that take a very practical approach to this issue.

BBEdit 4 for Macintosh

Mark R. Bell

Berkeley, CA: Peachpit Press, 1998.
(http://www.peachpit.com). 240p.
(Visual Quickstart Guide series).
ISBN: 0-201-69659-2. Softcover, $17.95.

More and more people are becoming Web authors today. People are realizing that HTML is not so hard to learn. Along with the proliferation of Web authors comes the growth of software to help with the HTML code. There are any number of popular programs, from basic HTML editors, to graphical user interfaces where you never even have to see the code, to hybrids that do both (let you create without using HTML but also allow you to access the HTML source code). BBEdit started out as a tool that programmers used to write software code for applications. It has now evolved into the premier text editing program for the Macintosh operating system. What makes it so popular is the ability to control the HTML code generated. This is not possible with graphical user interface programs.

There are two versions available: a free downloadable one called BBEdit Lite and the commercial version (BBEdit 4.5.2 at this writing) that sells for about $100.

This guide, from Peachpit's Visual Quickstart series, introduces you to the commercial version. Following the same visual approach of other books in the series, you can learn how to use BBEdit with minimal discussion along with pictures to illustrate the explanations. This book is for the beginner who may be completely new to BBEdit or an experienced user who wants to learn some of the more advanced capabilities of the program.

The guide is divided into four major parts. Part One, "Getting Comfortable with BBEdit," describes what the program is, hardware and software requirements, how to get a copy of the program, and how to install it and customize its features. After setting it up, you'll learn all about manipulating and working with text features such as searching for and replacing text—a really nice feature of this program. Think of the time saved for replacing tags and changing attributes when you have to maintain HTML documents.

Part Two, "Creating a Web Site with BBEdit," contains an HTML primer in case you are new to writing with HTML code. If you're already familiar with HTML you can skip this section or just read the parts to know more about it.

BBEdit uses a series of plug-ins to create and change HTML code simply. You'll learn all about BBEdit's HTML tools palette—how to configure it and use its features in sophisticated ways. Among other topics are templates, placeholders, and how to create tables with the Table Builder. Part Three, "Extending BBEdit," takes you further into the capabilities of the program to describe utilities, plug-ins, and how to use Internet Config and set preferences for e-mail, news, and the Web, among others. Maybe you are really ambitious and want to do a little scripting on your own. If so, the final chapter of the book, "Scripting," will take you through how to use AppleScript.

The book contains seven helpful appendices. "Menu Items" lists and describes what's available. "Preferences" helps you see what's possible so that you can customize BBEdit for your needs. "Additional Tools" describes additional "companion programs" that you may choose to add to your program. "Special Characters" lists the various characters from the "HTML Resource Guide." "Color Chart" highlights the hexadecimal code; "HTML Resource Guide" gives basic information about tags.

Written in a friendly style with easy-to-understand language, you can use this guide as a tutorial or pick it up to find a specific answer to a question about using BBEdit. If you are new to BBEdit, there's a certain learning curve when it gets to some of the more complicated aspects of the program. You'll also have to purchase the software, as there is no CD or floppy disk with the book. BBEdit is one of the most popular HTML tools for the Macintosh. If you're serious about learning how to make the most of its features, this guide will allow you to do just that.

Beginner's Handbook: Developing Web Pages for School and Classroom

Susan Hixon and Kathleen Schrock

Westminster, CA: Teacher Created Materials, 1998.
(http://www.teachercreated.com). 256p.
ISBN: 1-57690-195-5. Softcover, $19.95.

There are a lot of HTML books out there to help learn how to get started with Web pages. This one is written especially for educators who want to develop Web pages for their school or classroom. For educators who have been thinking about doing some Web publishing for their class or school but aren't exactly sure how to get it off the ground or convince administrators of the benefits, this book provides all the ammunition necessary to get going.

Kathy Schrock and Susan Hixon are two educators who know what they are talking about. Schrock developed a form for evaluating Web sites that is used by many people to teach how to evaluate and know what to look for in Web sites. Susan Hixon developed an Internet resource site for teachers. Both have been around the classroom and Internet for a number of years.

The book is divided into eight parts that cover background information and then delve into the actual hands-on practice of creating Web pages. Each part contains several sections devoted to specific topics. Part One, "Reasons for Having a Web Page," is an excellent introduction to all the benefits derived from beginning to publish on the Web. Why should students publish on the Web? Think about what it might do for their creativity and interest in learning. Imagine having people other than just your teacher read your work! Getting feedback from readers is exciting and motivating to children.

What about teachers? They can publish resource sites for other teachers and share in the benefits of creating Web sites that help others. The authors include online links that help show exactly what other educators and schools have done. There are screen shots of school pages and descriptions of teaching projects that help illustrate the background information.

The authors list specific reasons for having Web pages, such as telecommunications projects, facilitating communication, and enhancing home-school communication. Within these discussions are more details about specific projects and activities. The material is really a gold mine of information, illustrating why getting a class involved in Web publishing is worth the effort.

Part Two, "Questions to Answer Before Beginning," describes how schools can benefit, offers suggestions for deciding on a direction, tells how Web pages can enhance student achievement, and more. Again, Web sites serve as examples of successful implementation by schools already publishing on the Web.

Besides the big picture, it's important to have a focus on the class or project home page as well. What is the benefit to creating a home page? How does it help integrate new resources?

Once you decide on creating a Web site, it's important to decide how to administer it. Who will decide about content matter or contribute material? What about the quality of the content? Design? There are many questions that may arise throughout the process. Part Three, "Planning Pages," offers ways to effectively plan the content and layout of Web pages. Here are details on naming pages, with templates that assist in the overall design. Web addresses of exemplary sites are available as further resources. This section is very helpful, with lots of good information about those important details so necessary in the beginning of the process.

Part Four, "Collecting and Organizing Information," gives a step-by-step approach to collecting material and creating graphics. Scans of ready-made graphics can work. Teacher-created or student-created graphics are another option, along with free graphics. There are details on all of these choices. Part Five, "Creating a Web Page," moves through the basics of HTML, using templates, HTML, and editors to create Web pages. The step-by-step directions tell how to look at the source code for a Web page and alter it to particular specifications. Getting a feel for what a Web page looks like, in its HTML format, creates confidence to go ahead and create original pages. HTML topics include tags, graphics, hyperlinks, creating a new page, text colors and background colors, and tables. There are troubleshooting tips as well.

Another option is to use a Web page editor to create pages easily and without knowing HTML. This chapter lists suggested editors and offers examples of the various programs that do this. The section on HTML codes and tips presents the various tags with examples.

Part Seven, "Showing Your Page to the World," discusses how to publish pages locally as well as on an Internet server. There are also tips on how to get people to visit your site. After all the hard work, that's an important factor. Part Eight, "Appendices," offers evaluation guides for students, a glossary of terms, bibliographic citation formats for various grade levels, an index of URLs, and suggestions for the next step. A bibliography of books and resources is included as well, along with several pages that can be used for notes.

This is a well-organized and well-written book. The approach is practical and obviously comes from people who understand the educational environment. Throughout the book are screen shots and sidebars called "Snapshot from the Classroom," which present first-hand descriptions of actual classroom examples. These snapshots help illustrate how a point under discussion was actually implemented.

Some books may take a more research-oriented or theoretical approach; that's fine, but they are often not very practical. This book supplies both the theory and practical material. Educators can read it and say "I can do that." It's the kind of book that teachers can use because it's full of details—things that might have been overlooked. It's easy to see the authors know what they are talking about. They've thought of just about everything involved in creating Web pages in an educational environment.

The Complete Idiot's Guide to Creating an HTML 4 Web Page, 3d Edition

Paul McFedries

Indianapolis, IN: Que, 1998. (http://www.mcp.com/publishers/que/). 352p. (The Complete Idiot's Guide to ... series). ISBN: 0-7897-1490-6. Softcover, $24.99. (Includes CD-ROM).

After learning how to "surf the Web" and looking at great Web sites, some people are inspired to create their own Web pages—but don't have a clue how to do it. Here's a book that takes you through the entire process so that you'll be a Web publisher before you know it.

Maybe the first hurdle is buying a book that seems to say "*I'm* an idiot." This successful series has sold many, many books. Here's yet another written with the customary friendly approach to teaching a computer topic. The approach is light and casual. This is not to imply that the guide is a "lightweight" at all. It covers everything you need to know to start creating interesting Web pages.

This third edition expands the previous one by including updated HTML codes (style sheets and codes supported by Internet Explorer, Netscape, Java, JavaScript, and more) plus an introduction to Personal Web Server, Office 97 HTML features, and more.

The book's purpose is twofold: to provide you with a reference tool if you already possess some level of HTML experience and as a source to be read cover-to-cover if you need a tutorial from scratch. Three main parts make up the book. Part One is "Creating Your First HTML Web Page"; followed by Part Two, "A Grab Bag of Web Page Wonders"; and Part Three, "Painless Page Production: Easier Ways to Do the HTML Thing."

Beginning with an overview of HTML—what it is and what it does—the material moves along to basic tags and creating a very first home page. Moving through the components in a logical and organized manner, the topics build upon each other. There are features to help catch your attention when an important point is made. "Check This Out" and "Technical Twaddle" help you recognize tips, notes, and asides as well as technical points along the way.

As mentioned, humor runs throughout the book. Take a look at a few chapter titles, such as "From Buck Naked to Beautiful: Dressing Up Your Page," which tells you how to add some zip to a page with headings, spacing, and text features. "A Picture Is Worth a Thousand Clicks: Working with Images" takes you through the steps to add images to a page. "A Fistful of List Grist for Your Web Page Mill" explores how to create several types of lists. "Making Your Web Pages Dance and Sing" covers animated GIFs and multimedia topics.

Subsequent chapters take you through links, tables, forms, and frames, plus more. The chapter called "Netscape and Internet Explorer HTML Extensions" gives you a look at some of the attributes used by these two browsers. Basic design to create effective and interesting work, something everyone needs to know about, is taught in another chapter. For the more industrious, you can learn how to run your own Web server using Microsoft's Personal Web Server.

Several chapters that describe HTML editors and Web page software are particularly helpful. It's nice to know about the options available if you want to go to a program that takes some of the repetitive coding out of the creation of Web pages. The author has selected a nice variety of products, including Netscape Composer, Office 97 HTML tools, and Microsoft FrontPage.

Throughout the guide, the step-by-step directions help you cover the material in a very self-paced manner. McFedries does an excellent job of always mentioning how to obtain the software used in a particular chapter, whether it's shareware or not.

The accompanying CD-ROM contains a Web page publishing toolkit with software for Web managers, Internet Explorer 4, many Web graphics, Internet Knowledge Base, Web page/HTML editors, graphic software, Adobe Acrobat Reader, and other helper applications. The book also has a home page that offers updates and supplementary material not included in the book.

Appendices include "Speak Like a Geek Glossary," "Browser Basics: Surfing with Navigator and Explorer," "HTML Codes for Cool Characters," and "The CD: The Webmaster's Toolkit." The approach taken by McFedries may not be for everyone. Many of the other HTML books out there take a more serious approach to the topic, and if you don't want humor in your learning material, then this book isn't for you. But if you want to have a smile on your face as you increase your knowledge of HTML, and like a good laugh now and then, pick up a copy. You won't be disappointed.

Creating Web Pages for Dummies, 2d Edition

Bud Smith and Arthur Bebak

Indianapolis, IN: IDG Books Worldwide, 1997.
(http://www.idgbooks.com/). 380p. (...for Dummies series).
ISBN: 0-7645-0114-3. Softcover, $24.99.

Another title in the entertaining and informative "...for Dummies" series. This one will teach you all about how to publish a Web page. Targeted to almost anyone, whether a beginner or with some experience, the book is meant to be used more as a reference tool than a cover-to-cover read. You can pick and choose chapters depending on your level of knowledge. With the same easy-to-read style and humor as others in the series, it makes the process of learning Web publishing fun.

Divided into six parts including the appendices, Part One is an introductory "Getting Started with Web Publishing" that covers Internet basics and the World Wide Web. It presents issues you need to consider when starting out as a Web author and points out the importance of deciding what you want your Web site to be. Also covered are the basics of HTML and why it's good to know a little of it. There are step-by-step directions for creating a basic Web document, including tags, making lists, links, and more. But you may find you need another HTML reference guide if you want to get serious about learning HTML code, because this is not an HTML book.

Part Two is titled "Put a Résumé or Home Page on the Web" and really covers using a Web publishing service to get a résumé. Using GeoCities free personal Web pages, the authors take you through the process of creating a Web page. It's in the form of a tutorial, so you'll need to have a connection to the Internet to follow along. The remaining chapters discuss using other online services for getting published.

Part Three helps you make "Better, Stronger, Faster Web Sites." Learn how to spruce up your site by adding forms, tables, and additional pages, as well as how to set goals for your site. Even though the focus is a business site, the information can be applied to any site as far as adding pizzazz and making your Web site noticed.

Part Four, "Web Publishing Tools," is very helpful in introducing you to the many excellent choices for a Web authoring tool. Beginning with an explanation about the various types of tools and how to evaluate them, there are detailed chapters on Netscape Navigator Gold (now known as Netscape Communicator), PageMill, HotDog Pro, and BBEdit. High-end tools such as Microsoft FrontPage are discussed in a later chapter. All in all, this section is a jewel for learning how to select, evaluate, and use a Web authoring tool. As in other Dummies guides, there is a part called "The Part of Tens." In this book it's all about the do's and don'ts of Web publishing. Part Six is a compilation of useful appendices, including a glossary, Web service providers, a quick guide to HTML, and a description of what's on the CD.

Another title in the Dummies series, *Web Publishing for Teachers*, targets the education community, whereas this title does not. The software selected here and the options for creating and publishing your Web site are not geared to the teacher. Still, there is a lot of useful information; depending on what your goals are, you may want to consider a more general title like this.

Dreamweaver 1.2 for Windows & Macintosh

J. Tarin Towers

Berkeley, CA: Peachpit Press, 1998.
(http://www.peachpit.com/vqs/dreamweaver). 375p.
(Visual Quickstart Guide series). ISBN: 0-201-35339-3.
Softcover, $18.95.

Producing Web pages today can be complicated if you want to add some of the jazzy new features to your site. A few years ago, all you needed was a text editor and some knowledge of HTML to create a very nice Web page. It's the way a lot of people began. Next, along came some helpful HTML tools that made creating pages simpler. You could do it even without learning HTML. Dreamweaver has taken the next step by introducing a package that lets you take a WYSIWYG (what-you-see-is-what-you-get) approach where you never have to look at HTML code—or you can choose to work with the code as well. *Dreamweaver for Windows & Macintosh* is another entry in the Visual Quick Start Guide series produced by Peachpit. It takes a visual approach to teaching a topic, with lots of illustrations accompanied by step-by-step directions. If you've decided to try out Dreamweaver, then having a concise, easy-to-follow tutorial guide will help you get up to speed in no time.

The book can be used by just about anyone who wants to learn to use the tool. Whether you are a beginner with no HTML experience, or a veteran HTML author who simply wants to automate some of the work, or a designer who wants a tool to create HTML documents, this well-written and practical book will give you all you need. If you're just starting out, move through the chapters one at a time in sequence. Otherwise, use it as a reference tool if you already have some experience with Dreamweaver. Just locate the topic and go right to work on the area you want to learn about. The companion Web site makes it easy to locate further resources, more examples, and links to Web sites for additional help.

The book's 16 chapters cover the very basics needed for understanding Dreamweaver's environment; then they move on to opening an HTML file, working and saving your file, opening in a browser, and creating templates. "All about Text" helps you work with fonts, colors, and the various text styles of HTML, such as logical and physical styles. You will learn how to create tables, forms, links, and frames the Dreamweaver way. Besides the working of Dreamweaver, there are also little tidbits about HTML as you go along. What's a gif or a JPEG when working with images? How do you pronounce them? When working with links, there's an explanation about relative and absolute links. All of this can help when creating a page. If you understand what's going on in the background, things sometimes make more sense.

The more sophisticated topics, such as style sheets and dynamic HTML, are also treated. JavaScript is a programming language, but you'll learn how to use Dreamweaver's Behavior tools to apply JavaScript actions without having to write any script yourself. As you get into these more complicated components, there is a learning curve. Obviously, if you've heard about style sheets and JavaScript and have a notion as to what they are, you'll better understand what's happening. But the directions are very straightforward, walking you through the necessary steps for each action.

If you've chosen Dreamweaver as your HTML authoring tool, then having a guide like this will get you going as quickly as you want. The self-paced organization lets you work at your own speed, as fast or as slow as you like. Just prop this little book up next to your computer and go to it.

Easy Web Publishing with HTML 3.2

Jonah Neugass

Indianapolis, IN: Que, 1997. (**http://www.mcp.com/publishers/que/**).
181p. ISBN: 0-7897-1143-5. Softcover, $24.99.

This book seems to promise a lot, with its step-by-step directions and colorful illustrations laid out on the pages. It looks like a wonderful way to teach beginners about HTML. Unfortunately, there are some glitches along the way. As happens too often with changes to software and programs, step-by-step directions don't necessarily fit anymore.

Beware. The author does not say you have to use a Windows machine, but the whole guide is geared to that platform. Saving files, using WordPad and other software, plus all key combinations are all Windows conventions. There is no reason a Macintosh user can't learn HTML with this book, but you will need to be comfortable with simple text, saving files, and translating directions to the Mac environment (Command-C for copy), because no Mac equivalents are given in the book. You won't be able to upload files in the chapter on downloading if you aren't familiar with a Mac version of FTP software.

The book begins with the very basics of HTML tags, working up through the more complex topics like frames, image maps, and animations. Explanations are simple and easy to understand. Directions are numbered and contain screen shots to illustrate the directions. But you may need to pull out your magnifying glass or reading glasses to read what's on them; the print is tiny.

One thing to watch out for is the carriage return symbol that appears to be inserted after some of the step-by-step directions. If you truly know nothing about HTML, you may try to figure out what that symbol is, to type it, or you may think you have to put in a carriage return. There is really no need for this, as HTML does not care about line spacing. It would have been helpful if the author had covered this fact in the introduction and explained about the symbols.

There was also a glitch when it came to inserting graphics and then viewing them in Netscape. The exercise takes you through inserting the image and indicates that your screen should look like the example, with the bright shining graphic appearing at the top left of the page. This won't happen unless you have that image loaded on your computer. The author never tells you this. The page simply showed the dreaded question-mark graphic that indicates the browser can't find the image. The problem is that there is no explanation anywhere telling you about images having to be on your server when inserted without a complete Web address.

Each exercise builds from the previous one using the HTML files created. So, if you want to try the frames part, but have not done the basics, you will have to reconstruct those HTML documents. This book is really a basic introduction to HTML, as implied in the title "Easy Web Publishing...." However, sometimes there is just not enough information to help if things don't work out when you follow the exercise.

Home Page: An Introduction to Web Page Design (A First Book)

Christopher Lampton

New York: Franklin Watts, 1997. (**http://ig.grolier.com/**).
64p. ISBN: 0-531-20255-0. Library binding, $6.95.

HTML (Hypertext Markup Language) sounds like a programming language and the word "programming" can strike fear into the hearts of grownups. How hard can it be if there is a book that teaches children nine and up to create Web pages using HTML?

Learning HTML is really very easy. It's also fun, and kids will enjoy the thrill of seeing something they have worked on come to life.

Beginning with the parts of a simple HTML document, the author explains the concept behind it and demonstrates the code. Colorful screen shots make it possible to view the results of the work when opened in Netscape. With this book's tutorial-like approach, children can follow along and learn step-by-step how to create basic Web pages. Though written for children, the book does not talk down to its users.

Assuming some basic computer skills, such as using a mouse, saving files, and opening programs, the author does offer tips on how to get help if users get stuck. Computer concepts such as multitasking are explained. Also, Lampton points out that creating Web pages does not require being connected to the Internet. They can be stored on a hard disk.

Lampton takes kids logically through the process of Web authoring. Using the idea of a template, a simple document is created, saved, and opened in Netscape. Basic tags, such as creating paragraphs, making headings, and formatting text, are covered first. Then kids are encouraged to "go for it" and create some of their own pages.

In the next chapter, a few more advanced features allow children to jazz up their pages with some hyperlinks and images. Although sound, animation, and other advanced features are not covered, this well-written little book is a jewel for kids who want to learn to build a home page. Actually, as a parent or teacher, you might want to read along with your child, so you too can master the skills for HTML authoring. The same concepts taught here are what anyone learning HTML needs to master—just packaged in a kid-friendly wrapping. A glossary, suggestions for further reading, and an index are included.

Home Sweet Home Page and the Kitchen Sink

Robin Williams with Dave Mark

Berkeley, CA: Peachpit Press, 1997. (http://www.peachpit.com).
208p. ISBN: 0-201-88680-4. Softcover, $24.95. (Includes CD-ROM).

This book isn't just a book of Web design and it's not just a guide to the Internet. So it was more problematic deciding where to put it. But since the goal is to create a family Web page, the design chapter seemed the best place.

The authors wrote this book to help families learn to use the Web as a communication tool. The five main parts of the book include Part One, "What's It All About?," featuring chapters on electronic mail, the Internet, and the World Wide Web. Here is where the authors present an introduction to the Internet, explaining all about service providers, how to access the Internet, and how to use the World Wide Web for e-mail, FTP, and browsing. The goal is to make people comfortable with the exciting vehicles the Internet offers for communication.

Because e-mail is still the most popular use of the Internet, a nice discussion and breakdown of how to use it are featured, with sections on addresses along with examples from online services to illustrate what e-mail looks like.

The Web illustrates another means of communication by allowing people to publish and distribute information. The discussion of the main concepts of hypertext, finding links, and understanding Web addresses provides a good foundation. Locating information with search tools, as well as navigating and keeping up with sites, are also covered. The friendly, conversational style will appeal to beginners who may perceive the Internet as a scary place.

Part Two, "Before and After," introduces how to get set up to create a Web page, the tools needed, how to get organized, and how to publish your Web pages. The Web is treated as a publishing tool. It's now possible for people to publish whatever they want, and the author sees this as a boon to families who want to keep in touch. To create a Web page, it's necessary to use certain tools. HTML can be learned, but the authors believe that using HTML authoring software is the way to go for most people who want to get a site up and running. Other topics covered include graphics programs, helper applications, file formats, how to organize and name your Web pages, good Web design, and what to do when you finish your creation and want to get it published. Part Three, "Get Ready, Get Set," gets down to some of the details involved in creating a Web site. Here are tips such as creating a map of your site, with examples of what one might look like. Next comes writing the text that you want to include, creating graphics, and designing the pages. The chapters look at how you can spruce up a Web page with special fonts and color. Essentially, you'll learn what makes a good Web page and what doesn't.

Part Four, "Simply Great Projects," actually provides step-by-step directions for creating several projects, including a first home page, a family history, a photo album, a family newsletter, a calendar of events, recipes, family reunions, special occasions, and more. These are a great way for the novice to get started. The projects provide a look at what's possible. The directions are easy to follow and the CD that accompanies the book provides access to much of the software needed to get started. Part Five, "The Stuff at the End," focuses on advanced projects as well as how to get connected using the software on the accompanying CD-ROM. A handy review of the entire process is also featured. You can locate the exact steps necessary and go back to the pages where they were described. It's a nice summary of what went on. If you already have a connection, then you can skip the final few pages. They're there to tell you how to make the connection, with some tips on specific things to remember. There are specific directions for using various online services. Both Macintosh and Windows access are presented.

Besides the information presented in the five main parts, the CD-ROM has connection software for several online services, a collection of clip art designed for this book, graphical icons, bars and buttons to spruce up pages, fonts, and a Macintosh demo version of PageMill. There is also a Web site you can visit for updates.

The focus is family and the language is very friendly and jargon-free. With this book in hand, a family can work together to create their own Web site, making it a family affair. The projects are simple yet creative, making the learning experience fun for all members of the family.

How to Create Great School Web Pages

Ann E. Barron, David H. Tai, and Brendan Tompkins

Lancaster, PA: Classroom Connect, 1997. (http://www.classroom.net).
248p. No ISBN available. Looseleaf, $89.00. (Includes CD-ROM).

Many schools are becoming aware of the benefits of creating a school Web site. But it's often difficult to get started or to know how to begin. Here is a guide that takes you through the whole process of creating school Web pages. Divided into 12 chapters, this step-by-step guide covers everything from beginning HTML to advanced topics such as Java and publishing your pages.

The book begins with an overview of the World Wide Web, the growth of school-based Web sites, advantages of creating Web pages, and issues to be dealt with (such as copyright, safety, security, and control issues). The next 10 chapters cover all that's necessary to build Web pages, beginning with the concept of HTML and discussing options for creating Web pages using WYSIWYG HTML programs, text editors, and converters. Written in 1997, there are now more examples of editors to choose from, including Microsoft FrontPage and Claris HomePage, along with newer versions of the tools mentioned in the book.

HTML is introduced step-by-step, starting with the simplest step: putting text on a page, formatting the styles, adding space, and changing the font. As each concept is introduced and explained, sample HTML is shown, along with how it would appear when viewed in a browser. Hyperlinks are covered in detail and treated in a very easy-to-understand way. Internal links, linking to different protocols, design guidelines, and choosing colors are all covered. A quick reference guide follows, with examples of links for a local page, remote page, target, e-mail, and more. This is a handy source to have and to look back on for quick help.

What makes Web pages exciting is the ability to use images and even multimedia. This may be a bit advanced for some, but is worth the extra time to master. Here, the process is explained and illustrated so that it flows along with the rest of the material covered and fits logically into the process of learning to design pages. The multimedia section offers a quick tutorial on the various formats and converters used for each type. A very helpful resource section provides links to sites that offer sound archives, MIDI resources, movie archives, and players. Tables, frames, and forms are also covered. Java and JavaScript are introduced but not discussed in detail, as these are programming languages and need a lot more effort to learn than this guide can supply. Still, there is a nice introduction and explanation so that you have more information to decide if it's something you wish to invest your time in. The bonus WebPage Creation CD-ROM that accompanies the book contains a great deal of Web-ready clip art, Web page examples, and other resources to get started creating Web pages.

At $89.00, this guide is quite pricey. There is not much in it that can't be found in other sources at less cost. However, there are some pluses, such as the way it is organized and builds upon each concept along the way, just as if you were creating a Web page. And, of course, it is geared to the school environment, with sources and resources for educators.

HTML Activities: Webtop Publishing on the Superhighway

Karl Barksdale, Eugene Paulson, Gary Ashton, and Earl Jay Stephens

Cincinnati, OH: South-Western Educational Publishing.
(http://www.swep.com). 192p. ISBN: 0-538-67458-X.
Spiral notebook, $24.95.

The World Wide Web is an important communication tool today. Creating Web pages is something that more and more people are learning. It's a skill that can help you communicate information. *HTML Activities* is a book in spiral notebook format that guides you through the process of learning HTML. The notebook format makes it easy to keep the book next to your computer while you go through the activities. The lessons don't require a lot of software or fast Internet connections to learn HTML. To use this book, you simply need a text editor, such as NotePad for Windows or SimpleText for the Macintosh. An Internet connection is not required but is beneficial. It's possible to create the files and display them locally. The "Introduction" explains some facts about Web publishing and how it fits into publishing in general. There's also a look at what Web publishing can do and the benefits of learning it.

The material is divided into three "sectors." Sector 1 is "HTML Quick Start," which gets you up and on the Web in no time using basic HTML. Here is where you will learn all the basic tags for creating a simple page, and then move on through creating space or formatting the look of your document with lists, headings, etc. As you progress through the other chapters, you'll learn about hyperlinks and images and how attributes work with tags.

Sector 2, "Tools of HTML Professionals," takes it a step further by introducing HTML editors as tools for creating Web pages. The goal is to build up your confidence level and skills at the same time. This is a good section on analyzing various HTML editors, and looking at how they work in relation to word-processing software. You'll also be able to evaluate editors to see which type is best for you. A detailed tutorial for using Internet Assistant for Word is provided. However, the Web address to download the software has changed. You can still find it by going to the Microsoft site and then searching for Internet Assistant. If you try the address in the book, you'll get the dreaded error message.

To complete the next section, you'll need to have Internet Assistant installed. Sector 3, "Webtop Publishing on the Superhighway," goes beyond basic Web page creation to look at design issues and learn how professionals do it.

Each sector has several chapters along with hands-on exercises containing step-by-step directions. You'll be guided by a little cartoon character, Mark Web, Investigative Reporter for *HTML Webtop Times*, as you work through the chapters. There are numerous easy-to-read screen shots. Each chapter states a set of objectives at the beginning. At the end of the chapter are "Debriefings," which allow you to reflect on what you've learned. "Extensions" give you a chance to move beyond the material and try something extra; a "Table of Tags" summarizes the tags discussed.

The chapters move from the basics on up through using an editor to create pages and finally to a more sophisticated look at designing Web sites. The chapters are written in a straightforward way—no "techno-babble" here. If a step-by-step approach to learning HTML is your cup of tea, this guide will get you up to speed with HTML tags, editors, and the elements of good design. A couple of things are out of date, such as the name Netscape Gold (it's now Communicator), and there's a definition of the tag <IMG SRC> that seems suspect to me. I've always seen it stand for image source, but in this book the authors say it's image "search."

There is an accompanying Web site for the book, too. Appendices include a "Summary of Table Tags" and "Getting Your Pages Published or 'Posted' on the World Wide Web." A glossary is also included.

HTML for the World Wide Web, 2d Edition

Elizabeth Castro

Berkeley, CA: Peachpit Press, 1997. (http://www.peachpit.com).
263p. (Visual Quickstart Guide series). ISBN: 0-201-68862-X.
Softcover, $7.95.

Authoring Web pages is something anyone can do. It really is. But if you are intimidated by the thought of HTML, try this user-friendly book with its simple-to-follow directions and you'll be ready to go with your own Web pages. Even if you know something about HTML tags and code, this makes a handy reference tool.

First, the author goes into some background information about the Web and HTML and how they work together. You'll learn how HTML works in relation to a browser, as well as a little about HTML standards versus new features added by browsers like Netscape and Internet Explorer.

Castro's guide covers everything you'll need to get started creating Web pages, beginning with the basics of a Web address and HTML tags and moving all the way up to inserting movies/audio and using style sheets. There's also a section on getting your Web page published.

Information is presented in a clear, concise, and—most importantly—easy-to-understand manner. Castro uses very helpful screen shots alongside the material she is teaching to illustrate many of the tags. This is an effective method for reinforcing the material. But beware: you may have to pull out your reading glasses, as the graphics are a bit small and the print on them difficult to read.

Several valuable appendices include HTML editor tools, a chart featuring available HTML editors, special symbol tags, colors and hexadecimals, and a handy HTML compatibility guide. There is an extremely nice index to show you the colors along with their hexadecimal equivalents.

This capable guide serves a dual purpose: as a basic, step-by-step tutorial for new Web authors or as a very nice reference tool for more experienced ones. Be sure to get the latest edition. By the time you read this, a later edition will already be out.

HTML: The Definitive Guide

Chuck Musciano and Bill Kennedy

Sebastopol, CA: O'Reilly & Associates, 1997. (http://www.ora.com/).
552p. ISBN: 1-56592-235-2. Softcover, $32.95.

This second edition of this popular guide to creating HTML pages was released in 1998, with only minor changes. *The Definitive Guide* is what its name implies, an in-depth treatment of HTML 3.2. It's not simply a reference tool, nor is it really a tutorial. The book is written for anyone—from the absolute beginner with no HTML or even Web experience, to the experienced Web surfer with no HTML background, to the experienced designer. However, beginners may find the writing style a bit boring. There's really no humor and it's certainly not a lighthearted approach to the subject. No cartoons, no comical chapter headings. For those who like humor along with their technical learning, the Dummies or Idiot's series of books will probably better meet your needs.

To use the book, the only requirements are a computer, a text editor to create simple ASCII files, and a copy of the latest software of either Netscape or Internet Explorer. What makes the book "definitive" is that it "gives details for all the elements of the HTML standard, plus the variety of interesting and useful extensions to the language and some proposed standards the popular browsers have included." The authors caution about wandering too far from the accepted standard of HTML. There's a lot of interesting and useful information about the whole concept of HTML standards.

If you are a complete beginner, read chapter 1, "HTML and the World Wide Web," which introduces them and considers what HTML is, the question of standards, and a bit about HTML tools. Otherwise, skip to chapter 2, "HTML Quick Start," which introduces all of the HTML elements that will be covered in detail later on. The author recommends reading through this even if you have some HTML authoring experience. It's a nice overview of everything in a nutshell. The remainder of the chapters cover each topic in detail, working from basics about text elements to images, links, lists, forms, tables, frames, and the newer cascading style sheets.

Because Java is not part of HTML, it's not covered in depth. But there is a section on Java style sheets and JavaScript in chapter 13, "Executable Content." Applets are also described here. These are, obviously, more advanced features and will take a little time to learn. The chapters progress from the basic concepts up through the more advanced features if you read through chapter by chapter. There are not a lot of examples of HTML put into use, and it's not a tutorial with step-by-step directions. It's more of a reference or sourcebook.

If you just want to put together a few Web pages, and want some basics or need a step-by-step tutorial about HTML, or need some advice about which editors to use, then don't buy this book. If you want a lighter approach with a more casual writing style, you will probably not like this book. But if you want a straightforward, no-nonsense reference source that covers HTML in depth, then consider purchasing this book.

HTML 3.2 Quick Reference, 2d Edition

Thomas Cirtin, ed.

Indianapolis, IN: Que, 1997. (http://www.mcp.com/publishers/que/).
234p. ISBN: 0-7897-1144-3. Softcover, $19.99.

If you are looking for a tutorial or step-by-step guide to learning HTML, this isn't the book for you. However, it is a book for anyone who wants a complete reference to HTML tags and standards. The book is a quick and easy-to-use tool for learning some basic knowledge of HTML.

The book contains five parts, including "Quick Tables," "HTML Reference Section," "HTML Reference Tables," and a glossary. The "HTML Reference Section" is the meat of the book, containing an entry for every accepted element or tag plus those that appear to be on the way to acceptance. The entries are in alphabetical order and contain a compliance part, syntax, a definition, category (when applicable), and syntax example. The "HTML Reference Tables" provide HTML references for elements and symbols, with the binary as well as textual code, plus a description of the element and what it displays on the screen. In other words, if you want an ampersand to appear on your Web page, here's the table to give you the code to do it. This is a handy table if you want to insert specific characters and symbols into your Web document. Color tables and their hexadecimal codes plus text name are also part of this section. You'll have to guess what the color looks like—no colored pages are included. If you want an up-to-date compendium of HTML, including Microsoft and Netscape extensions along with the newest tags to keep by your computer for those Web page updates, here's a thorough and well-organized book that seems to be updated regularly.

Instant HTML: Programmer's Reference (HTML 4.0 Edition)

Alex Homer, Chris Ullman, and Steve Wright

Chicago, IL: Wrox Press, 1997. (http://www.wrox.com/).
448p. ISBN: 1-861001-56-8. Softcover, $19.95.

Designed as a quick reference tool for HTML authors, this guide takes Web developers from the basics of HTML (such as text formatting) through more advanced topics (including tables, forms, and even more sophisticated concepts such as inserting objects into a page) to dynamic HTML, JavaScript, and Java. It covers all versions of HTML, including 4.0 (the latest at this writing, and now recommended). The book does assume a knowledge of and familiarity with the Internet and the World Wide Web. It also covers extensions from Netscape and Internet Explorer. The book can be used either as a tutorial or as a reference source. Beginners will want to cover the material in a pretty systematic manner, as it moves from simple basics to much more advanced topics. Those with more experience using HTML can read it as a quick guide to HTML code.

Appendix A is the reference section and includes all HTML element tags in alphabetical order. The versions of HTML, which browsers use them, and all attributes associated with the tags are included. This is a handy reference source for those who want to look up something quickly.

The 12 chapters contain step-by-step directions taking you through the concept being taught, with helpful screen shots to illustrate points. This is a serious book with no gratuitous illustrations, cartoons, or photos. It keeps to the material necessary to teach the subject and uses a clear writing style. Other appendices include "HTML Element Tags by Category," "Special Characters in HTML," "HTML Color Names and Values," "The VBScript Language," "JavaScript Reference," and "Style Sheet Properties."

It's not geared to educators. It really has a more professional feel to it. But don't be put off by the "programmer's" in the title. Although the topics do expand to very complex HTML concepts, anyone who is past the basics of Web design and ready to move on to more meaty stuff will also find this reference guide an excellent source.

Internet Web Pages for Teachers and Students with JavaScript

Richard J. Kitto

London, Ontario: KS Publications, 1997. (**http://www.kspub.com**).
171p. ISBN: 0-9682790-2-3. Spiral notebook, $32.95.

This self-guided workbook is written for teachers who want to begin creating their own Web pages. It uses Windows 3.1 as the platform (Windows 95 will work as well), Netscape 3.0 (any browser is acceptable), and in several chapters employs the programs Paint Shop Pro, Web HotSpots, and GIF Construction Set. Trial versions of all these are available for downloading on the Web. A "Shopping List" on the first page of the chapter supplies the information about the tools necessary to complete the exercises.

Chapter 1, "Checking It Out," begins with an explanation of the Internet (of course) and includes a brief history to show how it evolved to where it is today, with the World Wide Web as the essential tool for exploring. Next, Web pages are explained, as well as how the Web works. A nice graphic illustrates the hyperlinks concept visually and effectively. Browsers and their features, along with some of the buttons and menu bars from Netscape, are briefly described. Other topics include client-server relationships, search engines, and other tools accessible with the Internet, such as mail, downloading files (FTP), and Internet Relay Chat (IRC). Finally, a brief set of Netiquette rules and a timeline of the Internet complete this chapter. As introductory chapters go, the information seems to flow in a very well-organized manner. Understanding how things began and evolved and knowing the basic facts about the Web are necessary if you are going to create Web pages. There is not a lot of information about each topic, but enough to give you the essentials. The language is very readable and easy to follow. Explanations are nontechnical.

Chapter 2, "Starting Your Own Web Page," explores HTML. Again, this is a well-written and well-illustrated section. Remember that if you are using another version of Netscape or another browser, some of the directions for opening, viewing, and saving files may be slightly different. As basic HTML tags are introduced, screen shots reproduce the results as seen in Netscape. The next chapters, beginning with chapter 3 on "Adding Effects," increase your skills for building Web pages by introducing more sophisticated code and tags. Backgrounds and text colors, hyperlinks, and graphics are covered in detail in chapters 4 through 6. The author supplies a good explanation of how colors work, hexadecimal numbers, and how hexadecimals convert to decimals and visa versa. It's rather technical in nature, so remember that you don't *have* to know all of this to create simple background colors or font colors in a Web page. The author just feels it's important to understand the BGCOLOR attribute if you want to create colors or understand why they look a certain way.

Chapter 6, "Modifying Graphics," is essentially a basic tutorial on the Paint Shop Pro program. You can download a demo version from the Internet. Corel PhotoPAINT is also used in this chapter.

Beginning with chapter 7, "Image Maps," the topics get a bit more involved. Chapters 8 through 11 teach how to create tables, frames, and animated GIFs and how to use sound. Chapter 12, "JavaScript," introduces JavaScript (not to be confused with Java), which permits building interactive Web pages. Included is a brief look at the concepts of object-oriented language, methods and functions, object properties, and language statements. You will also practice inputing data, perform mathematical operations, check data, and build an interactive application. Learning this may take a bit of work, as JavaScript is like a programming language; if you have no experience, some of the material may seem a bit complicated. Still, the exercises do give a good look at what's involved.

Chapter 13, "Setting Up a School Page," presents how to create a directory, how to use frames for file linking, how to update, and how to upload your files. Java is introduced in this section, as well as creating a simple applet.

The workbook is meant to be used chapter-by-chapter for those who are new to HTML authoring. But for anyone having some knowledge and who wants to begin with one of the more advanced features, that's fine, too. Each chapter has step-by-step exercises to enable you to work at your own pace through the concept being taught. Screen shots demonstrate the final results so the work can be checked.

This book is a beginning tool for learning HTML. The addition of Java and JavaScript makes this something for beginners as well as those with more HTML experience. Includes a glossary.

Kids Webkit: The Coolest Way to Create Your Own Web Site!

Lisa Lopuck

Berkeley, CA: Peachpit Press, 1997. (http://www.peachpit.com/ or http://www.kidswebkit.com). 64p. ISBN: 0-201-88675-8. Booklet, $22.95. (Includes CD-ROM).

Creating Web sites is not just for adults. In fact, kids seem to take to the idea faster than some adults. They see the inherent fun in creating something themselves and being able to show it to the world. HTML is simple enough for children to learn. But why not have some fun, too? This book/CD makes creating a Web site an adventure. The CD is the main tool for creating the Web pages, but the booklet is a companion piece that allows kids to preview the process as they move along. The book is designed for the 7- to 12-year-old audience.

Bright yellow pages with a spider web as background are really flashy. They are also a bit more difficult to read, but will a kid care? They will be fascinated by the colorful graphics and entertaining cartoon characters. The book and CD are led by "Spinner," a construction worker/spider who leads them through the Web building process. Using the CD is a multimedia experience with sound and animation. The book is equally colorful.

The author has a word for parents in the introduction—a word of caution but not alarm about children and the Web. She offers tips on keeping safe when putting children's Web pages up on the Internet.

Building the Web site takes three steps. First, choose one of several blueprints to work with. The book describes each one, and the CD presents a visual description along with audio for each. Next, choose a graphic for the pages. This can be cartoons, pop art, animals, an island getaway, etc. The graphics are designed to go along with the particular blueprint you select. The final step is to decorate and check out your Web pages and then upload them. Directions are given for uploading to America Online, so those who do not subscribe to this online service will have to use a different method to publish their pages.

One caveat: On the inside of the package cover, it implies that PhotoShop is supported, but in the Read Me file, it says it is not. So make sure to choose one of the other paint programs listed. You are responsible for purchasing your own paint/graphics program. The CD instructions assume that a paint/graphics program is located on the computer somewhere.

The Non-Designer's Web Book: An Easy Guide to Creating, Designing and Posting Your Own Web Site

Robin Williams and John Tollett

Berkeley, CA: Peachpit Press, 1998. (http://www.peachpit.com).
288p. ISBN: 0-201-68859-X. Softcover, $29.95.

If you just looked at the design of this book, you'd say, "These people know how to design a good-looking publication." This book is very eye-catching, with lots of color screen shots and illustrations throughout. The page layouts are easy to read and the color really enhances the learning experience. The book is well organized and very logical in its presentation.

Organized into five parts and assuming no experience with Web design or even much with using the World Wide Web, the book begins with Part One, "Using the World Wide Web," a basic introduction to the Web and Internet that contains information about navigating as well as searching for information. You may ask why a design book has to explain this, but creating Web pages requires a certain understanding of how the Web works and the authors realize this. The introductory material is brief but contains enough to give you a foundation. If you already have Web skills, just skip this chapter. You might want to take the quiz at the end. Fill in the blanks and see if you know as much as you think you do. There is also a guided tour that presents some things to think about when exploring the Web.

Part Two, "Making Web Pages," goes into the concept of just what Web pages are, as well as how to create them with authoring software. There is actually a step-by-step set of directions that can apply to whatever software you are using. The exercise begins with creating a folder and beginning a document that will form the Web page. It relates this experience to creating a word-processing document, making it easy for a beginner to understand. An important part of the design of Web pages is to be organized before you sit down and start creating material. It's crucial to set some guidelines for holding the files, naming them, and saving them. Also, you must think ahead to service providers, domain names, and Web addresses, as well as thinking about what audience you want to reach. A handy checklist of things to do before you begin is worth keeping handy.

Part Three, "Design Issues of the Web," teaches you the differences between print publication and Web publication. Many are technical in nature. It's necessary to take into account some considerations in designing Web pages that aren't relevant to traditional print media. Topics include cost of publication, using color, revisions and updates, distribution, customer response, file size, using sound and animation, and accessibility of the information. The quiz for this section lets you test your knowledge by deciding about a situation and whether it would call for a print or Web publication.

After learning the pros and cons, the authors settle down to design issues. Here basic design is introduced, with examples of good and bad Web sites to illustrate the four principles covering alignment, repetition, proximity, and contrast. Next, the interface design is considered. Although this sounds very boring and "program-like," it's really not. It's all about how the pages look and how they work and interact with the browser. A crucial part of interface design is how people find things on your Web site—navigation design. Beginning with a simple plan for your Web site can help you successfully achieve the results you want. There is a fun chapter on recognizing good and bad design, with examples of both. Hopefully your Web pages aren't here! A "Not-So-Good Design Checklist," as well as a "So-Much-Better Design Checklist," helps you be aware of things to avoid as well as what to include.

Part Four, "Color, Graphics, and Type," prepares you to work with graphics on the Web. First there is a chapter on color, including various color models (RGB, indexed, etc.), monitor resolution, bit depth, browser colors that work, and much more. It's important to understand how graphics work on the Web, so there are sections on file formats and features of graphics as well as on preparing image files, alternate labels, and thumbnails. There is a good section on using software to create images. The authors are aware that not everyone wants to spend a lot of money to buy expensive software, so shareware and inexpensive software are described. Of course, you don't have to create your own images if you don't want to. Understanding this, there's a section on getting images from the Web to your computer and how to scan images or use a digital camera. For those who are creative, step-by-step directions tell you how to make a gif, JPEG, image map and background graphics, and animated gif. Next, typography is explored, with suggestions for staying safe and making your pages legible. Understanding what goes into creating colors will help you create Web pages. Much of the information is technical, but the color illustrations and user-friendly writing make it easy to digest. Part Five, "You're Done, Now What?," tells you how to get your site up and running, as well as how to test it and make any necessary adjustments.

There is so much in this book. It's a real joy to read. For anyone who wants to learn about design issues, pick up a copy and enjoy yourself as you learn and create exciting Web pages. The book is excellently organized and beautifully designed (what else would you expect!). The color adds so much to the overall excellence of the book. It's easy to read this cover to cover or just to turn to the chapter for whatever your Web design needs are.

PageMill for Macintosh

Maria Langer

Berkeley, CA: Peachpit Press, 1997. (http://www.peachpit.com). 233p. (Visual Quickstart Guide series). ISBN: 0-201-69402-6. Softcover, $16.95.

If you need to learn how to use PageMill in a hurry, this book will give you a very easy-to-follow visual approach to learning all about it. Another in the series of Visual Quickstart Guides from Peachpit Press; the author has written more than 14 computer books and regularly writes for *MacWEEK* magazine.

For someone completely new to the Internet and the Web, there is an introductory chapter covering some basics. Just skip this one if you are already knowledgeable about them.

With lots of illustrations and easy, step-by-step directions, learning to use PageMill is easy with this guide. Beginners may want to read it cover-to-cover and follow each of the lessons. If you are more experienced, you may want to find the topic and go directly to it. The book is set up to work either way. Handy "thumb tabs" allow you to flip through chapters. Along the way are handy tips that provide additional information.

The 12 chapters and 4 appendices cover just about anything you might want to know to use PageMill to create Web pages. Topics range from the basic concepts of text entry, formatting, applying paragraphs, and links to more complex ideas such as creating tables and using frames and forms. After creating pages, there is a chapter on testing and enhancing your work as well as setting preferences for using PageMill. The appendices tell all about PageMill's features, including menus, shortcut keys, buttons, switches, and icons; PageMill's Inspector feature; and an HTML reference guide.

If you're a Macintosh user and have chosen PageMill as your Web authoring tool, this guide will be a practical resource for learning PageMill or just refreshing your memory about various features. It's a well-written tool that's easy to use.

Publish It on the Web 2d Edition (Windows Version)

Bryan Pfaffenberger

Chestnut Hill, MA: AP Professional, 1997.
(http://www.apnet.com/approfessional). 607p. ISBN: 0-12-553160-5.
Softcover, $37.95. (Includes CD-ROM).

Though not written expressly for educators, this book is for "any ordinary person" who wants to learn how to publish on the World Wide Web, including those who want to do so for schools, churches, small businesses, or organizations. It's geared to people who wish to have a Web presence but do not have the financial resources to hire someone to do the design and creation of a Web site. As a guide, it takes you through the entire process involved. What separates this book from other Web design books is that it is not just about HTML. In fact, HTML is only a small part of the book. The author wants to teach his audience everything from how to decide on the reason to create a Web site to how to put together the kind of site desired, all the way through to enhancing the Web site with graphics and other eye-catching possibilities.

The book is for the Windows crowd, including Windows 95 and NT. It's nice to know this up front. The accompanying CD-ROM includes Web publishing tools and a lot of software used by Web publishers.

To get started, Part One, "The New Opportunities in Web Publishing," introduces the World Wide Web and how it fits into the publishing environment; what the Web is all about (hypertext, URLs, CGI, Java, etc.), and why it's so well suited for use as a publishing tool. Part Two, "Designing Your Web," is all about how to choose a Web server, develop a plan, and decide on the target audience, along with what level of commitment you have for the site. Software and operating systems for servers, as well as the importance of selecting a domain name, highlight this section. "Understanding Web Architecture" delves into hierarchical webs, choosing the architecture for your design, and understanding the options. Part Two finishes with helpful fundamentals for design and how to choose software to create the pages. Here's where you'll learn about the various options, including HTML editors, WYSIWYG editors, and simple text editors. Lots to choose from for a beginner. Although some of the information in these chapters is somewhat technical, the language is friendly and the material provides a necessary background for Web publishers who also want to run their own servers.

Part Three, "Creating Your Web with HTML," goes over the basics of HTML for creating a Web page. The fundamentals of HTML and how to build documents using various formatting tags are presented. There is somewhat more detail about HTML components—such as physical vs. logical formatting, attributes, elements—than is found in other books about Web design. Done in a tutorial style, the chapters progress through adding graphics and even providing a script to create a form of getting feedback from visitors. The more complex component of adding Java applets is covered in a chapter as well. All in all, the HTML covered will provide enough information to produce a very nicely designed Web page. You'll also learn about HTML editors, using HotDog as an example. Finally, testing, publishing, and publicizing your Web site are also important aspects of Web publishing. Part Four, "Producing Dynamic Content," tackles multimedia and producing graphics such as animated GIFs. The author provides some tips and hints for producing successful graphics on a Web page. Also included is how to add video as well as how to produce Adobe Acrobat documents. Part Five, "Web Publishing Issues," introduces topics that must be faced by every Web publisher, such as security, copyright, and standardization issues. These topics are often left out in most basic Web design books. Part Six contains appendices, including an HTML 3.2 reference, ISO Latin-1 Special Characters, color codes, and one about the CD included with the book.

For those who just want to create a simple Web page for a class, this book may be overkill, but for anyone serious about learning how to publish on the Web and learning more than just HTML, this book seems to cover it all.

Roger C. Parker's Guide to Web Content and Design: Eight Steps to Web Site Success

> Indianapolis, IN: IDG Books Worldwide, 1997.
> (http://www.idgbooks.com/). 271p. ISBN: 1-55828-553-9.
> Softcover, $39.95.

Once you've learned the basics of HTML and are ready to start designing your own Web site, this title will provide all the essential information about planning your site, developing content, and promoting, maintaining, and improving your Web site. Along the way you'll also pick up tips about choosing a Web address, involving visitors by using registration forms, e-mail forms, and more. Although this book is aimed more at the business community, there is plenty here to help any Web designer make the most of building a Web site and avoid the pitfalls that trap most untutored Web designers. This is not an HTML tutorial. It only briefly touches on HTML, so you'll need to acquire those skills first.

The text is easy to read, with lots of white space and bold to highlight headings. Along with the plentiful information are worksheets to help organize your thoughts as you read the material.

If you are responsible for coming up with a high-impact Web site, spend some time reading this book. Your boss will certainly be impressed with your knowledge and your Web site will more than likely reflect all the useful tips and suggestions you've learned.

Teach Yourself Web Publishing with HTML 4 in a Week, 4th Edition

Laura Lemay

Indianapolis, IN: Sams Publishing, 1997. (**http://www.samspublishing.com**). 652p. ISBN: 1-57521-336-2. Softcover, $29.99.

At more than 600 pages, this is a book that can provide anything you would ever want to know about HTML and designing Web pages. It's a book for beginners as well as those with some experience in creating Web pages. Laura Lemay's fourth edition is an excellent tutorial as well as reference.

The book is divided into 14 chapters, which means if you cover 2 a day you will have completed it in a week. Good luck. For some, it may be a bit of information overload to cover the material in only one week.

The book covers basics about HTML, Web design, and editors, as well as all the components of HTML you'll need from the basics up through CGI and creating forms. Lessons consist of objectives to be covered, explanations of the component to be learned, and examples, followed by an exercise to put the material into practice. A screen print of what the HTML looks like is a good aid to checking your work. Lemay is very good at providing illustrations of the more complex material, which really helps you visualize the process. The fourth edition expands previous ones by including the newest HTML 4.0 and extensions in Netscape Communicator 4, as well as Internet Explorer 4. Any changes in elements such as tables, forms, or frames are also included. Dynamic HTML is new to this edition, along with cascading style sheets. An especially helpful section includes the latest tools to help you get started creating exciting Web pages.

The combination of background explanation and well-written exercises makes it a very user-friendly tool. Screen shots illustrate the design effectively. It's easy to recognize what is the "input" required by you and the "output" as interpreted by a browser. A "New Term" icon alerts you to new vocabulary coming your way.

There are many HTML books out there, as well as online resources that can teach you HTML, but this book is one of the best and worth the money to have as a reference too. If you are an experienced HTML author and just looking for what's new with HTML 4.0, this book may be overkill, but for anyone who wants a solid foundation in HTML plus the latest in 4.0, this book is an excellent choice.

Using the World Wide Web and Creating Home Pages: A How-to-Do-It Manual

Ray E. Metz and Gail Junion-Metz

New York: Neal-Schuman, 1996. (**http://www.Neal-Schuman.com/**).
286p. (How-to-Do-It Manuals for Librarians Number 67).
ISBN: 1-55570-241-4. Softcover, $63.75.

The purpose of this librarian-oriented guide is to provide information on how the World Wide Web can be used as an important information tool. It's also about how to connect to it or upgrade current access, as well as how to create a beginning Web site and train others to be proficient in using the Web. Practical in nature and written to cover the Web in a broader sense than just how to navigate, the goal is to help librarians begin to make decisions about using the World Wide Web. The target audience is the library community, administrators, staff, and even interested library patrons.

Chapter 1, "In the Beginning—Web Basics," covers the World Wide Web and Internet tools. It contains a timeline of interesting facts, the main concepts of hypermedia and URLs, plus browser basics and more. When appropriate, screen shots illustrate the material under discussion. Chapter 2, "Think Big—Look at the Issues for Libraries," presents material to help staff members begin a dialog about how to use the Web. Suggestions for considerations for planning and meetings, as well as a sample "issues" outline, provide a very practical look at getting started using the Web in a library setting. When applicable, the various library settings (K-12, academic, and public) are considered in the recommendations made. Other introductory chapters include getting connected and learning and teaching the Web.

What distinguishes this title from other Web-related books is the combination of information about the Web and why it's important, along with a considerable amount of information on designing, creating, testing, and maintaining a Web site. Setting up a Web site requires considerable thought and skills. Here, the authors have isolated those skills and presented a comprehensive overview of what's involved in creating a site on the Web.

If you are new to the idea of designing a Web site, you will find plenty of helpful suggestions, including how to plan your Web site, basic design, and creating the pages. "Authoring a Web Site" is designed to introduce you to the concepts behind Web authoring as well as choices in HTML editors or tools for creating pages. The most common HTML tags, along with examples, are covered. Directions are step-by-step when introducing a specific tag. You may still need a good reference book if HTML is entirely new to you.

One aspect that may be overlooked in the process of setting up a site is testing your initial creation. A valuable evaluation sample test questionnaire is very informative and a good way to get feedback before going live with your site. The authors suggest giving it to testers to obtain valuable feedback.

The book manages to put technical information into an easy-to-understand style with step-by-step directions when necessary.

If you are a librarian ready to embark on the creation of a Web site, this clearly organized manual will take you from the planning process through the creation, evaluation, and maintenance of a Web site. A glossary of Internet terms, accompanied by an extensive bibliography, provides further reading along with some online resources for all the material covered in the book. An appendix supplies sample Web sites mostly for academic and public libraries.

The Web Page Workbook

Dawn Groves

Wilsonville, OR: Franklin, Beedle & Associates, 1996.
(**http://www.fbeedle.com**). 176p. ISBN: 1-887902-05-8.
Softcover, $19.95.

Would you like to get started designing your own Web pages, or have your students learn? This handy little guide can set you on the way to Web design in a few hours. Structured as a text for a six-hour hands-on class, it provides a detailed tutorial on Web page creation plus design considerations, home pages, and HTML code. Half of the book is a tutorial providing exercises and information about the basics of HTML. The second part presents practical advice about Web design issues. Several helpful appendices offer a resource for further information as well as reference guides. The table of HTML tags is especially handy. Another helpful section is the Web Site Development Form that helps you conceptualize a Web page.

EarthLink software, which comes with the book, provides Internet access, although it's not necessary to go online to learn to create Web pages with the tutorial. All in all, this workbook makes learning Web design painless. If you need to develop basic skills to get going, or to help your students learn HTML, this little book may be all you need.
(*Courtesy of Multimedia Schools Magazine, Information Today, Inc., Medford, NJ*).

The Web Publisher's Illustrated Quick Reference

Ralph Grabowski

New York: Springer-Verlag, 1996. (http://www.springer-ny.com/).
266p. ISBN: 0-387-94831-7. Softcover, no price given.

This reference tool is a combination of two elements in writing Web pages: VRML v2.0 and HTML v3.2. Except for a very brief description of HTML and an example of a bit of HTML markup, this is not a guide or tutorial for novices in HTML. However, it does contain an alphabetical listing of the HTML components found in version 3.2. There is also a list of tags that have been removed from the standard 3.2.

Each HTML entry contains the following elements: "Description"—what the purpose of the tag is, whether it's obsolete, meaning of the abbreviation, and whether unique to Netscape, Internet Explorer, or HTML 3.2. "Required Attributes"—tells when a tag requires one or more attributes. "Example Markups"—samples of the actual code show how to implement the tag. "Screen Grab"—helps you to see the effects of the tag on the document. "Optional Attributes"—lists any optional attributes you may use with the tag. "Tips"—includes any tips that can save you time in authoring pages. "Related HTML Tags" is a cross-reference.

The VRML section includes the following elements: "Description"—the purpose of the VRML node, the meaning of its abbreviation, and the node type. "Screen Grab"—lets you see instantly the effect of the node on the scene. "VRML 2 Syntax"—the node syntax and default field values. "VRML 1 Syntax"—the node section specified in an earlier version of VRML. "Node Geometry"—information about every field in the VRML node. "Related Equations"—geometry-related nodes such as surface area and volume. "Texture Mapping"—describes how texture maps are applied. "Tips"—hints on using the node that can save time. "Related Notes" are for cross-references.

Entries are clearly labeled and easily read. Sometimes there are screen prints to help illustrate a tag more effectively, as with the <IMG SRC...> tag and the use of the ALT attribute. It really helps to see what it looks like. Also, the author points out problem areas when necessary, as with using the <U>...</U> tag to indicate that something is underlined. This can be confused with a hyperlink sometimes, so in the "Tips" section the author cautions against using it.

If you are comfortable with HTML tags, have experience with authoring Web pages, are still using standard 3.2, and want a reference guide to HTML as well as VRML 2.0, then this will provide you with an appropriate source. If you aren't into VRML, then you may want to consider other books, as more than half of the pages are devoted to that topic. Several helpful appendices include "URL Syntax," "HTML Character Codes," "Language and Country Codes," "HTML Color Codes," and "VRML Field Codes." No index.

Web Publishing for Teachers

Bard Williams

Indianapolis, IN: IDG Books Worldwide, 1997.
(**http://www.idgbooks.com**). 382p. (...for Dummies series).
ISBN: 0-7645-0111-9. Softcover, $24.99. (Includes CD-ROM).

Bard Williams has written other IDG Dummies books for teachers employing the same user-friendly approach; this time it's for Web publishing. Williams's book is for educators ready to take their interest in the Internet one step further and become Web authors. Whether for the classroom or for students, the book provides teachers with everything they need to get started creating Web pages.

The accompanying CD-ROM contains software such as a trial demonstration of Claris Home page, WebWhacker, and AT&T WorldNet Service. Using a Macintosh as the platform, Williams makes sure to present alternatives for Windows users when necessary. This makes the book useful to anyone who wants to learn Web publishing.

If you already have a working knowledge of the Web and Internet and don't need any history or description, skip the first couple of introductory chapters. In reality, you can use this guide as a reference tool. Just choose the chapters you need for the kind of help desired.

This is not an HTML guide. Aside from a glimpse of HTML code, some tables with common tags, and an appendix of HTML code, you will not learn to create pages by writing HTML with this book. Instead, you'll learn about the importance of planning, designing, and developing a good Web site.

There is an excellent chapter on HTML tools which Williams has divided into five categories: WYSIWYG (what you see is what you get) editors, which include Claris Home Page, Adobe PageMill, and FrontPage; cut-and-paste editors, including Web Weaver, HotMetal Pro, etc.; word-processor utilities, which points out that many word-processing programs come equipped with the capability of converting documents to HTML code; and hybrid tools that take you one step further and offer more than just basic editing features. An example is Tango and conversion tools like Myrmidon that let you take an already existing document and convert it to a Web page. A chart with the tool, platform, comments, and source helps you to see them all in perspective. And the author inserts his own comments about which tools he likes. Whatever you decide, Williams suggests sticking with one so that you get familiar with it and can make the most of its features.

You'll learn how to use Claris Home Page to create a Web page. Williams feels that this tool is a good choice for educators because it is easy to use and available to schools, plus educators may also be using other Claris products. In this part, you can explore how to open, edit, and format pages using Claris Home Page. Once comfortable with the basics, the author moves on to show you how to spice up your Web pages by using forms and inserting sound, movies, and even some Java. Once the pages are created, it's necessary to get them up and running. A handy set of tips and options on how to publish your Web pages can be found, as well as some very interesting projects recommended for classroom use. Several appendices include a glossary, a summary of HTML commands, and some tips for acceptable use policies. Finally, there is an "About the CD" section to let you know what's available and how to access the programs and files.

There is a nice balance of Web publishing information, along with projects and activities teachers can use in the classroom. Lots of tips, techniques, tables, and charts help illustrate the material, and the casual writing style makes learning how to publish on the Web a fun experience.

Author/Title Index